The Bridge

MWIZENGE S. TEMBO

Published by Linus Publications, Inc.

Ronkonkoma, NY 11779

Copyright (C) 2015 by Mwizenge S. Tembo

Cover Design and Photography by Mwizenge S. Tembo

All Rights Reserved.

ISBN 10: 1-60797-332-4

ISBN 13: 978-1-60797-332-4

No part of this publication may be reproduced, stored in a retrieval system, or transmitted, in any form or by any means, electronic, mechanical, photocopying, recording, or otherwise, without the prior permission of the publisher.

Printed in the United States of America.

Print Numbers 5   4   3   2   1

Author's Note

The author would like to acknowledge Mr. Evan Mbozi who was the editor of the first edition. The late Mr. J. J. Mayovu was instrumental in the storage and distribution of the first edition in Lusaka in Zambia. MHSRP.

Also by Mwizenge S. Tembo

- ❖ Satisfying Zambian Hunger for Culture, Indiana, Xlibris Publishers, (2012)
- ❖ Zambian Traditional Names, Lusaka, Julubbi Enterprise, (2006)
- ❖ Legends of Africa, New York, Michael Friedman, (1996)
- ❖ Titbits for the Curious, Lusaka, Multimedia Publications, (1989)

First published in 2005 by Julubbi Enterprises Ltd, P.O. Box 50016, Lusaka, Zambia.

Second Published in 2013 by Linus Publications, Inc., Ronkonkoma, NY, 11779

First printing in 2005 by Zambia Educational Publishing House, Lusaka, Zambia.

Table of Contents

CHAPTER ONE 1

CHAPTER TWO 8

CHAPTER THREE 18

CHAPTER FOUR 29

CHAPTER FIVE 42

CHAPTER SIX 59

CHAPTER SEVEN 68

CHAPTER EIGHT 78

CHAPTER NINE 88

CHAPTER TEN 130

CHAPTER ELEVEN 142

CHAPTER TWELVE 150

CHAPTER THIRTEEN 159

CHAPTER FOURTEEN 178

CHAPTER FIFTEEN 201

CHAPTER SIXTEEN 214

CHAPTER SEVENTEEN 221

SUMMARY 236

CHAPTER ONE

The African man grimaced as he clutched his left hand in pain when the taxi hit a bump on the Irish dirt road. The hand was put in a temporary sling in the emergency room at the hospital the previous night. He gingerly rested it on his knee. He was always a patient man. But this time, he couldn't help it. Gesturing with his left hand impatiently in front of the windshield, he told the taxi driver to drive faster. The taxi driver was clearly uneasy driving this black stranger to the Irish countryside. He was making small talk like rapid machine gunfire to hide his nervousness. The African man was not in the mood for small talk. He was a man on the last seconds of a possibly life or death mission. He was looking for landmarks.

The rendezvous point was about half an hour drive north of Belfast, west of a small town village named Gandy. There was a peninsular on the left and the dirt road would meander around several times, over three bridges, up to a place where there would be five big ancient rocks. He couldn't miss them. The taxi had passed the peninsular and the three small bridges all right. But there were so many rocks. How could he tell the group of five? He was getting flustered. Never in his wildest fantasies had he imagined the encounter would be this way – with pain, anxiety, nervousness, and a taxi driver whose rapid verbal fire was heightening his anxiety. In what seemed like a distant voice, and with a heavy rural Irish accent the African man could barely understand, the taxi driver yelled something about "it's going to cost you and whoever is your friend?"

What the African man saw one hundred yards in front of him almost made his heart stop. It looked like an Austin Morris car. The African man immediately gestured the taxi driver to stop. He gingerly opened the car door with his right hand anticipating pain from his left arm as he stepped out of the taxi. But the painkillers he had taken before he sneaked out of the hospital ward must have finally kicked in. He could barely feel pain in his sling-wrapped arm. His heart was pounding with excitement. Although not exactly under these circumstances, he had waited and dreamt of this moment for one hundred eighty days or maybe for thirty-one years. Would his buckling knees carry him the last eighty yards? He took five steps and paused. He shaded his eyes on this bright Irish sunny morning to see whether anyone was coming out of the parked car. Was there, in fact, anyone in it? He glanced at his watch. It was ten forty in the morning. He was supposed to have been there at ten thirty.

* * *

The Irish woman woke up that day relieved and excited that that was the day it would happen. As she lay in bed smoking, she momentarily felt a thrill as she realized this was how the American Apollo Eleven astronauts might have felt when they woke up the day they were to leave for man's first trip to the moon in 1969. Is this how robbers felt on their way to rob a bank? She also wondered, and shuddered, if that was also how Mohammed Otta and the hijackers felt when they woke up that morning to hijack the huge Boeing passenger planes, slamming them into the World Trade Centre towers in New York, killing thousands. The rush of pure anticipation and excitement was killing her. But she was enjoying it.

She kicked her covers off and went to the bathroom to get ready. She took a shower and dressed like she was going to her dead end job at the supermarket where she worked as a cashier at the checkout register. She wished she could dress to kill – a gorgeous red dress, matching golden earrings, smooth nylon socks, black high heels, and special glossy lip stick. But she didn't want to give her plan away. This was an opportunity of a lifetime. She knew she would be too nervous to drive. So she pretended not to feel well and asked her daughter Jill to drive her to the doctor. They were not going to be too long. Jill would be at work in good time. She didn't suspect anything.

The Irish woman had felt trapped her entire adult life. Her husband had left for work early at seven. He did that everyday. He never even kissed her goodbye. Their marriage had been lifeless and on automatic pilot for God knows how long. There was nothing she could do about it for as long as she could remember. She had only a twelfth grade education and could not get a better job. She was in a small town village of Gandy in remote Northern Ireland where nothing happened. But that day she was going to venture out towards the City of Belfast. Thanks to the secrets of modern technology, no one knew anything about what was going to happen, except her. Would it change her life? Was it really happening?

At ten that morning, she got into the passenger seat and Jill drove. They drove along what counts for the bustling main street in a sleepy rural village town. There were pairs of elderly white-haired people, who were neighbours, walking their dogs. They drove past her supermarket work place. Jill hit the left blinker to turn right into Crescent Street to the family doctor, when her mother stopped her and impatiently gestured for her to drive on.

"Let's go to Belfast," she said, "I am sick and bored of this little village."

That was not new to Jill. Her mother was always moody and had constantly joked that she wanted to be free to do things; to travel, to have some adventure, to relax, 'to be myself'. To Jill's surprise, that morning her mother looked serious. But with no luggage, Jill knew her mother was not running away to Timbuktu. Maybe she just wanted a nice country drive and to go to lunch. Because her mother looked so serious and intense, Jill suddenly got very nervous. She began firing questions at her mother.

"Where are we going?" she asked, "to lunch, just for a drive? Ha?" she glanced at her mute mother who was stoically staring through the windshield. "Are you a KGB agent? You are not leaving us are you?" Jill pretended to giggle to bait her mother to say something. She gave up and was very quiet and serious.

They had been driving for half an hour on the dirt road surrounded by picturesque scenes of green rolling meadows, distant knolls, and some mountains in the far horizon. There were farm horses, sheep, and cows grazing in the open pasture.

"I will explain later when it's probably all over," she suddenly said to her daughter, "that is if I come out of it alive," she added as if for effect.

Jill slammed the brakes causing stones on the dirt road to shoot like missiles on both sides of the road. As she jerked forward, her mother instinctively put her hand on the dashboard to brace herself. She was not wearing a seat belt because she did not care any more to be alive.

"Mother, are you crazy? What are you going to do? Tell me now. It's not too late to stop, you know!" Jill was afraid for her mother. The joking and the smile were gone from her face.

Her mother continued to stare straight through the windshield as if trying to compose her thoughts. She was too tense, too nervous, too anguished, and too excited to talk. At that moment, through her tear-glazed eyes, she saw a car drive up. It was a taxi. She expected it to move on. But it suddenly stopped and pulled over and parked just beside the five large rocks. That was it. Her heart pounded fast and hard. Could she handle it? She was engulfed by emotions that had built up for almost one hundred and eighty days or maybe twenty-four years. Her daughter's voice seemed distant and insignificant, like a pesky insect whining in one's ear at a picnic. She kept asking, "Mother what are you doing? Where are you going?"

The Irish woman slowly opened her passenger door and stepped out; her eyes were transfixed intensely on the taxi in front of her. She had to watch forevery small move. She saw that a black man had come out of the taxi. He walked towards her and stopped. His left hand had something on or around it. The black man hesitantly walked several yards and stopped. She gingerly took a few more steps towards him and stopped. For a moment they were like wild prey stalking each other, not sure whether to attack or retreat. Then it happened.

"Is your name Trish?" he yelled, putting his hand around his mouth to project his voice.

"Are you Kamthibi?" she yelled, putting her hand around her mouth to project her voice.

They yelled the question at the same time. The answer came simultaneously from their lips.

"Yes!!" they both yelled. Their loud screams of joy echoed between the big rocks.

Arms stretched toward each other, they ran like colourful birds in a courtship ritual. Before Trish's knees could completely melt under her, they locked their arms around each other in a bear hug. Kamthibi rapidly kissed Trish repeatedly starting from her neck, then her cheek, until they looked each other in the eye, slowly, and hesitantly locked lips. Trish was a small woman but Kamthibi could not support her body with only his one arm and buckling knees. Then they stumbled as Kamthibi tried hard to maintain his balance. As she kissed Kamthibi passionately, Trish felt them sway and something buckled. The inevitable happened. They stumbled on a galley and both crashed onto the embankment. They landed onto the green grass on the edge of the road above the embankment. Trish inadvertently ended up on top of Kamthibi. Their hearts raced with heightened nervous excitement.

Kamthibi waited helplessly lying down facing the blue sky because he couldn't brace himself with his left hand. 'Let this moment not end', he thought. She wanted to get up but he drew her to him with his right uninjured hand. Against the bright Irish blue sky, he noticed her purple shirt with a small silver chain around her smooth neck. Her red lips were trembling and practically begging to be kissed some more. Her long brown hair had a mild silver streak in it and was gently caressing his cheek. He wanted to touch and pass his fingers through the hair with his left hand. But he could not. Her eyes were small and sparkled, darting mischievously all over his face, and the arm in a sling. She had a luscious soul.

Trish realized she was practically on top of him. She didn't care. She loved it. She didn't want to hurt him so she braced herself to get up. But he drew her to him. That's when she noticed his large white eyes and teeth, which sparkled against the dark smooth skin. The contrast was such a mesmerizing novelty to her. His lips were wide and full. He had short kinky hair with a slight touch of grey in it. His nostrils were so big you could drive a bus through each one of them. She wanted to rub his hair and find out what it felt like. She was yearning to kiss him again. 'These are sweet lips. I wish this moment would last forever,' Trish thought. They both laughed hysterically and giggled at the spontaneous fun and awkwardness of everything that was happening. She noticed the hospital patient gown under Kamthibi's shirt. Tears glazed in his eyes as he looked at Trish against the blue sky above her again. He was overwhelmed. The teardrops were suddenly so big they streaked at the corner of his eyes and trickled on both sides of his head on to the grass.

Trish gingerly helped Kamthibi up as she wiped her own tears with the back of her hand. She sat beside him on the embankment. He put his right hand around her small waist over her blue jeans long pants. She wrapped herself around him as they hugged and kissed. It was at this moment that it happened. They wept in each other's arms uncontrollably. The floodgates that had been closed for months and possibly years were suddenly open.

"I love you, Trish," Kamthibi said in an emotion-soaked whisper with a surprisingly light African accent. "I will never love another woman the way I love you. I don't care now if I die this second."

"You are my man, Kamthibi," whispered Trish, "I was an emotional virgin until I met you. This is the real meaning of love. Love can truly be blind," she paused. "Just look at you."

Trish was lovingly rubbing the back of her hand against his black, smooth, clean-shaven face. Kamthibi closed his eyes as his heart melted from the sensations from her sweet soothing voice and smooth fingers slowly and lightly rubbing his face. He closed his eyes. He had never smelt such sweet soft perfume before, which was accentuated by the powerful natural scent of a woman. Kamthibi was startled by what he saw when he opened his eyelids. Trish suddenly felt a tap on her shoulder. It was Jill.

"Mother, are you out of your mind?" Jill asked with utter consternation in her voice. She grabbed her mother's hand and tried to tag her away toward the parked Austin Morris. She had just witnessed the unthinkable.

"Let's go home! Mother," Jill said, "this is insane."

"Wait honey," Trish replied hesitantly.

She was torn and anguished. She didn't want to go that minute. Not just yet. She loved this black man deeply. But it was so dangerous. Her first instinct was to pick up her shoes from the ground and leave. But she wanted to talk to him, to ask him so many questions. She wanted to laugh with him. Maybe to hug and kiss him passionately good-bye.

A plume of dust was visible on the far horizon behind the taxi and the sounds of fast approaching police or emergency vehicle sirens could be heard from a distance. In a matter of seconds, a Belfast Police squad car and an ambulance right behind it pulled over and stopped next to Kamthibi with the blue and red lights left flashing. The taxi driver's jaw dropped at the unfolding events. 'I am not going to get my fare now,' was his first thought, 'this looks like a major crime bust.'

"Oh! My God!!! Mother," are the only words that Jill could utter with her hand over her mouth. She was so dumbfounded.

CHAPTER TWO

The two police officers from Belfast number two prencit patted down Kamthibi thoroughly, all the while asking him if he was selling drugs or had any knife, gun, or weapon on him. They couldn't slap handcuffs on both hands as he winced and cried in agony when the officer grabbed his arm to remove it from the sling. They might have thought the broken arm was some type of hoax or trick. You never know with these blackie criminal types. One of the officers had worked in London in a tough West Indian neighbourhood and was only recently transferred to Belfast. He had seen all the criminal tricks in the books. Kamthibi was shoved into the back of the police car. The one uninjured hand was handcuffed to the metal caging at the back of the squad car with a threatening admonition from the officer that Kamthibi should not try anything stupid like escaping. He was to be questioned and charged at the police station.

The taxi driver was asked what he knew. Did he see any money or drugs or anything exchanged with the lady? The taxi driver in his rapid-fire style of speaking was clearly exasperated to be in the middle of an apparent crime bust during his routine attempt to earn a living. He had seen the blackie and the lady fall down kissing. But it was from a distance. He might have slipped something to her. The taxi driver shook his head swearing he hadn't seen anything and he wasn't part of any plan. He had never seen that blackie until that morning when he waved him down for a ride just by the back alley behind the City hospital.

The other officer walked to the Austin Morris car. Officer O'Malley casually talked to the two presumably local innocent-looking village women; an older middle-aged woman and her daughter. He walked around the car and took a causerie look in their car and the empty trunk.

Officer O'Malley asked and wrote both women's addresses and names down and briefly interviewed them. He noticed that the younger woman looked sad, dejected, and embarrassed. He felt sorry for these rural naïve village women who had no idea about how sophisticated criminals are often the best conmen. Both police officers agreed that common sense on the crime scene strongly showed that the two women were innocent. There was no sense slapping handcuffs on them and hauling them to the police prencit. They both mentioned that their boss would be angry with them for the lack of common sense judgment. Since they had taken down the women's names and addresses, and the village of Gandy was not too far away, they could always come back to pick both of them up for any further questioning. The taxi driver was a different case. He was to drive behind the police car to offer a formal statement about information he knew or anything he had seen.

Kamthibi's arm was throbbing. The painkillers and the adrenaline were wearing out. He didn't want to spend a night in jail with that throbbing arm. As the squad car cruised at a casual pace through the Irish picturesque countryside, the possible gravity of what was happening began to hit him like a ton of bricks. But he did not care since he had not expected to live to this point. The events after the memorable experience with Trish were unchartered territory he had not planned for. He felt he was supposed to be a black male body being driven to the City Hospital of Belfast Morgue for tagging and identification. He could be tortured, shot, framed and, God forbid, lynched.

Nobody would know. He was beginning for the first time to get a knot of fear and dread in the pit of his stomach. The dust was beginning to clear. Nobody would believe that had all that happened because of a deep romantic love he had developed for a woman. Not even his best friend from twenty-five years ago in college, who now lived in Manchester, would believe what had happened to him, nobody would, except maybe Kamthibi's wife. Kamthibi badly wished he could die or just disappear to take all the pain and emotional torture away. He could not bear all those painful thoughts and especially the throbbing pain in his arm. The strong temptation was to tell the cops that he was a harmless guy just in love, that he was not dealing in drugs, that he was a respectable man. But he knew from experience that would be pointless. Whenever he was stopped for any of those minor driving infractions like a broken tail light or one time when he had been mistakenly arrested for unpaid parking tickets in the United States, pleading and explaining to the officer did not work. You were arrested or had to go and see the judge. The law, especially for black men, is like a train. Once it begins moving it might take a while to stop or in some cases it never stops. Kamthibi thought he would be lucky if his train would ever stop.

He couldn't understand most of the jumbled lingo of female and male voices amidst beeps and swishes on the police walkie-talkies in the squad car. But Kamthibi could tell that he, black male suspect, was apprehended near the village of Gandy. Surrendered without struggle. He was in custody and being taken back to the base in Prencit 2 in Belfast. What about the hospital?.... anything missing from there? Maybe narcotics.... Swish...swish...positive over. This both shocked and angered Kamthibi. He did not steal any drugs from the hospital! What was all that no sense? This was a worsening nightmare. They had to check if drugs were stolen? Not money, not files, fraud in a health insurance scheme. No, blackie could not do that just for love. Blackie had to be a drug addict or dealer or pimp especially if involved with a white woman. It had to be something criminal. Kamthibi seethed. Something was brewing deep in his heart. A slow anger and a creeping humiliation began to fog his mind. He thought he was always a citizen with a clean nose. He had to make a statement. He was in love with a woman. And that's it. Why does it have to be complicated? Why are people such racist bigots all the time? But don't pile all your worst hostility, hate and evil on me.

During the drive, the two officers occasionally glanced in the caged back of the squad car with "are you all right back there?" Kamthibi had only nodded in spite of his throbbing arm. As they approached the Prencit 2 downtown Belfast, the two officers could see that Kamthibi's demeanour had changed. He had been calm but now looked angry with a defiant scowl on his face. Defiance is not good for a black suspect. That is seen as concealing criminal guilt. Calmness is all right because that is being cooperative and less threatening. But Kamthibi didn't care. Plenty of humiliation and danger was coming to him anyway in the days, if not weeks and months to come. But at least he could use it if only in a small way for something positive; dignity for one lone, powerless, and small African man.

The blue sunny sky earlier in the morning might have been a good omen for Kamthibi and his romantic escapade. But as the squad car sped a couple of blocks toward the Police station on Galledon Street, it started to rain steadily. No wonder it was so green in the countryside. The Prencit 2 Police Station was wedged between two dingy-looking buildings with graffiti marked all over it. Since it was raining, the squad car pulled into a side alley closest to the entrance. The officer opened the back seat door and unlocked the part of the handcuff that was locked onto the metal cage divider. Soon after, the taxi driver pulled right behind. Kamthibi and the taxi driver were led into the police station.

Once inside, Kamthibi could not stand the noise. There were handcuffed men sitting on the benches, leaning against the wall, or lying down in various poor shapes; drunks, petty thieves, the homeless, the winos. One dirty ill-shaven man reeking of alcohol and drooling yelled something about blackie causing trouble here in that town. One of the officers, Officer O'Malley, yelled at Scottie to shut up, "You are hurting everyone's ears!" Kamthibi's sight caused quite a stir as he was led through a long dark hallway to room 26 where a statement was to be taken.

Two detectives walked in very business like with a tape recorder. One of them had a writing pad with some official forms that had printed on them "Belfast Police Prencit 2." The two arresting officers and the detectives sat on one side of the table in the small room. Kamthibi let out a loud sigh as he gingerly sat down grimacing and holding his arm. The room also had a small video camera in the top corner of the wall near the ceiling and a telephone in the middle of the small foldable rectangular table. There were no windows in the small room. 'There are four police officers on this case. This must be quite a big case in Belfast or the officers must have been bored hauling drunks off the streets,' Kamthibi thought to himself.

"My name is David Flannery, ehhh, Chief Detective Flannery of Prencit Number 2 of Belfast Police," said Flannery in a brisk business tone. He gestured to his left, "and this is my assistant Detective Bradfield, and these are the arresting officers, Officer O'Malley and Blake both of whom you have already met."

Flannery was probably six feet, two inches tall with a long slender face. He had a slight grey touch in his brown hair. He had small but reassuring eyes that conveyed being in control. He was wearing a turtleneck shirt. He kept clicking his ballpoint pen in and out in his palm.

"Is there anything you want before we start?" Flannery asked Kamthibi in a surprisingly calm and friendly tone. This time he played with the pen in his hands fingering it round and round.

"Am very thirsty," Kamthibi said breathing out loud, "may I have some water? Also do you have any pills I can take for this pain? My hand is killing me." Flannery leaned over and whispered to arresting Officer Blake who walked out of the room.

"We will give you water. But unfortunately we can't medicate you unless authorized by a qualified medical physician," Flannery made the statement sound like it was straight from the interrogation rulebook, "look, this will not take too long. We want to take your statement and tie a few loose ends and you will be on your way."

At this point, Officer Blake came into the room with a pitcher of water and a glass into which he proceeded to pour the water.

Kamthibi quickly swigged the water down, his Adam's apple moving in big rapid swings up and down. He barely suppressed a huge burp and breathed out with obvious satisfaction with the glass of ice water.

"What is your full name?"

"Dr. Kamthibi Sungununu Simbazako," replied Kamthibi enunciating his name slowly.

"Could you spell that, please?" Flannery asked looking to rescue his assistant who paused at a loss as to what to write on the official police record and statement form. Kamthibi spelled his name out slowly. He was used to this. He had been doing it all his adult life.

"Do you have any identification on you?" asked Flannery, "passport?"

"I only have my driver's license. My passport is in my hotel room," Kamthibi said as he reached out to get his wallet from the pocket and with his one hand took out his license and gave it to Flannery. Detective Flannery raised his eyebrows as he looked at the license and then handed it over to his assistant. After a while it made its way over to the arresting officers who looked at it also with a bored expression as if saying this could be fake.

"How old are you?" Flannery resumed his questions.

"Forty-five years old."

"What's your occupation?"

"I am the Chief Seed Specialist with Mid-West Seed International."

"Where is that?"

"The office and research facilities are located in the Mid-West of the US, one hundred and fifty miles west of Chicago in Illinois in the small town of Clarksville."

"Sir," Flannery said with a deliberate pause, "I will call you Sir since I can't say your other name, *Si-mba – z*"

"*Simba-zako,*" Kamthibi corrected, "Sir is ok."

"Am not sure *Simba* would be appropriate – always reminds me of the character in that animal movie." Everyone smiled. Kamthibi was calm.

"Are you an American citizen?"

"No, but I am a Permanent Resident."

"Where are you from originally?"

"I belong to the Tumbuka people in Eastern Zambia."

"Did you say Gambia?" Flannery corked his face.

"No," Kamthibi said with obvious irritation, "Z – ambia in Southern Africa."

Flannery whispered in Officer Blake's ear again who stood up and walked out again.

"Now," Flannery paused, looked at the ceiling and then back at Kamthibi, "Can you tell us or explain what happened."

"Well, I was admitted in the hospital probably with a sprained arm. I was at the hospital ward this morning. I had gone to meet a woman I love so much. I got into a taxi and met her near the village or small town of Gandy north of here in the outskirts of the city. Then I was arrested and brought to the police station."

Flannery nodded slowly during the whole explanation. The look of disbelief and scepticism would have made even Jesus Christ give up his evangelising. At that point, Officer Blake walked in with a file and gave it to Detective Flannery.

"Look," Flannery leaned forward, "don't make it hard on yourself and everyone else. Just tell us everything then you can go and get treatment and everyone can go home. Are you Mohammed Akpari from the Gambia?" Flannery flipped through the file rapidly and began to run his forefinger along one page.

"No," Kamthibi replied, "I am not Mohammed. I don't know even anybody of that name and I wouldn't even have friends with such names."

"He was arrested last month at the same hotel you are staying at in town, the Hotel Cardigan. Ten pounds of cocaine powder and six ounces of heroin were found in his bag. The hospital is right now reporting that large amounts of medical narcotics are missing from the ward you were admitted in. They found three bottles of morphine under your hospital bed pillow this morning while you escaped. Were you arranging to deliver anything to the woman in Gandy? Money, drugs, a message?"

"What?" Kamthibi yelled, as he tried to stand up in protest, "I did not steal any drugs and I did not escape from the hospital either. What's going on here? You clearly have the wrong man! I want to contact the Zambian Embassy. Why don't you believe me?" Kamthibi asked a rhetorical question. "So, Detective Flannery, a black man cannot meet a woman he loves deeply on a country side in Ireland, ha!"

Kamthibi was emphatic and Flannery was clearly taken aback. He had expected Kamthibi not to ask for an embassy official or lawyer at this point, but to show a conciliatory tone. After all, the evidence was all around the suspect. This was an open and shut case. This looked like an obvious case of drug trafficking. Kamthibi leaned forward and said slowly.

"I love this woman. Her name is Trish. I met her on the Internet six months ago. I would have done anything to meet her. Nothing you accuse me of or frame me with is going to change that. I am not talking as an intelligent, educated, rational person who has a PhD. This is my heart. Why won't you let me have a heart?"

In the process of leaning forward, Kamthibi must have inadvertently put some weight on the bad arm and pressed a nerve because he felt very sharp pains that suddenly moved from his wrist to his armpit like sparks of lighting. He couldn't breathe as he grimaced holding his breath. Detective Flannery and Bradfield reached for him over the table. It was too late.

Kamthibi had visible sweat on his forehead as he tried to sit back down on the chair. He missed and kicked it over as he slumped to the floor.

"O'Malley, run to the dispatcher and call an ambulance! Quick!" barked Flannery. "Damn it, we don't want another international incident and the Home Office all over us again. And this is all on the bloody videotape! Let's keep him alive! Blake, get a wet towel!" Blake shot out of the room and ran to the bathroom. Shortly, he came back with a cold wet towel and placed it on Kamthibi's forehead.

Detective Flannery and Bradfield knelt down and lifted Kamthibi's head and tried to talk to him. Maybe lying flat pumped blood to his brain again because Kamthibi blinked and looked around mumbling, "Where am I? What's happening? My arm....."

"You will be all right.... the ambulance is on its way," Flannery reassured Kamthibi.

The phone rang and Officer Blake picked it up. He said yes a couple of times into the phone and said room 26 then hung up.

"Sir, that's the ambulance," said Bradfield, "they should be here any minute."

"Bradfield," called Flannery as Kamthibi was being wheeled past the front desk into the ambulance, "I will accompany the suspect to the hospital. It's important I find out how he broke his arm. Check with the FBI in the United States, the Illinois State Police, and the Clarksville Police Department to authenticate his statement. Have officers search his hotel room and luggage. I will talk with the hospital. If anything turns up after he has been treated, we will bring the suspect back to the police station to be charged and locked up." Kamthibi overheard the conversation.

Kamthibi felt like all of that was a long nightmare and he was just waiting for the awful dream to end. He stared at the ceiling of the ambulance as the IV was inserted, and the now familiar jumbled walkie-talkie communication with the police and the hospital emergency filled the air. After all he had been through, Kamthibi dared to think he would see Nurse Agnes at the hospital ward. She had helped to smuggle him through the back door into an alley, and called a taxi so that he could meet the woman of his dreams in time. Why did she help him? She risked her job. At least he could then go and thank her if she was still there. She could have been fired. He had heard Flannery loud and clear. With all the evidence so far, planted or not, he could be in jail in Ireland for a while or even for life. When the wheels of justice begin moving for a black man, they move slowly; or they never start at all. Kamthibi was going to enjoy every breath of his apparent temporary freedom, although he would be lying in bed in a hospital ward.

CHAPTER THREE

Jill and Trish drove slowly back to Gandy. It felt like they were in a funeral procession driving a hearse to the cemetery. The women were both sombre, perhaps in their own thoughts realizing both the gravity and shame of what had just transpired. Trish stared out of the window; suddenly waves of anguish rising through her bosom brought the glaze of tears to her eyes. She leaned her left elbow against the car window and rested her cheek on her palm. One tear droplet quickly slipped at the corner of her eye and disappeared on her blue jeans pants.

"Jill," Trish said in a wistful but emotionally charged tone of voice, "please pull over next to the pharmacy."

"What now mom?" Jill responded, startled out of her own thoughts, "what do you need from the drug store? I thought you just filled your prescription only last week."

"I don't need anything," Trish responded, "I just want to tell you something."

Jill drove into the pharmacy parking lot and parked. She slowly shook her head, turned off the ignition, and slumped her forehead on the steering wheel in obvious exasperation.

"Jill, I am sorry for what happened," she tried to compose herself, wiping her tears.

"You better be sorry, just the humiliation of it all. You are my mother for God's sake."

"Jill, could you listen for a while and let me talk, ok", Trish said suddenly in a defiant tone, "it was wrong for me to let you come along and see what you did. You are my child and it's wrong for me to put you in the middle. But I was too scared. I needed a friend to come along. But I am not apologizing for what happened. This is the first time in my whole forty something years of life and twenty-five years of marriage, that I have truly loved a man and he truly loved me."

"What about Dad?" Jill asked, "Are you going to leave him? You mean you never loved Dad?"

"Jill, oh, what's the use, you can't understand," Trish threw her arms up in desperation, "you will never understand until you are my age. To be locked up in lifeless marriage, two kids, household chores, a husband who is always drunk, gone and has no idea what romance is. And now I have an opportunity to live a full life; even if it's just for two minutes. All you can talk about is am I going to leave dad? Life should never be black and white, either or, to be in love and not to be in love!"

Jill burst out sobbing. Trish held and consoled her.

"I am terribly sorry," Trish said, "am terribly sorry. I am getting angry with the wrong person. I don't want you to be in the middle of this. But since you were a child, you have always been my friend. I don't mean to hurt you. I am really confused and worried right now. Tomorrow I am going to see the doctor about the chest X-rays they took last week. I have had this persistent cough and bronchitis for the last couple of weeks. It's probably nothing. You know I have smoked all my life. My health has always not been very good."

"But of all the men, Mother", Jill said, "you had to kiss that .. that….that blackie!"

"I don't want you ever to refer to that man as blackie!" Trish angrily said wagging her forefinger at her daughter. Trish was in a defensive mode. It's as if Jill had suddenly touched a very sensitive spot. "This is a man who loves me and I love him. He just happens to be black or African or whatever you want to call him. I have chatted with this man for months for thousands of hours, on the phone and on the Internet, sharing our most intimate feelings, thoughts, hopes, and dreams. He is the first man ever to make me feel excited about life."

Jill was clearly stunned about the depth of devotion her mother had for that totally strange man whom she hardly knew. That was a new side of her mother she never saw. Jill had never known that side about her mother. It dawned on her for the first time in her life that her mother was a fighter in her own way.

"Jill, it's no use," Trish said, "I don't expect you to understand this. And I am sorry that I have put you in the middle. You are still my child. I won't tell your Dad because it would devastate him. He would kill me. It would be cruel. He would kill me. Since we got married out of high school twenty-five years ago, I have been like a material possession to him. I am like a house you own; you can paint it, ignore it, come home to it drunk, you wake up and leave. But you never consider its feelings. People treat their pets with more love. After twenty-five years, even a house will begin to leak and break up if you don't give it proper attention…"

"Mother," Jill interrupted, "you are ranting and not making sense. Take me to work. I am already late."

"Wait," Trish said in an eerie whisper as she placed her hand on Jill's arm, "I never told you this. Your father has a dark side. When he is drunk he will sometimes get into a murderous rage. You remember when you were five; I told you your cat had been run over by a car? Your Dad…" Trish paused, "had smashed the poor creature against our living room wall late at night during one of his drunken rages."

"Why are you telling me all this?" Jill gasped in disbelief. There was silence. After dropping Jill off at her work, Trish drove home with a flood of thoughts about the conundrum she was in and the whirlwind that was twirling around her threatening to violently hurl her into a chaotic abyss or even death. She lit a cigarette. Her daughter always forbade Trish to smoke in the car. She couldn't get Kamthibi out of her mind. In her wildest dreams and the steamiest Internet chats, she had never imagined that being held and actually kissed by that man would make her feel this way; warm, tingly inside, weak in the knees, and most of all wet and juicy all over. She now had an even deeper yearning and irresistible desire to submit herself to him; to be with him all the time -maybe even for the rest of her life. But there was also reality to deal with. She hated reality right now.

What would the doctor say about the X-rays the following day? Of course she couldn't tell her husband Richard about Kamthibi. He would go into a murderous rage. He would never give her the type of love Kamthibi gave her. Her husband would never compete successfully against such love even if he wanted or tried to. Too many ugly and deeply painful things had happened between them in their marriage over the last twenty years that killed forever any notions of rekindling any romantic flame between them. She contemplated for a millionth time the possible dreams she could live out with Kamthibi; the dreams Richard always dismissed as by a woman who had depression, because she didn't have enough to do, but had the simple luxury of just watching kids and cooking all day-the exciting dreams she and Kamthibi had chatted about for hours on the Internet. Most devastating for her husband would be the humiliating thought that of all the men, it would be blackie or an African man who got his possession. His girl! His woman! His chattel! If anything Trish was sure that alone, would so demasculate, so overwhelm her husband with so much humiliation and contemptuous jealous, that it would ignite in him that murderous rage she had seen once when he had violently howled the poor sleeping family cat against the living room wall. Trish had spent hours washing the blood off the walls in the middle of the night while overcome with anger and fear. She thought, 'What is it with men possessing women that way as objects anyway? And then white men and all this business of racism?' She had read now and then over the years, with shock, that black men in America were lynched if a white woman merely said as much as the black man had looked at her in a certain way.

Once she got home in the house, Trish all of a sudden felt exhausted. She collapsed on the couch stamping out the cigarette butt on to the ashtray on the coffee table by the couch. She was thinking of getting up and walking into the bedroom and crawling into the already dishevelled bed. But that would be too much trouble. She didn't want to think or worry anymore. She coughed several times and finally drifted into sleep.

It must have been a deep sleep because she was aroused many hours later with the opening of the front door. She heard rapid footsteps like someone in a hurry. She glanced at the living room mantle clock. It was four thirty. It was too early for Richard to be home from his construction job of sixteen years. Sure enough she saw Richard dart between the living room and the kitchen, into the basement of the house. After a few seconds, the steps were rapidly thumping up from the basement.

"Rich," Trish called. Earlier on in their young marriage, they had jokingly agreed she would not call him "Dick" because they did not want to confuse "Dick" the man and the other "Dick" who was always unthinking and demanding. They had laughed and laughed. But it was as prophetic at the time as the separation of the two names would later in their marriage reflect the parallel of how they drew apart the longer they were married. But they both got used to "Rich." Relatives and other people never understood why she never called him "Dick."

"I didn't see you there on the living room couch. I thought you would be asleep in the bedroom," Richard said. He was carrying a bag, "I had forgotten my bowling ball for tonight. If you can't sleep some more take the tranquilliser pill. I have got to run. Will see you later."

"Rich, wait," Trish called as Richard slammed the front door shut, "are you coming to the doctor with me tomorrow?"

Trish became irate. She was tired of being ignored by her husband everyday and always having her feelings trivialized. She stood up in anger and frustration and violently slammed the small pillow on the couch. The pillow bounced off the couch, knocked a lamp and it crashed to the hardwood floor shattering the bulb into pieces. She ran to the front door and opened it violently. Richard's car was just disappearing out of the driveway.

"Rich, you are a real Dick!!!!" she screamed after Richard out of the open door, stomping her foot, "how can you take me so-so-so for bloody granted! You don't say hello! You don't even care that I am scared? I could fall off the cliff tomorrow and your little world wouldn't stop. You are happy for me to chain smoke, feel depressed and pop pills and tranquillisers to fall asleep? You are so-so-so dim? Why do you always trivialize my feelings? You dismiss me as just a woman who has nothing to do? Well, Dick, I am tired of this. I want a life!!!!! I want a life!!!!!" Trish screamed and slammed the door shut.

She ran back into the living room and dropped and buried her face in the couch and sobbed. As she calmed down, Trish was surprised at her anger and rage. She found it amazing how experiencing true passionate love with Kamthibi, even for those few minutes earlier that day, made Richard's treatment of her look so much more starkly cruel and insensitive. How could she have stayed in this marriage for twenty-five years? She cleaned the broken glass on the floor. She walked into the kitchen to make some coffee. She lit another cigarette. She bet that just as he had done virtually everyday for twenty -five years, Richard was going to come back at midnight drunk, staggering, with a slurred speech and reeking of alcohol. He was going to jump on top of her demanding sex. He had often shoved it inside her with his dead weight and the stench of alcohol almost suffocating her. It felt like a hard piece of plywood was violently shoved inside her. She would clench her teeth, hold her breath, shut her eyes tightly, and grimace until the horrible ordeal was over. She would then finally desperately breathe out and shove the dead weight off. She was sure in his drunken state he assumed that all her desperate sounds of pain and discomfort were because he was such a great lover. Then he would sometimes just fall asleep. It was always disgusting and hardly a romantic experience. But they were married and earlier on in their marriage, she felt it was her religious and marital duty to give him sex. But much later it was just to keep the peace. There were times in his drunken state that he would taunt, threaten, and argue with her for hours. It was loud. She was afraid the commotion would wake up the kids who would hear them arguing loudly. Earlier on in their marriage, he would slap her because that did not leave marks on her body. She kept the dirty secrets from relatives. The children certainly knew. But that night she was going to resist him. She didn't care anymore. The kids were grown. She needed to get a life. She coughed persistently as she sipped the coffee and smoked and flipped through the TV channels without pausing to watch anything.

Later that evening, she prepared some salmon with a Caesar salad for dinner. Her daughter came in from work. They had a quiet dinner and engaged in small talk. Both of them knew that things from then would be different. Jill went to bed early because she did not want to be there when her father came back late from bowling. She could not bear the thought of talking and facing her father and not telling him what had happened that morning. But that was also her mother's business, which she had been careless and irresponsible enough to expose her to. That's why she really wanted to move out. But she was concerned about her mother being fragile. Both her parents had not necessarily chased her out of the house. So she stayed.

Later that night, Richard came home. Trish heard the front door click open and shut. She heard the shuffling steps of a drunken person wading and staggering through the living room. The lights had all been turned off except for the small night-light in the kitchen and the bathroom light in their bedroom. Trish was lying under a blanket on the living room couch nervously waiting for the big dangerous battle that was going to ensue. Richard did not see her. He didn't expect her to be lying on the couch. The sickening heavy stench of alcohol hit her as he staggered and shuffled past the living room to their bedroom door. He paused and she could see his long shadow and silhouette from where she was lying on the couch. Any minute he was going to turn around and begin searching for his property, his woman, in the rest of the house. Maybe he would even wake up his daughter to ask her. Trish held her breath. Something unexpected happened. She heard the bedroom door slam shut, the shuffling of feet, and loud thump on the bed and the fading squeaking of the mattress springs. She waited for what seemed like an eternity. There was no movement in the bedroom.

After a while, she gingerly stood up and tiptoed to their bedroom door. She put her ear to it. She heard light snoring. She slowly turned the knob and cracked the door. The snoring was deep and loud. Richard was comatose, drunk, and asleep. The dishevelled covers on the bed in the half darkness may have looked like his woman ready for him like she always had to be. He must have thought he was easing himself on top of her for another one of those after heavy-drinking-and-bowling-romantic escapades when he slumped on the bed covers. Maybe the bathroom light made him think she was using the bathroom and would be back in bed any minute. He must have been too drunk to stay awake let alone do anything as physical as having rough sex or raping her for that matter. 'A bullet in his head right now could end my torture', the thought crossed her mind for just a split second as she stood there. Trish slowly tiptoed backwards and carefully shut the door.

"Mother," Trish gasped and jumped out of her skin placing her hand on her bosom. It was Jill. The sudden whisper behind her had scared Trish. Her daughter must have heard the entire goings on.

"Shhhhhhh!!!!" Trish placed her forefinger on her lips, "Richard is asleep. Why aren't you in bed?" Trish asked her daughter like she was a five-year- old.

"He is drunk isn't he? I am worried about you mother." Jill whispered.

"It's late, go to bed", whispered Trish as she put her arm around her daughter, "we will talk tomorrow."

Trish slept on the couch that night. Before she fell asleep, the split moment thought of putting a bullet in her abusive husband's head scared her. It was so unusual for her to ever think like that even for a split second. That thought had never entered her mind before. She also remembered a woman in America who poured gasoline on her drunken sleeping husband

and lit the bed. He had abused her for years. Trish knew this was the time to leave the marriage. But how was she going to do it?

The following morning, Trish felt triumphant enough to face the day. She had slipped into the bathroom to take a shower and Richard was still in his clothes on top of the bed. Trish had always undressed him in the past. Richard had no clue or could not remember what had happened the previous night whenever he was asked the following morning.

"Richard, can you come to the doctor at noon today?" asked Trish as Richard was about to walk out of the door, "I need someone to be there."

"Here we go again," replied Richard in a tone that signalled that they had gone over this thousands of times before; the sign of a long troubled marriage, "you know how my boss and the boys are at work. Why be there when your woman has womanly problems with her doctor? Besides, I would have to come home, remove my overall, take a bath or at least dress up. Then for one minute the doctor will say your X-rays are ok. What's the big deal? Women always like to make a big deal of everything. Your timing is always wrong. You have seen too many Soap Operas and Hollywood movies."

"No, Rich, this is not a Hollywood movie", retorted Trish, "this is life. Besides, the doctor called yesterday and said I should go with someone," she lied. She wanted someone to be with her. She was anxious and scared. She had not been feeling well lately. She couldn't possibly ask her daughter again to accompany her. She had always been nervous about doctors since she was in high school.

She and Richard were high school seniors. They both felt like outcasts. It seemed like everyone else was paired and were trying sex. She and Richard were hanging out innocently, frequently smoking and doing some drinking in the car. They both felt left behind and needed to catch up with experimenting. One night in the back seat of the car, one thing led to another and she and Richard had sex. She felt after that less than great experience that sex was tremendously overrated. But at least she had finally lost her virginity. She felt mature. She missed her period for three weeks and was worried sick and told her mother. Although she saw Richard, she refused to have sex with him again. But that was too late because it was like closing the barn door when the horses have fled.

Trish went to a doctor by herself to have a pregnancy test. She didn't think she was pregnant. She waited in the doctor's room for the results. Finally, the doctor called her.

"The test is positive. You are three weeks pregnant."

The words were like a sharp spear piercing her chest. Her world had changed instantly. Her freedom, a chance to go to college or just to even dream about it, her childhood, and her teenage innocence were all instantly thrown out of the window. She remembered the melancholy song of the legendary Irish singer Melvin Evans playing. She remembered the time and date as twenty-sixth April 1976 at 2:15 pm; only three months from graduation from high school. Her life had changed forever. She had felt so alone. Her mother and her boyfriend were not even there. Since that day, she had grown weary of going to the doctor alone to receive test results. But it looked like that morning, and that day, it was going to happen again. She dreaded and hated being alone. But probably there was nothing to worry about. In her more than thirty years of smoking, she had had many X-rays because of coming down with constant serious bouts of bronchitis. But all of them had always come back negative.

Trish walked into the office of the only family doctor in the village with apprehension and nervousness. The building, the sights, the smells were familiar. She had been there since she was little. She remembered coming in for immunizations and their mother would buy her candy afterwards to make the pain go away. She remembered the fevers, thermometers, some of the dreaded injections before oral antibiotics became more common. Although the doctor was a warm familiar figure, he now had grey hair and moved a little slower. Most young doctors went to larger cities such as Belfast and Dublin for more lucrative careers. He still had the charm of the country village doctor who had known his patients since they were newly born babies. He knew for example, that Trish's father had died at the age of forty when Trish was fourteen years old. He knew that Trish and her husband did not particularly have a warm and close marriage. So he was not surprised when Trish came alone to be told the results of the X-ray.

As soon as Trish walked into the waiting room, which had five people seated, the ageing doctor approached her and warmly put his arm around her and led her to his office. Trish heard him say, "I wish I could have told you over the phone but the news is not good. You have two white dots on your left lung. We don't know that it's cancerous yet. We will have a biopsy done and sent to Belfast Hospital lab." Trish felt as though the doctor was talking to someone else and not her. The doctor said he was sorry and had called her mother. She should have been there any minute. "You need to have someone with you."

Her mother walked in with haste and somewhat out of breath. Trish was in tears. The doctor had already told Trish's mother the bad news on the phone and she had rushed over immediately. They embraced and cried. The doctor left the room. Mother and daughter held each other for a long time and wiped each other's tears.

"Oh!! My baby." Trish's mother cried over and over again with anguish as she held her daughter tightly, as if her daughter would suddenly disappear and be gone the very next second if she let her go.

CHAPTER FOUR

Kamthibi was rushed into the emergency room in severe pain and barely conscious. The emergency medical personnel gave him a tranquilliser and the doctor looked at his X-rays again. The doctor determined that Kamthibi had a hairline fracture on one of the bones, but the pain was from a severe contusion and sprain of the fibula ligaments that connect the hand to the wrist. The doctor thought that Kamthibi had incredible pain tolerance. He had never seen anything like that in his several years of experience in the emergency room in the City of Belfast main hospital. Contrary to what he had thought earlier, Kamthibi would not need surgery. Instead, his severely sprained wrist with a slight dislocation of the hand and stretching of the ligaments would have to be reset and put in a soft cast. Kamthibi was given some extra sedative to his arm and the medical team went to work. He could see the blinking small lights, could hear the constant beeps of monitors attached to numerous mesh of wires on his chest, and several Ivs connected to his arms. He could feel the pressure on it as the doctors and nurses worked on his arm but didn't feel any pain. He was like in a half dream. The people around reminded him of what negatives looked like when he first developed black and white film as a member of the photographic club in high school more than twenty years earlier. Kamthibi suddenly felt tired and drifted into that comfortable sleep that is induced by drugs. He felt like waves of soft water drifting through a waterbed, and he was forever floating gently on the soft, comfortably warm water. He suddenly felt carefree and very comfortable. Is this how a near-death experience felt or maybe that is what drug junkies experienced?

When Kamthibi next opened his eyes and blinked, he saw all fuzzy white around him. He could hear sounds and voices. A fuzzy white figure was standing above him. He blinked several times and tried to shake his head. This was neither a dream nor a near-death experience. There were the familiar sounds of the hospital ward; the characteristic smells of hospital medicines. Kamthibi remembered those smells when his father took him to the local clinic for malaria fever as a child in rural Zambia in Africa. They made him swallow a tablespoon of quinine. He didn't know it at the time. It is the bitterest substance known. No wonder Kamthibi could taste it in his mouth twelve hours later. He had survived so many such medications. There was a time as a boy when he endured twelve injections in twenty-four days for the tropical disease bilharzias or schistosomiasis.

Kamthibi's eyes twinkled a bit and his heart jumped with joy when he saw the figure above him was Nurse Agnes. He didn't know how to thank her for what she had done, risking and putting her job on the line.

"Thank You," Kamthibi barely mouthed and half whispered with his dry lips. He wanted to mouth out more words but Nurse Agnes had a plastic smile and looked anxious and afraid. She nervously looked around the small ward enclosure. She quickly put her forefinger to her lips gesturing Kamthibi not to say anything. She warmly brushed her hand on Kamthibi's forehead as he briefly closed his eyes.

"It was my pleasure," Nurse Agnes finally said sensing that Kamthibi might have many unanswered questions, "listen, you don't have much time," she whispered as she nervously looked around the small enclosure and peered out making sure no one was nearby.

"Why?" Kamthibi whispered.

"At first I wanted to do something for another desperate human being. I could tell once you began to talk the glow and the anguish that I could see in your soul about this lover. What's her name? Starts with a T -."

"Trish," Kamthibi whispered.

"Yes, Trish. You are in danger," Nurse Agnes hissed, giving him as much information quickly before someone came, "I overheard some bits of talk among the doctors and nurses. Richard…"

"But that's Trish's husband," Kamthibi interjected placing his hand on Nurse Agnes' hand.

"Yes," Nurse Agnes whispered. She hastily continued "he hired some men to put an overdose of the colourless rape drug into your beer at the hotel lounge. Your passing out, falling and spraining your arm saved your life because you didn't finish your glass of beer. And you were taken to the hospital."

"Yes, I remember the two men at the bar," Kamthibi said, with his eyes popping out and a puzzled look on his face.

"Richard is Dr. Butler's son," Nurse Agnes whispered, "Listen, the doctor will be here soon to make the rounds. Someone was trying to kill you and now they are framing you with all these drugs. They are out to get you. If a man ever loved me the way you love her, I would want someone to help me meet that special lover. I know you did meet her because it was all over the local news. Besides the town rumour mill has been wild. I knew sneaking you out of the hospital was unprofessional. But I had no idea it would turn out to be a criminal offence to meet your lover. I could tell from the way you are that you are a very sincere man. I admire you. I wish my husband were like that. I know you don't sell drugs. Detective Flannery was here. I pray you have some good news. Dr Butler is coming. Remember you are in danger."

"They will amputate my arm so that I will bleed to death?" Kamthibi whispered trying to cut the tension.

"No, no, Kamthibi," Nurse Agnes said with a nervous smile, "I hope it's not that kind of news. I trust Dr. Butler. It looks like he may not be involved in this whole thing."

Dr. Butler walked into the small curtain enclosure. He said good morning in a cheerful manner. He was short with a slight bald spot near the top front of his head. He was well groomed with short trimmed dark hair. He grabbed the clipboard at the foot of Kamthibi's bed and began to mutter to himself.

"So you are from Zambia and not Gambia", he said looking at Kamthibi, "you are in good shape. You were here for such a short time the other day I forgot to tell you that I was born in Zaire where my father was a missionary doctor. But I came back to Ireland when I was still too young. I wish I had stayed longer. I just remember playing with some of the African kids there. They once begged me to steal some sugar from my house. I got into trouble with my parents for that." Dr Butler stared at the clipboard again. He seemed to be checking a list. He signed it.

"K-a-m thibi," he said slowly trying to enunciate the vowels and consonants, "that's a difficult name for an Irishman. The Chief of Police talked to me on the phone and Detective Flannery was here while you were still asleep. They couldn't find any evidence against you. If I were you, I would be careful because someone planted some bottles of morphine under your hospital pillow. The police are still investigating. There are no charges made at this time. You are free to go as soon as you can walk. The cast can be removed once you get back to the United States, London, or any hospital in Africa. If I were you, I would leave the country immediately. Good luck." Dr Butler shook Kamthibi's hand, tapped him on the shoulder several times and left.

Nurse Agnes had a big smile of triumph and pride on her face as she stood next to Kamthibi's bed with her hands crossed. Kamthibi smiled a smile of relief as the two looked at each other as though they were two siblings who had just fooled their parents. Nurse Agnes' walkie-talkie asked for her to report at the nurses' station desk. Kamthibi felt nervous immediately. Whoever was framing him could be back to finish him off. Why would anyone want to kill him? Who could it be? Was he merely at the wrong place at the wrong time? Kamthibi wanted to leave. But where would he go? Ireland was surrounded by water.

Something important had been troubling Kamthibi since he had opened his eyes. His dearest teenage friend since college must have received the tragic letter in Manchester by now. Kamthibi had written the letter in the United States, mailed it at Heathrow International airport arrival lounge en route to his connecting flight to Belfast. Nurse Agnes was hastily walking out of the curtain enclosure.

"Nurse Agnes!" Kamthibi called.

"Please call me Agnes," smiled Nurse Agnes.

"Would you do me an important favour? Would you please telephone my best friend in Manchester?" Kamthibi said, "His name is James Lutula. His cell phone number is 390-430-5860. Tell him I am alive but in the hospital. Could he tell everyone, the Zambian Embassy in London, friends, relatives-anyone, that I am here and alive. Please do this immediately."

A short moment later, a shadow appeared on the curtain enclosure. It paused.

"Agnes," Kamthibi called nervously fearing the worst. This was the assailant coming to finish him off? Kamthibi thought. "Who is there? What did James say?"

The figure that walked in blew his mind. It was Trish. She was wearing a brown dress with yellowish stripes; black high heels with smooth nylon socks. Her round golden earrings gently dangled from her ear lobes as she turned her head to look around the curtain enclosure that was his hospital ward. Her matching golden thin necklace around her smooth long neck immediately brought memories of their first encounter on the roadside near Gandy. The two red roses in her left hand matched the crimson on her lipstick.

Trish stood there forever like a shy school girl holding the flowers in one hand and her black handbag in the other. She thought that Kamthibi's dark skin contrasted so beautifully with the white hospital sheets and walls. He glowed. His eyes and soul feasted, looking at Trish the way they had never feasted before. He stretched out his hand. She came to the edge of the bed and sat next to him placing the flowers on top of the covers and the handbag on the floor. He drew her to him as she leaned down to kiss him. Neither of them could believe the deep warm feelings that enveloped them.

"Sorry to disturb," Nurse Agnes said. Trish stood up quickly; acting like a kid whose hand had been caught in a cookie jar. Trish remembered that she and the nurse had crossed paths on the ward hallway, "Dr. Simbazako, your friend James is shocked and stunned. He thinks you are dead. I tried to explain. But he didn't believe me. You better call him immediately…"

"Oh, by the way," Nurse Agnes said turning to Trish, "I am Nurse Agnes. I take it you are Trish. You are a very lucky woman. This man is willing to die for you. He loves you so much." Agnes shook hands with Trish and excused herself.

"Kamthibi, who is that woman? Agnes or whatever? I know she is a nurse." Trish asked Kamthibi anxiously, "I don't like her. She is acting too familiar with you."

"You are right to feel a little jealous Trish," Kamthibi stretched out his hand again and beckoned to Trish to sit on the bed, "she is our guardian angel. She is on our side." Kamthibi pulled Trish to whisper in her ear, "she just told me a man poisoned my beer at the bar. The same person tried to frame me here in the hospital by hiding morphine bottles under my pillow. I am a marked man."

"What?" Trish whispered in disbelief.

"She said Richard might be behind all this."

"Oh, my God!" she said placing her hand on her bosom, "my husband, Richard?"

"Yes," Kamthibi nodded.

"I can't believe it. How did he find out about us?"

"Nurse Agnes is the woman who sneaked me out of the hospital to come and meet you in Gandy," Kamthibi explained, "She said she just saw me in distress wanting and determined to see you. She said I acted as though if I didn't meet you I would die. She said my heart, my eyes, my very breath, and my whole being said that. She said she had to help. She felt like if she didn't help she would feel like the person who failed to save someone out of a burning inferno when they had the opportunity to. But she thinks I am in danger."

Trish warmly caressed Kamthibi's black hand in both her small white hands. She could feel the throb in their hands like kindling charcoal that's about to burst into a glow of red-hot ambers.

"Why does your friend, James, think you are dead?" Trish asked as she leaned down and stole a quick kiss from Kamthibi, "what did you tell him?"

Kamthibi stared at the white hospital ceiling with flowery designs on it. Should he tell her or not? The anguish showed on his face. He knew he might never see her again. He was leaving Ireland immediately maybe never to come back. He really had nothing to lose. He would tell her everything for whatever it was worth.

"Trish, this is going to sound crazy," Kamthibi looked at Trish as he held her tender hand, "my love for you is so deep, I was willing to die to see you. I have never felt like this about any woman in my whole forty-something years. When I was planning the trip to come and meet you, I knew I could die." Kamthibi swallowed as tears welled in his eyes.

"Oh, Kamthibi" Trish softly cooed as she kissed him lightly on the forehead, "I'm not worth dying for. I have only a twelfth grade education. I am just an ordinary woman from a small village. I am not even a famous star."

"That hurts, Trish," Kamthibi responded, "my heart was searching for a special star all my life. It's found it and it's you. All I want is you. You ignite something deep in my heart. My heart sings when I talk to you or when I chat to you on the net. I was a black man coming to an unknown European city, small rural white village, to meet a white rural woman in a small village, and all of this for not just ordinary love, but for the very special and deep love I have for you, dear."

"Why do you keep harping on "white" this and European this", Trish commented, "You know I don't see you as black. All I see is your loving soul; lovely human being who deeply cares for me."

"That's just you, Trish and perhaps five other whites," Kamthibi said, "but you and I know that racism is still strong. People are hateful, hostile, and the neo-nazi will kill someone just because they are black or belong to the wrong race. Well, I don't want to dwell on this race thing; we have been over it so many times on the chat. But to cut a long story short, I mailed a letter to my friend in Manchester on my way here, telling him what to do if I died here."

"What? You mean sort of like a suicide note?" Trish asked incredulously.

Kamthibi looked at Trish for a while.

"It wasn't exactly that. But I can see how someone reading it might think so. But I was not going to kill myself. Do you understand, Trish? I have always worried about dying or disappearing where my parents, wife, and children did not know what happened. I just wanted everyone who was close to know if it became necessary."

Trish looked confused. She was in her own deep thought. She anguished and agonized whether to tell Kamthibi she was diagnosed with lung cancer or not. Maybe she should take a couple of hours, maybe even a day, to rethink. She had not intended to tell him. But something about Kamthibi's sincerity changed that. She didn't want to be the one to be the hypocrite. But she was still hesitating.

"I have to go", Trish said as she suddenly stood up wiping her tears with a Kleenex.

"Is it because you think I am suicidal?" Kamthibi asked in exasperation, "You can read the letter for yourself. Hand me my right shoe."

Trish grabbed Kamthibi's shoe. He reached inside the shoe for a sock. He turned the sock inside out and pulled out the folded and smudged yellow notepaper from a small sandwich plastic bag. Trish unfolded it slowly. Some of the ink had run but everything was still readable. That was the original Kamthibi had photocopied. He had sent a copy to his friend, James, in Manchester and he had left another copy in his office desk drawer back in America. Someone investigating his disappearance or death would probably have looked in his desk drawers first at work for any clues. The letter read:

Dear Trish,

This is to you in the event that I die on my pending trip to Britain, which is actually to visit you, my sweetheart, in Ireland. I have ceased to try to understand what is happening to me and especially my heart since I met you. My love for you is so deep and my tenderness of feeling so profound toward you that I have a deep yearning to submit to you. I never understood deep love for a woman through more than forty years on this earth until I met you. When I chat with you my heart sings. My heart sings when I think of you. My heart sings when I think of holding you tenderly in my arms and whisper to you sweet nothings. I want us to eat a delicious dinner by candlelight at the hotel-dining lounge. I want us to dance the night away and to smile and laugh at nothing and the same things.

I will meet you in the green meadows brightened by the blue sky in Gandy village in Ireland. Maybe enjoy a white snowy Christmas. But I want to hold hands with you and walk with you under the moonlight and bright stars of savannah Africa. I want you to hear the lone cry of the blue tiny titi *bird and see the bright coloured* mpheta *bird building nests in tall green elephant grass during it's mating rainy season. I want us to eat the sweet delicious mango fruits and the explosion of food delicacies that my mother cooks so well at Simbazako village. I have the indescribable bottled yearnings to enjoy the fruits of life with you. I have been waiting for you for more than forty years.*

I love you so much that I am willing to risk death and endure serious bodily harm just to see and be with you. I know I am going to a strange place, to meet a married woman whose husband drinks heavily and may be murderous, and deadly racism and hate are still a given among most of your people. But if I am too afraid to die, what is life without meeting you? We both realize we have never been truly and deeply in love before. We are emotional virgins. We all get married due to being young, or out of social desperation and loneliness. Sometimes people get married for money or material wealth or status. There is nothing wrong with all these reasons. If we were all interested in really marrying someone we truly and deeply loved, we would not get married until we were forty years old. Our existing for so long, having several children in loveless marriages, is akin to being in a cage or a bird that tries to fly off the back porch but.... one wonders. This poem in dedicated to you my love, Trish.

My Beautiful Bird

My beautiful bird
Has bright coloured plumes
Flaps barely a few feet
Off life's back porch
But it will not fly

It has a sweet melodious song
That I awake to early every morning
Come Summer, Fall, Winter, Spring
But my beautiful bird won't fly

Fly my beautiful bird, fly
I am afraid my beautiful bird
If it flies, will it come back?
Will I hear the sweet song again?
Early in the dawn of the day?

Sadness engulfs me
Fear churns the belly
For my beautiful bird
It may never know
The exhilarating thrill
Of flying out of life's back porch

To soar above the pine trees
High above the beautiful mountains
Of many Springs' sunny blue skies
And bright flowers of a thousand colours
Summer's rich green foliage
Fall's spectacular bright colours
Winter's bittersweet crisp air

Sadness engulfs the heart
Fly my beautiful bird
Fly
Fear churns the belly
Fly my beautiful bird
Fly

My love for you is eternal. If ever there is a heaven after death, our souls and spirit will for sure meet and commune in eternal happiness and jubilation.
Yours truly,
K.

"Oh, Kamthibi this is such a sweet letter. Can I keep it?"

"Of course," replied Kamthibi, "after all, I don't need it any longer. My life is a mess. I might be killed before I reach the airport. My marriage is gone since my wife already knows about you by now through James. My future without you is worthless. I feel numb inside. I don't know if I should even leave this hospital bed. But I suddenly feel so good to see you. I have a flight booked for London tomorrow. I might go home to Zambia to my village. I need to touch base with my roots. I need to renew my soul."

"Don't be hard on yourself, Kamthibi," Trish said, "You have always been an optimistic person. I was going to go now but I don't think it would be fair if I didn't tell you this."

"What? That you are going to dump me and go back to your husband after all, ha?" said Kamthibi sarcastically.

"No, it's not that," Trish paused for a while. Kamthibi was dying with suspense, "I have been diagnosed with lung cancer," she said looking squarely in Kamthibi's eyes, "I might die soon," she added for effect.

"You're joking, right?" Kamthibi replied with incredulity, "You are pulling my leg."

"Surely Kamthibi, why would I joke about such a serious thing?" Trish was clearly irritated.

Kamthibi noticed that she was serious. This was not a joke. He stared at the Irish painting of a farm in a picture frame on the wall. He looked at the hospital monitors beeping and flashing, and the brown cushions on the love seat and the lone empty chair. He sat up in bed and they both instinctively held each other for a long time as they both wept. They didn't know what to say. Something had died in their relationship. Words could not express what both felt. Despair, desperation, hurt, disappointment. Why me? Why her? There was emotional turmoil for both of them. It was worse for Kamthibi since Trish had already lived with this reality for a couple of days. But Kamthibi had just heard it. It was still so painful to think that life was going to be over for her soon. Kamthibi kept repeating that he was so sorry several times. He felt sudden desire to protect her. She felt a sudden desire to be with him. But both could not say what they felt. Something held them back. It's as if they intuitively realized they had reached an inescapable end.

"Smoking did it," Trish finally blurted, "you remember I told you I smoked now and then? Actually, I smoke at least a pack a day and I have been doing this since I was fourteen years old."

"Don't beat up yourself over something that happened in the past," Kamthibi tried to console Trish. He just did not know what else to say.

"Kamthibi," Trish finally said, "I have got to go before my mother freaks out since I am staying with her."

She briefly kissed him and quickly disappeared behind the curtain enclosure as if she wanted to escape the pain and devastating finality of parting with someone you deeply love but realize you will never see, or be with them again.

"Trish, wait!" called Kamthibi half-heartedly, "there is something I want to ask you."

It was as well she left when she did because Kamthibi needed to think. He stared on the bed blankly. Then he noticed it. He picked up the crimson rose she had left on his bed. Slowly, so slowly, Kamthibi put it to his nose and for the last time inhaled the sweet smell of the rose that was from her heart.

CHAPTER FIVE

Five years to the day he met Trish at the Five Large Rocks outside Gandy, something happened in Kamthibi's life that was to profoundly change his life forever, for better or for worse. Who could tell at the time?

When Kamthibi and his wife Nora Nkhata, and their three children emigrated from Zambia, they reacted typically like all new immigrants who had gone to the US during the last two hundred years. They were very euphoric and felt very optimistic about their new and fresh opportunities in the United States. They worked hard for long hours. They bought a new house in a good middle class neighbourhood in the small town of Clarksville in the middle of Illinois. Although they were the only blacks in the small neighbourhood, they did not mind and all the white neighbours welcomed them. Kamthibi and Nora hoped to educate their children; one girl and two boys, all the way to college. After all the serious economic problems of high inflation, low pay, poor medical facilities, and schools they had escaped from in their home country of Zambia, both were thrilled to get out of the country when Kamthibi got a job in Clarksville.

But what they forgot as time passed, was to take care of their marriage, too. They needed to pace their working schedule such that they would spend time together to talk, laugh, catch up on news from home, and eat meals together with their children. They should have nourished their marriage just as every couple does.

Since in Zambia they were able to still afford house servants and nannies on their middle class income, Kamthibi needed to help Nora more with the children. But he did not. But they assumed that since they were both African and Zambian and raised in the Tumbuka culture, their marriage would last forever. Nothing could shake it, especially in a small predominantly white town in the middle of rural Illinois three hours from Chicago.

Nora worked part time at the Clarksville Retirement Community. She could not get a decent full time job although she had a degree in Nursing, earned at the University Teaching Hospital in Lusaka. She needed re-certification. Even if a job had been available, the kids were still too small. Nora had to stay at home most of the day. She worked night shifts a few days per week. Kamthibi would then be home with the kids at night.

As the novelty and excitement of the new environment wore out, the gruelling daily routine began to get first to Nora and then later to Kamthibi. They were socially isolated as there were no Zambians and let alone Africans anywhere near Clarksville. Nora resented that she was isolated and alone all day long. She cooked, changed diapers, did laundry, and took care of the kids. Kamthibi just came home in the evening to eat and sleep. What got to her was that he always expected sex but was hardly loving or romantic about it. He would not even hold a conversation with her. When the "headaches" and "I am tireds" got to be too many, Kamthibi also grew angry, resentful, and withdrew into himself and communication ceased. After all, Kamthibi also felt he was putting in sometimes ten to twelve hours of work per day. Often he went to the office on weekends. He wished he didn't go in on weekends but Nora was increasingly nagging him to do laundry and when he did it she would tell him he was doing it all wrong. The normally otherwise happy-go-lucky, jovial, playful couple became mechanical and tense; each performing their chores with minimal talk.

Things got personally better for Kamthibi, but a turn for the worse for the marriage, when he had to work in the Chicago office for six months for his employers Mid-West Seed International. One of the key research specialists in that office had to go on an extended leave of absence to get treatment for melanoma. Kamthibi commuted most days and sometimes he spent nights in Chicago because he had too much work.

A few times, the temporary position in Chicago required him to travel to China, Hong Kong, Brazil, and Ethiopia. He stopped talking about his adventures on these trips because he could sense Nora's wall of resentment whenever he described his journeys. So if he ever talked about his job to Nora, he down played anything he enjoyed especially on the trips. Kamthibi at this point began to fantasize about a lover who would travel with him to visit these fascinating places. But he knew he could never act on the fantasies because of his marriage, the children, his extended family in the village that he supported, and worst of all, he didn't have the financial clout to support such lavish romantic escapades with a lover. So these just remained fantasies. He had many temptations but never once thought of acting on them.

One day, the Chicago office sent Kamthibi on another mission to Brazil to collect seed samples and technical information. He flew to Rio de Janeiro on a Tuesday. The following day, the Brazilian counterpart of the Mid-West Seed International drove with Kamthibi two hundred miles to Masenao, a muddy frontier town on the edge of the Amazon basin. The company officials had collected only half of the valuable seed samples and had an incomplete inventory of the technical information. There had been a miscommunication between the company officials in Rio de Janeiro and the field company office in remote Masenao. This was not unusual in Third World countries. Kamthibi was hardly surprised nor annoyed since he remembered the frustrating working conditions he had endured working in Zambia.

When Kamthibi returned to his hotel in Rio, he called his bosses in Chicago. He told them it would take another two weeks for the company to complete the inventory of the seed samples and information. Kamthibi was told to return to Chicago on the next flight. Chicago was contemplating terminating the contract or not renewing it since this was the third time they had trouble with the Brazilian company.

Kamthibi flew to Chicago's O'Hare Airport a day earlier at ten that Friday night instead of Saturday night. Before he drove out of the airport, he tried calling Nora several times but the phone was busy. Sometimes the kids knocked the phone off the hook and it took a while to discover it. Kamthibi jumped in the car with less than a half tank of gas and drove home. He was too lazy to fill up. He would gas up the car the following morning at home after a good night's sleep. He could even take the kids for a rare ice cream so that Nora could take a break.

After the long tiring drive and exiting off the expressway, he was relieved finally to turn right into 1202 Oakridge St. driveway, a three-bedroom bungalow. At first, he was surprised there was no car in the driveway. He double-glanced at his watch and it was just after midnight. 'Where would Nora have gone with three kids so late at night?' was his first thought. The front door was locked. He was reaching for his house keys in his pockets when the door opened and it was the fourteen-year-old baby sitter. She was rubbing her eyes having fallen asleep on the couch watching TV.

"Where is my wife?"

"She had gone to work. But she called a while ago that she would be late," the baby sitter replied.

"Where was she calling from? Did she tell you?"

"It sounded noisy in the background. She could have been at a gas station, I don't know."

"I will drive you home."

Kamthibi drove the baby sitter home. Many thoughts went through his mind as he drove slowly to the baby sitter's house. The baby sitter sensed that the situation was not good as the normally talkative Kamthibi was quiet. In his mind, he wondered what else his wife did when he was gone all those nights. Whatever happened, Kamthibi was very appreciative of Nora; she always deeply cared for the kids. She would never leave them alone. In fact, Kamthibi had wanted to stop having children for a while after their first-born daughter, Pyera. But she persuaded him to have another one and that was why there was a big gap between the first born who was ten and the next son who was four years old. The youngest one was two years old. Maybe Nora was motivated to have more children because she had a strong mothering instinct or was it because of being brought up in a traditional African family? He had only heard about her while she was attending St. Monica's Girls, Secondary School. Kamthibi was at Chizongwe Secondary School at the time. But he had later met her in Lusaka at a party.

When Kamthibi got back, he noticed that Nora's blue aged Oldsmobile Cutlass was parked in an oblique manner-like someone who had been in a hurry to get inside the house. Before he stepped out of the car to go into the house, he noticed their bedroom light go off.

Kamthibi was beginning to get a little upset. He had been brought up in a traditional African society in which when a husband returns from a long trip, the least the wife should do is greet and welcome her husband and give him some food before she went to bed. Nora lately seemed to have thrown by the side all these good and wholesome customs. After all, she now argued, Kamthibi could microwave himself something if he was hungry, and taken a shower on his own if he wanted to. As a wife, she didn't have to boil some hot water for him to have a bath, as women would do in the village in Zambia. After all, she was so tired after a long day alone with the kids. Nora was becoming more and more belligerent by the day. 'This marriage is going to the sewer,' Kamthibi thought as he slammed the car door to get into the house.

Once in the bedroom, Kamthibi clicked the bedroom light back on. Nora was obviously pretending to be fast asleep. That on its own was not unusual. But her clothes were scattered on the bedroom floor next to the bed. That was unusual as she always carefully hung her clothes. That was clearly someone who had been in a hurry to change into her pyjamas to jump into bed quickly. Worst of all, he could smell some cigarette smoke on her clothes. She must have been out somewhere.

Kamthibi walked into the two boys' bedroom. They were both asleep. He kissed them on the forehead and left the door cracked. He opened his ten-year-old daughter's bedroom door. She was also asleep. But he couldn't kiss her on the forehead. The custom from his traditional African Tumbuka tribe upbringing prohibited fathers or older males for that matter, from walking into their daughter's bedroom. Would he ever enter a girl's *nthanganeni* hut in the village? Never. Why should he do it because he is in America, to imitate Western culture? Should he do it because he was in America where fathers entered the bedrooms and hugged and sometimes horse played with their eleven, fourteen, and even sixteen-year-old daughters? After all, his daughter was already quite a young lady. Kamthibi shut his daughter's bedroom door.

'There was no sense in starting a loud argument this late,' Kamthibi thought. Their marriage had been on hiatus for so long. It didn't matter if he found out what Nora had been up to the following morning. He decided to get a beer from the fridge, go into the basement, listen to some romantic music, and unwind. He had had a long day. But there was no beer to be had in the fridge.

Since his car was practically on empty from the long drive, he decided to use his wife's. He drove to the twenty-four hour convenience store. He bought a six-pack of beers. As he was about to walk out, he saw a large, bright red, plump, and juicy looking hot dog slowly rotating on a metal skillet in the hot cabinet display warmer. Kamthibi was very hungry. He bought the hot dog that protruded on top as if defying the small split bun. He squeezed lots of ketchup on it just the way he used to like it on those late nights of drinking in graduate school. Kamthibi plunged into it, taking a huge bite as he plopped into the driver's seat tossing the six-pack on the passenger seat. A large thick drop of ketchup escaped from his mouth and dropped on the pants on his thigh. He groaned looking desperately for a paper napkin or anything to wipe it off. Nora always put some in the glove compartment to clean the kid's messes. That's when it happened.

Kamthibi clicked the glove compartment open. Something pink dropped to the floor. He picked it up to examine it and a small square-shaped plastic packet fell out. Then it hit him like a brick to his head; this was a woman's underwear with an unused condom wrapped in it. His mind raced, posing a million questions and giving only the one most alarming answer. His mind assumed the worst. His wife of more than sixteen years and three kids was having sex with some other man maybe in the car! Did his sudden return from his business trip cause a panic and interrupted something; maybe just that night? Who was the hunk, the imbecile? He drove with his anger building up as he bashed the steering wheel and swore a couple of times.

Kamthibi marched into the bedroom, clicked the light on, and shut the door. He tore off the covers from the sleeping Nora, and grabbed her arm between the elbow and the shoulder and lifted her up.

"What the heck is this?!" Kamthibi yelled angrily shaking the pink underwear and the condom packet in Nora's face; his eyes bulging out. "Ha! Answer me!"

Nora crossed and locked her arms in front of her chest with fists under her chin and turned ashen-pale. Kamthibi's eyes were dangerously barged out and his neck veins were taut. Nora was speechless, stunned, and shaking. She was in danger of a severe beating or even death. She had never seen her husband look this angry and scary before.

"What were these doing in the car?" he screamed again shaking her and staring barely inches from her face. He slapped her hard. Nora slid off the bed more out of shock than the force of the slap. Kamthibi was shocked at his loss of control. He had never hit his wife before. He stood up in panic to get out of the bedroom. But Nora thought he was coming around the bed to hit her again.

"L – o – o - k," Nora stammered crying with gashes of hot tears on her cheeks. She crouched on the floor searching for anything to say, "I…can…I can …explain." Words choked her throat. She buried her face in her hands and sobbed, "Stop!! Please Kamthibi, the father of my children," she pleaded, "You are going to kill me!"

Kamthibi sat back down on the edge of the bed with elbows resting on his thighs and head bowed down between his hands like a defeated hero. Tears of anger, shock, and deep disappointment welled in his eyes. It sank into his heart that after all those long years of marriage, his wife was having an affair; something that he had never expected from her. In his worst nightmares, he had never expected it would happen that way.

"I am sorry, I saw no way out…. and…." Nora said between sobs.

"Out of what?" Kamthibi yelled, angrily turning around and pointing his forefinger and lunging at Nora, "how could you do this!"

Nora cringed on the floor, crawled on the far side of the bed and dashed for the bathroom. She slammed it shut and locked it. She moaned, wept, and cried. Kamthibi angrily banged on the door loudly with his fist yelling for Nora to open the door. He heard the kids crying in between the pauses in the loud banging. He opened the bedroom door and what he saw across the hall in the kid's bedroom broke his heart.

The children were huddled in the middle of the room on the floor. The two younger boys were crying hysterically-the kind of deep crying and sobs that shake and rock the child's chest. Phyera was sitting and holding the two small children like a hen protecting it's young from a fierce hawk. She was crying too and looked very scared. Kamthibi felt like a monster to his own children and he felt awful in the pit of his stomach. He felt a deep disgust at himself at the chaos and turmoil. When he tried to console and reassure his daughter by placing his hand on her shoulder, she cringed in fear. He knew then that he did not want to destroy his children. They needed his protection as their father this moment more than ever. The voice of Kamthibi's mother echoed from his childhood past in the Tumbuka language: "*Kuchaya mwanakazi yayi. Sungani bana.*" (Never beat your wife. Look after your children). His parents were more than ten thousand miles away and wondered how they could intrude into his life at this time.

Kamthibi walked out of the children's bedroom back into their bedroom and softly knocked on the locked bathroom door.

"Nora," he said in a low voice that surprised Nora, "come out and please put the children to bed."

Nora gingerly cracked the bathroom door open, fearing this to be a trick. She wiped tears from her face with a tissue and walked out to the children. Kamthibi quietly lay down on the bed, crossed his legs, hands folded on his chest, and stared at the ceiling as his heart throbbed with unimaginable internal pain; the type of pain no one can see outside. This was the beginning of a long tumultuous year for Kamthibi and Nora in their sixteen-year-old marriage.

They did not have sex with each other for more than one year. They went to see a marriage therapist for four months. They slept in one room upon the recommendation and following some of the gimmicks of the therapy. Kamthibi hated that the woman therapist never blamed anyone for the affair his wife had had. He wished he was in the village where custom requires that blame be assigned publicly for such a tragic and hurtful incident in a marriage. The children kept them together as their innocence was as refreshing as it was contagious. They were also an excellent diversion from the serious festering marital problems just underneath and pressures of work. The few details of the affair were excruciating for Kamthibi to hear. Nora had slept several times with Peter, a white workmate at the Clarksville Retirement Community. Kamthibi cried day and night. He was teary-eyed for months on end, sometimes wondering how he made it through meetings at work.

* * *

Kamthibi was bedevilled by his experiences from his village life upbringing. His mind wondered down into those deeply emotional experiences that had touched him but were buried in his heart; both those that were painful to remember and those that exhilarated his soul. Eating meat was such a rare treat as a child in the village. Kamthibi and his cousins had the responsibility of herding the goats. His uncles never once slaughtered the goats just to eat. They were used for adult transactions like paying bride price for the young men's marriages. One day, one of the greyish-black goats had broken its *goda* or tether and was causing commotion hitting and attacking other goats.

Kamthibi's uncle lost his temper. He grabbed a medium-size log and delivered one blow to the he-goat's head. The goat immediately slumped to the ground lifeless and began to twitch as if he was having a seizure. His uncle instructed Kamthibi and the boy cousins to go and get some broad *musuku tree* leaves to spread on the grass on which to slaughter and skin the goat. They were going to eat it. Kamthibi excitedly ran into the bush chattering with the other boys about eating the juicy delicious meat they had long awaited. When they came back a few minutes later, however, and to their deep chagrin, the he-goat was up and walking, although with a slight stagger. They were not going to eat it after all. The best expectations can be given and taken away in a flash in life. Kamthibi had never forgotten such extreme swings of the emotions from those days just like the ones he was experiencing now.

Kamthibi could not explain why the next memory kept coming up in his mind again and again. It was a teacher who had inspired and ignited in Kamthibi his life-long intense desire to achieve his dreams. He had never, ever thanked the teacher publicly over the many years. He still vividly remembered him thirty years later after his PhD, having a family and now a career in America. He was an African Headmaster and his seventh grade English teacher at his boys' boarding primary school. He was short with dark skin. He had greased and shiny thick dark hair that he combed backwards. He always wore a tie, well-ironed pants, and shiny, well-polished black shoes. He had a stern no-

nonsense look with a permanent frown on his forehead when he walked in the school yard. His punishments were always severe and strictly enforced. If the punishment for breaking a school rule was one stroke of the cane, he gave you two and if it was two, he gave you four. Every student in the school knew this and feared, and some hated him. Rumours abound among students that the reason his wife had a miscarriage was because he was so cruel. 'It served him well', so they believed.

The school was located on a remote plateau literally on the British-colonial drawn border between Zambia and Malawi in Southern Africa. All the students had two pairs of khaki shorts and short-sleeved shirts for school uniforms. The students were barefoot, had two small blankets, and a bar of soap. In the classroom at the time, Kamthibi had only five old tattered textbooks for a class of forty students. They had limited facilities but the teachers gave them the best knowledge they could deliver.

The school routine was gruelling starting everyday from four thirty am. But it was particularly so on a chilly morning when Kamthibi decided to be tardy and skip his early morning chore of sweeping the school Assembly Hall. The floor was so dirty that as soon as the Headmaster and the schoolteachers entered the assembly hall, the first announcement from the Headmaster's lips was for Kamthibi to see him in his office immediately after the assembly. Kamthibi could have run away if he had had the time to plan and think. But he had none. In his office, the Headmaster sternly asked him why the Assembly Hall floor was not swept. Kamthibi had no answer. His tears did not help either as the Headmaster gave him two swift strokes of the cane on his rear end while telling him that laziness and irresponsibility were unacceptable. Kamthibi never skipped any chores again and didn't dare complain to his parents either because without doubt they would have supported the Headmaster.

One chilly morning class period, the Headmaster and surprisingly Kamthibi's most favourite teacher, digressed from teaching English, and asked the class what they wanted to be after completing school. The students looked at each other blankly in stunned silence. What could kids in a rural African village school dream about? Then the Headmaster gave the class his memorable talk.

"What's the matter with you!" he raised his voice. And then he said almost whispering and sweeping the class with his gaze: "You are young. The future for all of you is wide open. Our young, independent country of Zambia will need doctors to cure disease, pilots to fly planes, agricultural experts to grow more food and find better seeds, locomotive drivers to run trains, bankers, teachers, surveyors, newspaper reporters, architects to design homes, engineers. Any of you could even go to college at the new University of Zambia, get one or two degrees and become world renown researchers and professors. You need to know not just about our school, our chief, your village, or our country, but also about the whole world. Did you know that as we speak in the classroom now, on the other side of the world in Japan it's midnight and people are asleep?"

Kamthibi had smiled and looked around his classmates with amazement, excitement, and befuddlement. That was it! He didn't know about his classmates but that stuff was too fascinating for him; a kid who had only known about herding goats in the village up to this point. His imagination had been ignited and a seed was planted. Kamthibi went on to high school, and to the country's newly-built and only national University of Zambia at the time and later went to do his Masters and Ph. D in Agriculture in the United States.

Later that same year, the Headmaster received an urgent letter from Kamthibi's parents. He had to give Kamthibi the grim news in his office that Kamthibi's younger brother had passed away at home after a brief illness. He couldn't go home for the funeral as his home village was too far. As Kamthibi wept in deep grief alone lying on his dormitory bed that evening, he was summoned to the Headmaster's house. Students were often summoned to his office but never to his house. His wife made a cup of tea with some buttered scones. Kamthibi had wiped his tears and sniffed as he sipped the tea. In an unmistakably grief stricken voice, the Headmaster said he was deeply sorry about the loss of Kamthibi's brother. The Headmaster wanted Kamthibi to be strong, as only God took care of all of us including the grief we experience when we have lost people we love. Kamthibi could not believe that those kind words were coming from the widely-feared and fierce Headmaster. He had seen a side of him he could never tell the other students because they would never believe him. Before Kamthibi left the house, the Headmaster mentioned that the big, all important high school entrance exams were only three months away. He knew Kamthibi could pass the crucial exam, qualify to go to high school, and maybe college. This would be his only chance to go to high school.

Kamthibi could neither stop nor understand those powerful memories, which kept him awake at night, anguished, and churning his emotions, which were perpetually raw. 'What do all these memories mean?' he kept asking himself over and over. He could not make sense of their strong intrusion into his tumultuous life. For months, the pain was like a huge stake lodged in his heart day and night. The pain he endured transformed him and he began to experience life and emotions in a way he had never known he could. He spent months fighting and resisting deep anger, hate, resentment, despair and disillusionment. He began to have a constant burning desire for romantic love. He felt so alive. His heart was a magnet attracting anything romantic within miles of him - beautiful flowers, music, clothes, food, and especially women. His burning and engulfing romantic desires were always sizzled with the image of Lina Phiri, a girl he had encountered in his early teenage days in the village in Eastern Zambia.

Lina was a fifteen-year-old girl he had adored like no other girl since. Kamthibi was fourteen years old at the time. He had walked by Lina's house many times to try to steal a glimpse of the love goddess but to no avail. One late afternoon, he accidentally caught up with Lina walking to her home on the narrow dirt road.

Kamthibi shook Lina's small, soft, delicate hand. She greeted him in that high-pitched angelic voice instantly melting his heart and stomach. She had short black hair, smooth, soft, dark brown skin that decorated every curvature of her body. She had a radiant baby face with bright-white teeth, and milky-white eyes that twinkled. Her neck was smooth and had small, soft, baby-like folds in them, which begged to be touched and caressed. Her breasts were firm and sticking out of the bosom of her dress. Her stomach was flat. Her behind rose and fell in a tantalizing smooth mound-curvature. Her legs were straight, smooth, and had small dimples behind the knees just above her calves. She was the sexiest girl Kamthibi had ever seen. When she smiled, it took Kamthibi's breath away with sheer joy of being worthy of her smile.

But Kamthibi's mouth was dry and he was tongue-tied during the entire two-mile short walk. She engaged in a lovely monologue that bathed Kamthibi's ear like sweet nectar. She said she knew what his thoughts were and coyly looked at him with those milky eyes while he was enduring the torture of his life. She appeared to be sophisticated perhaps, her eyes set on older men; sixteen and seventeen-year-old boys. But oh! How Kamthibi yearned just to be with her magical spell forever. When they parted, Kamthibi knew her image would be singed into his mind and endure into eternity. How God could create such torture for poor boys like him, Kamthibi had thought at the time.

Kamthibi's yearning to relive that experience was rekindled more than thirty years later. His whole body and soul was begging and poised for a deep romantic experience. The saying "be careful about what you wish for" would soon come true for better or for worse for Kamthibi.

No sooner had these feelings been tormenting him for weeks and months than something very innocuous at the time happened. One night at his office located in a two-storey building downtown Clarksville, he was on the computer as he had been for thousands, if not millions of times. His friend James Lutula sent him an e-mail from Manchester. It had instructions that Kamthibi get on an Irish Chat Network (ICN) so they could communicate and goof around without worrying about an international long distance phone bill. Kamthibi was not only unfamiliar with the concept of chatrooms, but he had heard that most of it is really not what it is hyped up to be. The story was that maniacs were in chatrooms and did lots of trash talking. Kamthibi did not have time for that. He was a mature, old-fashioned, responsible adult man who enjoyed good conversation, either on the phone or best of all face-to-face. So it was with trepidation that he logged on to the Irish Chat Network. He and James chatted, joked, played, and goofed around in this somewhat new medium. After a while, both of them were bored and were about to log out. That's when it happened. As soon as he disengaged with his friend James, Kamthibi randomly clicked on the name "Trish" of the more than two hundred names that were in the chat room. He wasn't even sure what he was doing and why. He just wanted to goof around with some Irish girl or maybe she could even be from Rawapindi, Hong Kong, Tananarive, or Galapagos Island, who could tell? Who cared in this anonymous fake medium? He wanted to goof around for a minute or two and logout so he could go home. It was quite late.

<Kamthibi> *Are you Trish?*

<Trish> *Yes, r u Kamthibi?* lol (laugh out loud).

<Kamthibi> *Are you in Ireland?*

<Trish> *Of course, that's my real name too and I am not impersonating anyone.*

<Kamthibi> *How do I know you are not on planet Mars?* lol.

<Trish> *How wood I know English? Oopss, I forgot of course Martians know everything. Don't they? Dahhh!!* lol.

<Kamthibi> *Dahhh! Of course I'm slow tonight* lol.

<Trish> *Are u man or woman?*

<Kamthibi> *Why?*

<Trish> *I just wanna know.*

<Kamthibi> *Are u man or woman?*

<Trish> *Woman, u?*

<Kamthibi> *It's not necessary for u to know.*

<Trish> *That's unfair.*

<Kamthibi> *Ok, ok man.*

<Trish> *Where r u from?*

<Kamthibi> *Why?*

<Trish> *Your name is unusual.*

Kamthibi and Trish went back and forth. Trish told Kamthibi she was bored and her children were grown. She wanted to experience some adventure. She told Kamthibi her full name. But Kamthibi kept skirting the issue of his full identity after he indicated that he was a man, married and immigrated to the States. After they laughed and teased each other about so many things, Kamthibi felt he had never had so much fun meeting a woman since the hey days of going to parties when he was a teenager in college. Trish kept insisting on Kamthibi telling her two things: the meaning of his name and where he came from originally.

<Trish> *U better tell me, after all I have told u everything about myself* lol.

<Kamthibi> *What does it matter? We can just chat!* lol.

<Trish> *U r a mean guy* lol.

<Kamthibi> *The name* Kamthibi *has two meanings in my language. The first one is that it is a sweet traditional drink brewed with finger millet.*

<Trish> *What is finger millet?*

<Kamthibi> *It's a type of grain grown in my home area.*

<Trish> *That's interesting.*

<Kamthibi> Kamthibi *is also a sensuous traditional dance that women and men dance to in the village in the evening just after dusk.*

<Trish> *That's very romantic. Can u show me how to dance* lol.

<Kamthibi> *The dance is actually now dying out. My parents and grandparents danced it when they were young.*

<Trish> *Where r u from? It's obvious u are not American.*

<Kamthibi> *Why is this important? We can just enjoy the chat.*

<Trish> *No, tell me,* Kamthibi *please?*

<Kamthibi> *Promise me u will not freak out and faint* lol.

<Trish>*I promise, I promise, I promise, tell me am dying.*

<Kamthibi> *Ok, ok am Zambian, am from Africa.*

<Trish> *Big deal* Kamthibi *!!!* lol.

<Kamthibi> *I am African, am black. Aren't u shocked?*

<Trish> *No, I see blacks and Africans in Belfast and see them on TV. I like black American music.*

<Kamthibi> *I thought u might faint because u have never talked to an African before.*

They teased each other, goofed around, and Kamthibi found himself laughing so hard like he had never done in years. He was actually having fun with Trish-some impersonal make believe woman from Ireland- it could even be a man. What a new concept? Trish seemed to love it too.

For a while, the chat room conversations were harmless fun. But after a while, Kamthibi and Trish spent hours in very intimate conversations. The few hours changed to hundreds of hours and soon it was practically thousands of hours that they spent together in the chat rooms and on the phone. They felt very comfortable with each other. They shared dreams, their life stories, until it was inevitable that a mutual irresistible desire to meet face to face developed. For months they could not discuss and plan anything else besides and beyond their decision to meet at the five large rocks on the road from Belfast to Gandy.

CHAPTER SIX

More than forty years to the day Trish met Kamthibi at the five large rocks, she would have led a life no different from other millions of rural Irish women. The circumstances of her upbringing were hardly unusual, except for what one might call some events that created some meandering in her life which all of us share in one way or another.

Trish was born Patricia Fitzgerald. She grew up in a solid, working-class Catholic neighbourhood of Newbury in Belfast. The family's four room home was tightly sandwiched right smack in the middle of a chain of look-alike same-size box houses covering several blocks. They didn't have a front yard. Trish remembers playing with other girls in the street. Boys played separately from girls. That code was strictly enforced among kids until their early teenage years when "going steady" was a status symbol everyone aspired to. Everyone in the two-block area knew if a boy was going steady with a particular girl. They lived in the poorest section of Newbury. But Trish did not realize they were poor until after several years into her childhood. The discovery happened by accident.

The Newbury Catholic Church they attended every Sunday was located just six blocks north of their house. The street on which the church was located was the demarcation line between the poor section of Newbury and north of the church, the better off section. Indeed, anyone always noticed that from that church northward, the homes looked better with attractive front yards, less kids on the streets, and less graffiti. People always talked about whether one lived in the north or south section of Newbury. Although everyone wears good clothes when they attend church on Sunday, less obvious differences are always apparent. People from different neighbourhoods may sit in different sections of the pews. Their children may be more rambunctious or reserved than others. So it was the case with churchgoers at Newbury Catholic Church.

One Sunday after mass at her young age, Trish was marching out of church with her older brother, father, and mother when she heard a little boy point to her and say what amounted to the tail end of a conversation they might have had regularly at home; "Daddy, does that little girl live in the poor section, in south, south-xbury?"

The little boys' parents hushed him, warning that he should never say such bad things in public. That was being rude. As all children do when they hear something that they don't understand, they ask their parents.

"Mummy, do we live in the poor section?" Trish asked looking up and tapping her mother several times on her hand to draw her attention.

"What are you talking about?" Trish's mother asked defensively pulling her arm away. She was talking to her father.

"That boy over there said we live in the poor section of Newbury," Trish repeated, pointing to the boy who was also walking away to a parked car with her family.

"Nevermind, Trish," her mother replied impatiently, "we live in a nice house and we give you enough food. It really doesn't matter what people say about where you live so long as you have food on the table and a roof over your head."

It was not actually her mother's answer that had puzzled and peaked Trish's curiosity. It was her mother's defensiveness. Her father looked embarrassed and did not say anything either. His look said 'don't ask me either'. Trish sensed there was something wrong. She walked the few blocks home quietly.

As soon as she changed from her Sunday church clothes, she dashed into her older brother, Tommy's room.

"Tommy, what is the meaning of poor?" Trish asked, "Why did that boy say we live in the poor section?"

"Dummy, poor means you don't have a nice house, food, or nice clothes. We don't even have a car," Tommy answered sarcastically and walked out of the room.

There was no room for follow up questions or further explanation. Although Trish had read and heard folktales about being poor, she had never connected it to herself. As far as she had been concerned up to that point, her family had a nice house and their life was the best. But her innocence was suddenly and rudely shattered that afternoon. From then on, she began to look at her clothes, house, any toys, and wondered how better off being rich felt like if she was poor.

It was the beginning of a long painful journey of growing and learning about the outside world beyond her small house in South Newbury.

She eventually learned that she could not walk or play beyond the Newbury Catholic church as she and her friends would not be welcome by the kids there. However, she learned from her parents that walking many blocks further south of her house in Newbury could be very risky and even dangerous. This was a Protestant neighbourhood where Catholic people and kids would not be welcome. They could be in danger of being not just chased away by gangs of hostile Protestant youths, but they could be stoned, beaten up, and even killed, their parents had warned.

One day, Trish's father came home from work angry and agitated, which was unusual for him, for he was a quiet man. He had told the kids to stay indoors. There had been demonstrations or troubles in Londonderry between Catholics and Protestants, and thirteen demonstrators were shot and killed by the paramilitary police. The bad news that was spreading like a wild fire was likely to spark further protests and clashes in hot spot areas where Catholics and Protestants lived next to each other. Trish and her brother, Tommy, stayed home from school and were indoors for several days with very nervous, fearful, and tense parents and neighbours. Trish was very scared. Two days later as predicted, the protests spread to the South of Newbury at the Catholic and Protestant line.

During the clashes, the protests and counter protests, gangs of youth and some adults lobbed Molotov cocktails and threw rocks into the opposing, jeering, hostile, and screaming crowds on the opposite side of the demarcation line. For a while there was a stand off. The Belfast police restored order only after use of teargas to separate and disperse the groups. Thirty were arrested, fifty-one injured, and one Catholic youth died. For days after, Trish was afraid to play outside. Their mother and all neighbours escorted and walked them to school. She was afraid of sending the children on errands to the neighbourhood grocery store. For a while, Trish's mother walked to the grocery store to buy milk, bread, butter, sugar, and cooking oil.

In spite of all this, Trish had many pleasant childhood memories. Her father worked in a job in construction. He would wake up early every morning. Her mother would prepare him breakfast, and pack his lunch box. He would pick up his lunch box, rub Trish on her head several times, before walking out of the door to the bus station a street before the Newbury Catholic Church. Sometimes, he got a ride from one of the company construction truck drivers. Trish loved to be rubbed on her head by her father. He never said much else. But that rub was one of the few powerful gestures of love to the little girl from her father.

The most favourite though was when Trish's father came home from work during early afternoons every Friday. He worked half day that day. She would sit by her tiny bedroom window that faced the street and wait in anticipation. She would see him walking toward their house and would race to the front door. He would burst through the door, remove his helmet, rub his hair to air it, and yell something to her mother. He would remove his filthy overalls, which had fresh cakes of mud on them, untie the thick bootlaces, and remove the grimy heavy boots whose soles were clogged with fresh mud and dirt. The smell of sweat, dirt, and grime were all so powerful and manly to Trish. Then her father would reach into his pocket and pull out her favourite milk chocolate candy bar - the Obtan. Trish swears up to this day that she may have lost some of her teeth early to decay because of the chocolate candy bar her father bought her during her childhood. To this day, she loves the Obtan milk chocolate bar because it reminds her of the warm childhood memories.

Although he was married to his mother, as a young girl, Trish was convinced that her father loved her the most. She felt as though no one else saw her father rub her head every morning before walking out of the door and never saw him give her the Obtan favourite milk chocolate bar on Friday afternoons. She felt this was a secret love affair just between her and her father. She was his secret princess.

School was the best thing that happened in Trish's life. It exposed her young imaginative mind to a world beyond the narrow confines of her Newbury box-like house and neighbourhood. Geography and Nature Studies were her favourite subjects through all her school years. She wanted to be a traveller and a scientist when she grew up. As a child, Trish was drawn to, fascinated by, and often day dreamed about distant lands and the exotic looking people in those lands. She yearned to get away from her boredom and loneliness on the many days she could not go out to play because her mother would say it was dangerous outside. In her young childish mind, she couldn't imagine such a people being actually alive, walking, and talking. She day-dreamed about what it would be like to be in China, India, or to see the kangaroos leaping more that thirty feet in just one leap in the Australian wilderness.

But what made her imagination boil over and go absolutely wild was Africa; the people and the small village huts, the jungle, and the wild animals. She had a million questions for her teachers who did not seem to have answers to some of them. How did Africans avoid being trampled, say by the huge elephants, since they lived in such small huts? How did the children play? How come there were no Africans in Ireland? She was amazed at how black or dark they looked in the bright colour photographs in the books. The skin contrast fascinated her. Would the skin feel rough or just different if she touched it? Some of them ate insects for food! Yaks!! Trish had reacted with disgust at the very thought of eating insects. She always had a sense of wonder about Africa and the Africans. Secretly, she admired them, as they seemed to walk so free in the open wilderness. She compared this to her life in Newbury where she could not walk or wander anywhere she pleased.

Years later, Trish broke down and cried in the bathroom watching a classic American mini-series "Roots" on TV. This was a story of an African boy who was kidnapped and sold into slavery. He and his descendants lived a life of being whipped and worked like animals on plantations in America. She could not stand the notion of enslaving the free African and abusing him so severely, taking away his freedom. "Why!" "Why!" "Why!" Trish had wept softly in anguish in the family bathroom, thumping her fist on the top of the small bathroom cabinet sink and wiping her tears so that her father, mother, and brother did not notice anything. She could not talk to anyone about this, not even her parents, the few friends she had, or her teachers. Trish intuitively knew they would not understand why she felt that way. She was afraid they would dismiss her reaction as morbid. After all, the Irish never enslaved any Africans and the Irish were eight thousand miles away from Africa and scenes of the crimes. They would wonder why anyone would be so obsessed about the poor Africans.

During her early adolescence, something happened in Trish's life that would have a profound effect and would change her future destiny. Her father had by that time ceased rubbing her head in the morning because they agreed it was for small girls. And she was not a small girl any more. Instead, she was turning into a young lady. But he still brought her the Obtan milk chocolate candy bar every Friday. Her father began to talk to her more when he noticed she looked moody and down.

On this occasion, Trish complained to her father that she did not have too many friends. She was also having difficulty attracting or gaining the attention of this one boy in her class. She didn't expect her father to say anything since he had never been much of a talker with her. He just did not talk much. Trish was very emotional and looked very upset at that occasion. Her father had walked over and stood abreast to her with her teary eyes.

"You will know when the right boy comes to you," her father said putting his arm around Trish's shoulders and squeezing her against him for a matter of some seconds.

Trish was thrilled. She felt warm inside. She felt so happy and reassured that things were going to be all right. Her father had never hugged, kissed her, or ever said, "I love you." Those few simple words and a simple physical gesture meant a million I love yous to Trish at the time.

A week later, Trish's father came down with a high fever. From then on, he went to work sporadically and was home and in bed most of the time. He could not dress up and play on the bagpipes anymore, which he used to do with his friends in parades and other neighbourhood get togethers. He deteriorated from the robust energetic man Trish had known to someone gaunt and helpless. Life was slowly sapped from him. He was diagnosed with pancreatic cancer. He died two months later in the hospital. He was so young, just in his mid-thirties.

More than three dozen family relatives and friends attended the funeral and burial. Trish was surprised that she did not moan or cry so much. She was just very, very angry. She felt as though her father had suddenly abandoned her at a park without saying good-bye. In a strange way, she felt as though her father had left hastily for some place and would return any minute. It's as if she could wait outside her tiny bedroom window and see him walk up the street to their home again and give her the Obtan milk chocolate bar. She would feel this way about her father's death for most of her adult life.

Trish, her mother, and brother could not make ends meet on their own in Newbury any more without a breadwinner. So the family moved to the village of Gandy where they shared a house with Trish's maternal grandmother she barely knew. To say that Trish hated Gandy would be an understatement of the century. As an adolescent, she felt it was a great travesty and injustice that her mother moved her from the South Newbury fine working class neighbourhood, leaving her friends and a best friend, the familiar neighbourhood, church, and school to some small village where there was nothing.

At first, Trish didn't even want to go to the only village school. Gradually though, she had to reconcile with reality and swallow the bitter pill that she was to live in Gandy. She would go to school in Gandy, try to make some friends, and just learn to adjust. Trish never forgave her mother for the move. But her mother always explained that she was a widow with no income besides her dead husband's meagre pension check. Besides, the Catholic and Protestant troubles were getting so bad in Belfast that she had feared for both her children. Eventually, Trish's mother got a job as a cleaning maid at the Supermarket and the village butchery. Life was rough, but Trish's mother at least managed to hold the family together.

Trish was never one of the popular girls in her school. She blamed it on her mother and the move from Newbury for all her troubles. Because she was outside the circle of popular girls, she could not attract the popular boys either. She ended up hooking up with Richard Butler, another boy who was not in the circle of popular boys. Richard also lived with his paternal grandparents. His parents had been missionaries in Zaire in Africa. Richard and Trish more or less felt sorry for each other and were being rebellious at the same time.

Trish and Richard felt not only ostracized, but also that they felt they had to catch up and try some of the naughty things the popular girls and boys were apparently doing. Whether these were actually happening or not was beside the point. So Trish began to smoke, drink some alcohol, and hangout with Richard in his old beat up car. It was soon after their first meeting that they hastily experimented with sex. Trish had never planned on getting pregnant or becoming Mrs. Butler. After all, she had not even finished high school yet. She had exciting dreams about her future.

CHAPTER SEVEN

Kamthibi felt even more lonesome when Nurse Agnes's shift ended and another nurse took over. The nurse disconnected the monitor wires as Kamthibi's vitals were back to normal. Although Kamthibi was feeling much better, the realization that Trish was gone from his life probably forever was unfathomable. His being in physical danger did not seem to matter anymore. Something had changed. It snowed all night. He tossed restlessly as he wanted to get out of Ireland immediately. He knew his flight to London was at 6:00 pm the next day. He almost wished he had been jailed or could stay admitted in the Belfast City Hospital for a while. At least he would be safe and not have to decide anything for a while; not even what to eat. Kamthibi crossed his feet under the covers and placed his one hand under his head on the pillow. As he stared at the ceiling, furious thoughts churned in his head like waves in a violent storm.

Someone was trying to kill him and then frame him. But that didn't scare him as much anymore. Trish, the woman he deeply loved, was gone and would probably be dead soon. That hurt and deeply saddened him. He had a deep desire to protect her, but there was nothing he could do. That's life. It is never fair. He lamented that he would never hold and kiss her again. Maybe he would never talk to her again; not even on the phone. Maybe her priorities would now shift to spending time with her family during what may be her last days on this earth. Who would blame her?

He could go and visit his friend James the widower in Manchester. His wife had died of meningitis although people were whispering AIDS. He was raising their two young daughters alone. The younger one was eighteen months when her mother died. It was hard and lonely for him. James matured so much that in a way he was no longer the happy-go-lucky teenager Kamthibi was best friends with in college at the University of Zambia. But their friendship was always eighteen years old - young, fresh, and playful. Returning to his wife and two kids in Illinois was the last but depressing option. Not with the way his wife had treated him so badly, all the emotional baggage he had accumulated, especially now with all the love turmoil mess he was in. The village was the most attractive. Once in the village, how would he account for leaving his wife and children alone in America? Kamthibi had not spent Christmas with his parents and family for more than twenty years. He needed to heal. How he would enjoy the mango fruit, reuniting with some of his boyhood friends, the food delicacies of the December rainy season, the *Kulimizgha* Tumbuka ceremony, and the traditional village dances! His heart warmed at the lovely memories and thoughts. He did not have to decide what to do until he was in the tranquillity of London's Heathrow International Airport the next evening. When some thoughts cross the mind over and over again, they are like counting a million sheep. Kamthibi drifted into a deep sleep.

Kamthibi woke up feeling fresh and energized. He didn't feel like lying down in bed anymore. He brushed his teeth, washed his face, and sat in the love seat reading and thumbing through a pile of magazines. Nurse Agnes was off that day and Kamthibi wished he would see and thank her for going out on a limb for him. He wanted to know more about who was framing him and trying to kill him, and why? But he got the hospital's address. He would be sure to write her later.

The new nurse on duty went through the formalities of discharge. He was given some prescriptions of painkillers and antibiotics in case he had an infection. Kamthibi was escorted to the front desk lobby where he sat in the discharge lounge waiting for a taxi to take him to the hotel. As he was about to step into the taxi on the snowy pavement, a woman called his name from the car that had just pulled up behind the taxi. It was Agnes with a two-year-old in the car. She came out and they shook hands goodbye. Nurse Agnes slipped a crunched piece of paper in Kamthibi's hand.

"Read it later," Nurse Agnes whispered under her breath like a ventriloquist. "K," Nurse Agnes said aloud for the benefit of the standers by, "my daughter Meranda was anxious to see an African man. She had just been read a children's story about an African child who saved the village men, women, and all the children from marauding lions at night."

"That's good," Kamthibi said.

"The only African people she has seen are on TV. My husband had jokingly encouraged me to bring her to see you so she could brag to her playmates that she had seen an African."

As soon as he was in the taxi, Kamthibi read the tinny note from Nurse Agnes. It was hurriedly scribbled: "It's all over town. Richard Butler is going to kill you. Leave now. Take care."

Bells rang in Kamthibi's head as he realized what a close call and danger he was in at the hospital and what danger he was still in the next eight hours before the flight departure. How would he make it to the airport? Kamthibi was afraid of returning to the hotel to collect his belongings - a suitcase of clothes and a small carry-on bag with research papers in it from his work. This could be dangerous. He didn't want to be in a private room the rest of his stay. He had to avoid his hotel room. He expected his bags and room to have certainly been searched for drugs. He paid the taxi driver for the short ride from the hospital. As soon as he walked through the hotel lobby, it seemed like everyone was looking at him. When he asked for the room key acting as if nothing had happened, the receptionist did not look at him. Instead, he pointed to the manager's office with instructions that Kamthibi sees the manager first before his key could be released.

The manager was surprisingly cooperative. Maybe he did not want any more trouble from this apparent maniac. He told Kamthibi that he would pay for the first two nights. This included the night he passed out and broke his arm when he fell from a bar stool in the hotel lounge and had to be taken to the hospital. Kamthibi was shocked about this alleged incident.

"I don't remember falling off the stool," Kamthibi argued, "but I will pay since I guess I had not notified you that I would be spending the night in the hospital," he said with an obvious sarcastic tone.

"Sir, I am only telling you what I was told," the manager said, "The police also came and searched your room. I am not sure they looked through your belongings. There was nothing we could do when they are conducting investigations."

"I know, I know," Kamthibi said impatiently, "I will charge the room to my card and I don't catch the plane to London Heathrow until 6:00 this evening. I might stay or wait here or I might just go and visit a friend of mine." Kamthibi didn't know who could be in on the plot to harm or kill him. He wanted to spread some uncertainty.

"Certainly," replied the manager, "I will call the front desk so they will know what to do."

The manager picked up his phone and talked to the reception desk. Kamthibi went to the reception desk, charged his room and picked up his room key. The reception clerk collected his suitcase and the carry-on bag from the back of the office and gave it to the porter. They were so polite it was difficult for Kamthibi to be angry.

Kamthibi was very disturbed about the manager's story. Had he been so drunk that he had slipped off the bar stool and had severely sprained his arm? That had never happened to him before. That was a very unlikely story. How come he couldn't remember a thing beyond the moment he had left the bar counter to go to the bathroom? There was something fishy about this. But that's how the rape drug is said to work. The rapist slips the white powdery stuff into the unsuspecting date's drink. Since the drug is colourless and tasteless, the woman does not notice anything until she begins to lose her consciousness. The man rapes her. But the woman never remembers anything. Could somebody have laced his drink before he had gone to the bathroom or after he had come back?

Kamthibi had read in the news that the rape drug wipes your memory when administered with alcohol. Why would anyone want to do something like that to him? He remembered his excitement after drinking two beers. He had been asleep and cooped up in his hotel room all day. He was tense and wanted to talk to anyone. He was excited about finally meeting Trish the following day. He remembers two Irishmen sitting on both sides at the bar. He might have mentioned that he was in love with this sweet Irish woman. Maybe the two men were racist bigots. He couldn't remember. But he now knew they might have been hired by Richard. These thoughts frightened him. But he was relieved he would be out of Ireland before sundown.

Kamthibi sat around the Hotel Cardigan lobby and read some newspapers. His safety for the next six hours was to be in a public place. The hotel desk clerk approached him saying there was a phone call for him.

"It's me, *mwana*," the very familiar voice said on the other end of the line. It was James with the signature of "*mwana*" which is the Zambian equivalent of "buddy" or "close friend."

"Yes, *Mwana*, J", Kamthibi resumed the conversation, "I was just sitting in the hotel lobby. I will talk to you in Nyanja."

"Are you alive?" James asked half laughing because he was anxious, "I thought you were dead. I received your short love note to Trish. As a concerned friend, I called all over Belfast -the hotel, the police station -and I talked briefly to the nurse at the hospital. Are you okay or you have lost your mind?"

"*Nili bwino*, mwana, (I am ok my friend)," Kamthibi, said. "*uyu moma amene nikonda mwamuna wake afuna kunipaya, imwe a Bemba mukuti Chipeshamano*" (But it's just that this Irish woman

I am deeply in love with her husband wants to kill me. You Bembas say it is sad). *Sembe ninali ku village sembe banthu bakamba ati uyu mukazi ali na magic.* (If I was in the village at home, people would say she had bewitched me)."

They both heartily laughed on the phone at the boyish easiness and familiarity of the conversation. A listener would think the two men were fourteen years old and that nothing serious was being discussed. This is perhaps as close as two friends can be. James and Kamthibi had met as sophomores at the University of Zambia both majoring in Agriculture. They immediately came to like each other as they had a jovial approach to life and shared some of the most intimate experiences to do with both celebrations, successes, failures, and disappointments with grades, "*momas*" or young women as they were colloquially called at the University of Zambia. The young men were known as "*mojos*" in the campus lingo and student press at the time. They had gone to numerous parties and had participated passionately in student politics. But navigating the narrow and meandering adult lives after graduate school had brought both of them face to face with life's turbulences and a share of tragedy. James lost his second wife of seven years. Kamthibi lived in social isolation in a remote part of Illinois where there were no Zambians, let alone Africans. Kamthibi's marriage was in perpetual turmoil over the last five of the twenty years of being married to his wife, Nora. They were now practically estranged and maintaining a veneer of normalcy in the marriage for the sake of their three children.

"*Kwanja kothyoka kali mu* sling. *Chipeshamano sinizamuona futi mpaka ine nife*" (My arm is broken and in a cast. I will probably never see Trish again)," Kamthibi finally said in the phone wiping tears from the laughter. "*Mwana, sembe banipaya ine. Siniziba cocita.*" (Friend, they would have killed me. I honestly don't know what to do next.)

"*Ubwere kuno ku Manchester kuti upumule. Tibwere tikambe. Nabana bazakondwera kuona Uncle Simbazako,*" James suggested, "*Nanga bakazi bako Ba Nora nibauze ciani?*" (You can come here to Manchester to recuperate from your troubles. Besides, we can catch up on the last five years, and my children will be excited to see uncle Simbazako. What should I tell your wife, Nora, if she calls asking about your whereabouts? There was a long pause.

"*Mwana, ndiwe muzanga maningi. Sinifuna kunama. Pamene mukazi uja anali na* affair *yake yija papita myaka five. Cikwati sichiri mushe. Mavuto maningi. Siniziwa chocita. Uyu mkazi kuno amene nimkonda azafa,*" Kamthibi finally said. (Seriously my friend, you are my closest friend. I don't want to lie to you. Since Nora had the affair five years ago, our marriage has never been the same. We even had a fight just before I left. I am not sure of anything any more. I love Trish so much. But she is dying).

"*Azafa!* Oh, sorry *mwana. Azafa naciyani?*" (She is going to die. Friend I am sorry. What is she going to die of?)

"Cancer."

"But *mwana, uli nabana babili. Uziba kuti pamene ninangena ku* Church *maningi nicita* believe *maningi* in forgiveness," James replied in a more sombre tone. (But you have two children and you know that since I became a born again Christian, I believe in forgiveness). "You should hang in there with your marriage and try to make it work, at least for the sake of your kids if not anything else. Look, my wife is gone and my kids, especially the older one, miss her mother everyday."

"*Nimvera, Mwana.* But *nishupika maningi chifukwa mukazi wanga akhala* as if *ali mu* prison. So *tingasunge bwanji* marriage? *Mukazi wanga nimambala.*" Kamthibi said realizing that they had been through this conversation so many times before since his friend became a born again Christian. (I understand my friend. But it's hard when you try to care for the marriage and my wife acts as though she is in jail serving life imprisonment. My wife is very crooked). "Look, *Mwana,*" Kamthibi quickly said to close this painful subject, "*ngati nafika ku* airport *uko ku Mangalande, nizakumira foni. Tizakamba camene nizacita.*" (When I arrive at Heathrow International Airport in London tonight, I will give you a call to tell you what I will be doing next). "I might come to visit you, I might return to Illinois in the US, or I might go and visit my parents in Zambia in the village and spend Christmas with them."

Kamthibi checked out of the hotel late and boarded a hotel courtesy bus to the Belfast International Airport. Considering what he had gone through the previous days, he did not want to miss the plane out of Ireland that evening. He was walking as fast as he could through the long narrow crowded corridor toward Air Oceania check-in counter when his name resonated far behind him, loud, and above the crowd and airport bustle noise. A woman's voice was repeatedly calling, yelling and asking him to wait.

'Have I dropped my wallet, passport or ticket?' Kamthibi wondered momentarily.

He quickly patted his jacket and pants pockets. His passport and wallet were there. He noticed a woman jostling and parting the crowd as she pushed her way toward his direction.

Kamthibi felt a bright flash of lightening in his heart as it missed a beat. It was Trish. She excitedly grabbed Kamthibi's hand like a little child. She gave Kamthibi a quick kiss on the cheek. They were in the middle of the crowd of people walking back and forth. A few stopped to frown; squint and stare, and others were mesmerized with shock at such an unusual sight. The majority just walked on. An elderly man reacted as though the two were filth.

"Trish!" Kamthibi yelled with obvious apprehension at the total sudden and unexpected encounter, "You are the last person I expected to see. What are you doing here?"

"Kamthibi," Trish said with excitement, "I am coming with you to Africa!"

"What?!" Kamthibi asked in disbelief as he frowned, looking at her from head to toe, "Are you out of your mind? Are you crazy? Did Richard send you to keep stalling me until he kills me? Your husband is trying to kill me! He tried to frame me. Besides, you are ill. You have cancer. There is malaria, snakes, lions, AIDS and cholera in Africa. What do you want to go there for?"

"Yes, yes I know about my husband, I know I am sick. I have a few months to live," Trish said still holding Kamthibi's hand, "we don't have time. I had to run away and hide. He is out of his mind. Please help me Kamthibi? After all those thousands of hours of chatting on the Internet, I have come to love you, to know you, to trust you with all my heart. I want to spend my last few weeks of life with you. Please?" Trish gazed pleadingly into Kamthibi's eyes.

"How can I help you, Trish?" Kamthibi asked, "you have not flown anywhere before. You grew up in a small village. You don't have the money. Can you eat the Zambian food in the village, *nshima*, caterpillars, and mice? Ha? Can you run away from lions, leopards, and snakes? Besides, your maniac of a husband might kill both of us."

"He would never come to Africa," Trish pleaded, "I will be all right. If I am going to die anyway, I would rather die with you."

Trish was wearing blue jeans long pants and a jacket, light green blouse with gold-looking buttons, black ebony earrings, white sneakers, and she was carrying a large green back pack meant probably for back packing on an African safari.

"I am not world savvy and I admit I only know Africa from the National Geographic TV programmes," Trish had a long face with droopy eyes like those of a sad dog. She was about to cry. But she suddenly had a look of bright determination, "But I want to be with you. I decided during the last few days I don't want to wait around for Richard to kill me or for me to die of cancer. I love you and want to be with you during my last days on this earth. I want to know about your life, I want to eat some new different foods. See Africa. To experience life with you."

Kamthibi was caught totally off guard. He had tried to scare her. It was not working. Her husband was a jealous maniac. Could he follow them? He did not know what to say. He held her in his arms as he felt his heart melt all over.

"I love you, Trish." Kamthibi found himself saying, "I have dreamed about meeting and being with you for a long time. Except the way things are happening is not the way I had planned it. I had never imagined things would be this way."

"I never imagined things would be this way either."

Kamthibi and Trish held hands for a long time silently looking into each other's eyes and souls. Their faces were pregnant with emotion. They were enveloped by that irresistible magical attraction again. But this time fear, apprehension, and the pain of indecision were all over Kamthibi's face. Uncertainty and anxiety were all over Trish's face, as she intuitively knew things were exactly in the balance.

"Please," Trish pleaded never once letting her eyes leave Kamthibi's.

"Air Oceania flight 201 to Heathrow International Airport is now boarding", was the ominous loud message from the air terminal speakers, "all passengers are asked to proceed to the boarding area. This is the last call."

"Let's go, Trish," Kamthibi grabbed her hand as he gestured for her to go with him to the check-in counter.

CHAPTER EIGHT

Trish's world in rural Ireland had been small. When the plane was accelerating on the runway, finally taking off smoothly with the ground miraculously receding, Trish was gripped with anxiety. At the same time, her instinct was to scream like a child riding and experiencing the gentle pleasant ride of a Ferris wheel coaster at a country fair for the first time. But she fought hard to suppress the strong urge and she swallowed repeatedly. Instead, she peered through the small window of the sixty-passenger two-propeller plane, glanced at Kamthibi and smiled a twinkling smile of contentment. She wanted to be as dignified as other passengers but also to impress Kamthibi. She didn't want to appear as a *fontini* as Zambians would say or dork as Kamthibi's children would say in America. She was reassured and glowed and smiled with inner warmth when Kamthibi's hand sought hers.

Kamthibi felt turmoil inside himself. He felt the way he did when as an eight- year-old, he had been learning how to ride a bicycle for more than a week with his older sister holding on to the rear of the bike as he peddled awkwardly, zigzagging all over the place. One day his older sister, sensing that Kamthibi had gained enough skill, suddenly let go on a slope riding on his own for the first time without Kamthibi's knowledge. He had felt exhilarating triumph, thrill, and pleasure of the ride and gripping fear at the same time. This is how Kamthibi felt inside but did not want to show it to Trish yet. After all, she was depending on him.

The flight was a short forty-five minutes over the Atlantic Ocean. Both Kamthibi and Trish did not have time to even talk before they were already landing. Trish was surprised at how smooth the landing was. She had always imagined that there would be a violent bump. After all whenever she jumped from the steep steps on her front yard of the house or evening running, the landing is always jolting on the body; not necessarily smooth.

Once they got off the plane, they collected their luggage from the Air Oceania domestic flight arrival bay. Trish put her large backpack on a cart and so did Kamthibi, his on another cart. They chit-chatted in a surprisingly friendly manner as they negotiated the long hike through the mazes to the Heathrow International departure check-in. They paused to read directions at each fork in the maze and followed the appropriate arrows. The Heathrow Airport International departures check-in was bustling with people. The place was a mob scene as the early evening is the peak time for international flight departures to all over the world. Every few seconds, the airport was announcing the boarding of a plane to Moscow, last call for passengers on a flight number to Tokyo or Abudabi, or a named passenger flying to Bombay had to report to the courtesy desk immediately.

Kamthibi sensed that there was still an air of uneasiness between them since he had vehemently discouraged Trish and then had suddenly and hurriedly agreed at the airport in Belfast for her to go with him to Africa. Kamthibi pulled Trish to a bench that was positioned along the wall in the bustling large departure hall. They sat down facing each other.

"Trish, I know I was harsh in discouraging you to come to Zambia with me," Kamthibi said holding Trish's hand in his hands, "but I love you and I want you to know that I am really happy you are coming with me. Right now I know it's dangerous. I don't know whether your husband will come after us. I know it will be very exciting for both of us in spite of all the possible danger, problems, and obstacles we will face."

"Kamthibi," Trish replied, "I didn't expect you to jump up and down when I told you I would be coming with you. I wasn't necessarily asking. Here you are with a sick white woman who has a dangerous husband who tried to kill you, going back to your country, home, and family in Africa. It's a big burden. I know that."

"You make it sound like you are just some white woman randomly picked from a catalogue", Kamthibi interrupted, "you are special to me."

"But I hope you understand," Trish paused and looked at the wall and then stared at the empty distance searching for the right words, "how my deep love for you crossed with my terminal illness and my deep desire to live my last days and breath of my life to the fullest. I also want to make you happy. I know we love each other. That's what matters the most right now. Nothing else."

Kamthibi felt like the words were taken right out of his mouth. They stared in each other's glazed eyes for a while holding hands.

"Oh, Kamthibi," Trish said, "I'm sorry I didn't tell you everything about my husband. He is dangerous. But that's not the whole story. I will tell you on the plane."

They kissed each other lightly on the lips as if they were signalling with this affectionate gesture that the deal was done. It's as if they were saying, 'Let's go and do it!'

"Trish," Kamthibi said, as if reality had suddenly snapped them out of a fog of the romantic emotions, "how much money do you have?"

"My mother lent me three thousand dollars from her savings," Trish replied, "well, it was more like a gift because she probably knows I might not live long enough to repay it. She knows I was always unhappy, especially in my marriage from the very beginning. I would like to think it's my gift from her to enjoy myself for once and live a full life."

"Good," Kamthibi said more with relief than anything else, "that will take care of your round trip ticket. You know you wouldn't be let into Zambia without a round trip ticket. And I have this," Kamthibi wielded his credit charge card, "I will charge my round trip ticket and I have more than a thousand dollars for pocket money. We will eat with my relatives and friends and we will be ok. Let's go."

They both stood up and pushed their carts and bought tickets on the long crowded Air Zambia check-in counter. The plane was departing for Lusaka International Airport in the Capital City of Zambia at nine thirty that night. As they pushed their baggage carts toward the security check point along the huge walkway packed and jostling with people, that's when it happened. Trish's face turned ash-white. She suddenly grabbed Kamthibi by the shirt around his stomach, slipped her hands around him inside his long winter coat, as she pulled him between the merchandise shelves in the nearby gift store with his back to the bustling walkway. She kissed him hard on the mouth and buried her face on his shoulder.

"Quick," Trish said, "put your coat around me. Hide me."

"Why?" Kamthibi asked puzzled.

"It's Richard!"

"Your husband?"

"Yes! He is looking for us. Oh, My God!" Trish cried, "Don't look," Trish said when Kamthibi tried to turn around to look, "he didn't see us. He is probably watching the security check point. I don't know what to do."

"Do you think he has a passport and a ticket?" Kamthibi asked.

"No, I think it expired many years ago. Since he came back from Zaire many years ago, he has never travelled abroad. He drinks all his money."

"Quick, let's go through the security check point," Kamthibi said, "he can't get past the check point."

They quickly hassled along the walkway. They stood in line with Kamthibi covering Trish's back. They quickly checked through security screening.

* * *

The international departure lounge was a hive of activity. What struck Trish more than anything else were the many different types of people and their skin colours. Many were white, but then there were blacker ones than Kamthibi, brown, olive, and many colours in between. Some people had short, thick, kinky black hair, blonde, long, black hair. There were different nose shapes, the eyes, and the colourful clothes, and costumes. Some women were wearing veils. Many passengers were families with children. Some were clearly exhausted and taking naps. Others were sitting, reading, or talking and chattering in languages Trish would never have dreamed of hearing. Many were rushing to departure gates to board planes. The duty free shops were everywhere enticing passengers to impulsively buy last minute gifts. The glamorous shops were glittering with numerous choices of merchandise for Christmas and other gifts. Trish noticed small portable cameras, radios, clothes, toys, and chocolate. 'Oh, I love chocolate,' she thought. There were wines, cologne and perfumes, jewelry, speciality cheeses, jams, tea, coffee, and post cards that said "Greetings from London."

There were TV monitors everywhere you looked, constantly blinking and shifting as warnings and announcements for departing flights were constantly announced on the public intercom. There was a huge board up near the top covering half of the wall in the departure-waiting lounge. It showed forty flights in black and white large plastic letters. Every few seconds there was a huge continuous sound of flap, flap, flap as if dominoes were falling as the departing plane at the top disappeared and a new boarding plane was added at the bottom. Trish was overwhelmed and mesmerized by all this. Kamthibi had been equally mesmerized many years earlier when he had first flown from his country to London.

All of this created a special excitement and urgency to their journey and the anticipated adventure. They chose an empty seat and put their bags down to rest their tired feet. For the first time no one was staring at them. Richard was unlikely to find them for now. Who would have time to stare with so many different types of people from different parts of the world mingling? The announcement on the public intercom continued to constantly remind passengers not to leave any bags unattended. Such bags would be immediately taken away and destroyed.

Trish and Kamthibi plopped down with a big sigh of relief. They took turns going to the bathroom while the other watched the bags. Kamthibi used the pay phone to tell his friend James in Manchester not to expect him. He would be travelling to Zambia that night to spend Christmas with his parents in the village. But Kamthibi did not want to put his friend James in a position where he had to lie if Kamthibi's wife, Nora, called to find out about the whereabouts of her husband. Kamthibi did not tell his friend that Trish was travelling with him.

Trish nervously called her mother to tell her she would soon be on her way flying to Africa that night. Although her mother might already have suspected that, Trish did not want to burden her beyond what was necessary with further juicing up what was already the scandal of the millennium in Gandy. All the attempted poisoning of Kamthibi and framing had not yet come to light. The sizzling juice to the local gossip-scandal for now would be that Trish was not only travelling to Africa with the blackie she had met in a steamy computer chat room, but a happily married one for that matter. As it is, the scandal was bad or sensational enough that she had met and kissed a black man on the rural country road in broad daylight. Sensational rumour had it that it took two burley Belfast police officers to ply and separate Trish from the tight grip while she was locked with the black man's passionate French kiss. Over the few days, the village people stared at her and some of her work mates whispered and looked away from her. Her mother stuck by her through all of this sensational scandal. Trish did not tell her mother she was going with Kamthibi. And now here she was sitting with Kamthibi at the Heathrow International Airport about to embark on a trip of a lifetime.

After a while of people-watching, Trish and Kamthibi tried to relieve tension and played a game in which each one had to identify the nationality or the race of the next person they saw walk by. They wondered how one could tell a Briton, a Norwegian, or Irishman from a Swede or Italian; an African from an Indian or Sri Lankan. Trish confessed that besides TV, she had not seen too many people of different nationalities in Belfast, let alone in Gandy. Kamthibi said he had, of course, seen Africans of various skin colours; from light brown chocolate to blue black.

"I have seen *ba Mwenye* or what Indian retail traders are known as in Zambia, and the *ba Zungu* yourself."

"What is *ba Zungu*?" Trish asked anxiously, "Is it something bad like "devil people." I know that whites colonized Africa. I learned that in my history high school class."

"No," replied Kamthibi, "not at all. It's a term Zambians use for all whites. So don't be offended if you hear *"Muzungu, Muzungu."* It means "white man."

"M-u-z-ungu, M-u-z-u-ngu", Trish repeated the word with obvious amusement and interest.

"Ok, Ok, Trish," Kamthibi said excitedly tapping Trish on her thigh several times, "what race and nationality is this guy wearing this type of head gear?"

"Kamthibi, that's unfair. Let's just do race. I am so bad with geography. I am not the one with a Ph. D."

"But my Ph. D was not in geography. It was in seed genetics," Kamthibi retorted obviously having fun, "ok, we will do race first."

"I – think – this – guy is," Trish said slowly, "from Tajikistan. No, No, Lebanon."

"Wrong," Kamthibi said, "he is a Sikh from Northern India. The reason I know is I used to have a Sikh teacher when I was in high school in Zambia."

"How come you had an Indian teacher?" Trish asked as she played with Kamthibi's hand.

"At my country's independence from Britain, we didn't have enough Zambian teachers. So many teachers were hired from abroad."

"Were the teachers any good?"

"It was a mix," Kamthibi replied balancing and gesturing with his palm, "some were good and some were not so good. There was a physics teacher who had such an atrocious accent that none of us understood anything he was saying."

"Ok, Kamthibi, it's your turn," Trish tapped Kamthibi's thigh several times, "what about this woman with a baby, tell me her race, nationality, language, date of birth, exact town of birth, what she ate this morning…" Trish was laughing.

"Wow, stop. I didn't say I was God," Kamthibi feigned complaining and laughed. He scratched his forehead. "Oh, boy," he said making a sound of desperation from his twisted lips, "it's difficult because I honestly can't tell Koreans, Vietnamese, Japanese, and Chinese apart."

"No excuses or coping out," Trish insisted laughing and teasing Kamthibi, "you are the smart one."

"I have an idea. If we can't tell the person's nationality we should walk up to them and ask them," Kamthibi suggested, "and you should be the one to ask since they would be very suspicious of a black guy asking them about anything."

"I don't know about that," Trish said realizing they were just having a good time with the game.

"I will be darn," Kamthibi said slowly with a surprise look on his face.

"What, what?" Trish asked impatiently as Kamthibi was staring at a black man about eighty yards away walking casually heading in their direction.

"Trish, I bet this man is a Zambian," Kamthibi said standing up, "just by the way he looks and the way he is walking, his body language."

Kamthibi and Trish watched the man as he walked like the numerous passengers who had passed by. Kamthibi approached the man and greeted him in English. Then he popped the question. The man, who was in his early thirties, admitted that he was a Zambian. He said he was travelling home after attending a conference in the UK. He had gone to Secondary School in Ndola in the Copperbelt Province of Zambia. He was waiting to catch the same flight later that night to Zambia. Afterwards, Trish asked why they didn't talk in an African language.

"Trish, this is something that many non-Africans don't realize," Kamthibi explained, "there are so many Zambian languages in Zambia that those who are educated prefer to use English because it is the only official language everyone learns in school. That man, for example, speaks *Bemba* but I speak *Nyanja*. So we can only communicate in English."

"Well, that's so bad," Trish said, "it's a shame you can't speak the same tribal language."

Kamthibi looked at Trish with irritation and impatience. Trish was surprised.

"Did I say something wrong?" Trish asked, "Should I have said B—?"

"No," Kamthibi replied, "It's too complicated to explain and it's not your fault. Let's go and get a drink at the bar."

Kamthibi stood up pulling Trish's reluctant hand.

"No, Kamthibi" Trish insisted, "I am willing to listen. If I don't know or don't understand I will let you know."

"If you would like to know," Kamthibi finally said, "tribes don't exist in Africa anymore. But you guys in the West continue to use it. I don't belong to a tribe anymore. Does that man who was born and grew up in the city belong to a "tribe" anymore?" Kamthibi gestured with his forefingers the quotes around "tribe."

"But this is what everyone uses", Trish replied in what Kamthibi found to be a predictable desperate reaction, "who is going to be able to say *B-i*?"

"*Bemba* and *Nyanja*", Kamthibi curtly corrected with obvious irritation.

"I am sorry, Kamthibi," Trish suddenly said in a calmer voice, "I am probably saying things I don't understand. It's obvious this is something that bugs you, ha?"

"Like I said, it's not your fault. I am getting angry at the wrong person," Kamthibi stood up and pulled Trish's hand, "let's go to the bar and get a drink and snack before…" Kamthibi looked at his wristwatch, "we board the plane in about an hour."

CHAPTER NINE

The Air Zambia jumbo jet with more than three hundred passengers destined for Lusaka International Airport began to saunter on the runway. Kamthibi and Trish could see the blue lights demarcating the runway dashing by slowly. Then the London City street lights dashed by in a blur as the plane accelerated and seemed in danger of running out of ground as it took forever to finally take off. There were the usual loud bangs under the belly of the plane as the landing gear was immediately swallowed into the straining giant plane's belly. The bright twinkling city lights on the ground gradually receded into the distant, otherwise pitch-black night.

Too many things were a first for Trish. The entire plane's personnel from the pilots to the stewardesses were all black Zambians. At first, that had made Trish apprehensive. All her life, she had heard so much about how Africa and Africans are backward and primitive. How was she going to understand all of this with the images of African tribes always on TV documentaries? She was surprised that a third of the passengers were white and two thirds were Africans. The stewardesses and the Captain on the intercom spoke English with a Zambian accent. But Trish knew she would not have been able to understand anything had she not known Kamthibi.

The Captain introduced his crew and said we would soon be flying over southern France then on to North Africa then over Zaire to Lusaka in Zambia. Estimated time of arrival was seven thirty am Zambian time. He wished the passengers a good dinner and a pleasant flight. The stewardesses began to serve snacks and readying dinner. Kamthibi and Trish sat quietly for a while. He stared out of the window. But it was pitch black outside except for the red flash of lights on the tip of the protruding huge wing. The plane's loud droning combined with the continuous swishing sound filled the cabin, a sign that the plane was now cruising at a high speed.

After dinner late in the night, the cabin lights were turned off. Some passengers watched a movie. Most of them slept. Trish took the three different coloured prescription pills her family doctor had prescribed to her in Gandy for her lung cancer. She was to take them three times a day with meals. Except for being tired because of the long day, Trish was lucky that she felt relatively strong and well. She kept her fingers crossed that she would stay well most of the trip. She knew she would have some bad times. But hopefully those would be off set by the good times she would have, especially with Kamthibi. 'They already just had a hundred years worth of fun and enjoyment,' so she thought. She just felt so good inside. She grabbed her small plane blanket and leaned her head on Kamthibi's shoulder.

"Is this ok, Kamthibi?" Trish asked in a whisper.

"Yes, of course Precious," Kamthibi whispered.

'Did she hear him right? Did he call her "Precious"? Should she ask him to repeat? That would spoil things,' she thought. Trish glowed, felt warm, and tender inside. She leaned her head on Kamthibi's shoulder. Kamthibi put his arm around her shoulder and squeezed it. He felt so warm inside like he had never felt before. That's why he had whispered "Precious." His loins were hot and throbbing begging for action and relief. He could smell Trish's female scent that sets all men on fire. He did not want to do anything more. Besides he was sure all passengers around their seat were watching like hawks. He couldn't remember a woman having this effect on him ever - not even his wife of twenty years when they were first dating. He wondered why. Is this one of those mysteries of physical attraction and love? He closed his eyes and tried to sleep through the loud droning and swishing of the jumbo jet.

"I can't sleep because I have so many questions," Trish said looking at Kamthibi's with his closed eyes.

"I can't sleep either," Kamthibi replied, "but for a different reason." He smiled coyly at Trish.

"I know," Trish smiled back, "being a man, you have only one thing on your mind."

"And what is that?" they both laughed as he squeezed her.

He drifted in and out and through a million fantasies and thoughts all night. Trish was fast asleep. But Kamthibi was clearly tense and uncomfortable. At some point he fell asleep. When he woke up, he opened the small plane window and there was a bright red glow in the eastern horizon above the white clouds. This was sunrise, probably above the Central African Republic just before the huge country of Zaire. Kamthibi looked at Trish. She was resting on his shoulder asleep. Her shirt was loose. Her chest angle was positioned in such a way he could see through to her bra and two thirds of her right breast. Kamthibi let his eyes feast for a few seconds before he put his arm around her neck to her shoulder and shook her lightly.

"Look," Kamthibi said pointing outside the window.

"What?" Trish said lazily, opening her heavy, sleepy eyelids. She peered out of the window leaning over Kamthibi's knees. "Oh, what a beautiful African sunrise. What a beautiful red glow. I have never seen anything like this in my life. It's wonderful." She pulled up her shirt and buttoned it shut and sat up.

"Kamthibi, what time is it?" Trish asked yawning, "I had such a surprisingly good sleep. I'm already getting used to flying."

"It's about seven am. We should be landing in Lusaka in about two hours. You better go and use the bathroom and wash up before it gets crowded," Kamthibi said, "I know I am going since they will be serving breakfast soon."

Soon after breakfast was served, the jumbo jet slowed down and began the long gradual descent. When the plane broke through the thick white clouds of the Savannah December rainy season, the plush green vegetation was visible far below. Large brown rectangular patches of commercial farms, and smaller patches for subsistence village farms frequently broke the vegetation. This is where corn or maize crops had just been planted on farms and tiny village fields that dotted Savannah Africa. Although his village of Nkhorongo in Lundazi was hundreds of miles to the east of the plane's flight path, Kamthibi could always kid his parents and relatives in the village that he had seen and waved to them as they worked in their fields when he was flying in from London the other day. Kamthibi smiled at the thought of being back home after five years. This time he was back with Trish.

As the plane landed, Kamthibi could see the familiar airport terminal on the left, the barbed wire, the short green grass, and the *mphangala* and other thorny Zambian trees on the right along the bushes. Due to the landing of the jumbo jet, huge schools of birds were swirling around the trees. The grass and the trees were so green. It was a sharp contrast to the white snow and the dead looking brown disrobed trees now in Ireland and North American freezing winter.

"Welcome to Lusaka International Airport," the sweet words of the Zambian woman stewardess said on the intercom, "local time is nine thirty and the temperature is seventy-eight degrees." There was a murmur and cheer from the passengers who no doubt still had the freezing chill of the European winter on their minds. "You are required to remain seated until the plane has come to stand still at the arrival gate. Be sure to open the overhead bins carefully as your luggage may have shifted during flight. We enjoyed having you on the flight and hope you will travel with us again in the future. Have a pleasant stay in Zambia."

"I don't know why they have to say what the temperature is in Lusaka," Kamthibi said with obvious amusement and excitement, "it's always warm and pleasant here. They should just say the temperature is great. Take off your heavy coats and put on your t-shirts and you are free to walk bare foot. But not in here yet, until you step outside the plane."

The plane finally arrived in front of the terminal building and came to a full stop and everything was turned off. It was quiet suddenly. They could see a hive of activity as the pickup truck with disembarking steps was being driven towards the plane, and the little tractor trolleys for transferring baggage, too. Along the terminal building there was what looked like a motorcade. There were an unusual number of police officers and men wearing military fatigues with guns. There was obvious beefed up security.

"This is for you, Trish," Kamthibi joked, "the Zambian government knew this important Irish lady is coming. We should arrange for a motorcade to welcome her."

"I wish. Don't be silly," Trish said laughing as Kamthibi placed her arm around her shoulders and squeezed her to his body, "I don't know whether I would want to be that important. I could use a limo though to take me to the hotel for some rest." Kamthibi removed his watch from his wrist and put it in his pocket.

"Why are you removing your watch?" asked Trish looking befuddled.

"I don't want to worry about time," Kamthibi replied, "I don't come home very frequently. I probably come only once every five years. But each time I have come with my Western attitude to time, I have had so much frustration. Time is less meaningful here. Things are relaxed and laid back. So I just put my wrist watch away and take it out when I fly back towards Europe again."

"You are lucky you are with me," Trish said smiling and patting Kamthibi on the arm repeatedly, "I never worry about time because I was brought up in a small rural village. We will make good soul mates."

The doors of the plane were not opening. The activity outside increased. This time, a string of men and women wearing brightly-coloured Zambian traditional clothes came to the tarmac of the terminal. The men had drums. The older women were wearing bright *chitenje* traditional Zambian women's dress. The young girls were wearing short leopard skin skirts and tops that barely covered their breasts. Their smooth bellies were bare. Their chocolate brown skin looked gorgeous. Young men were wearing long colourful loose pants but had shirtless chests. Although the passengers could not hear anything from inside the plane, the people began to drum, sing, and dance. All the white passengers squeezed to the narrow plane windows to look at the action outside. The Zambian passengers looked bored, impatient and inconvenienced. Kamthibi overheard a Zambian passenger say in the *Nyanja* Lusaka language: "*Banthu bakuda, kabili ise ma passengers talanding'a first sembe taseluka. So tonse tizayamba kuyembekeza ba President bakalibe na kubwera*". (I don't know what it is with black people. We passengers arrived first. We should have been able to disembark. Now everyone has to wait for the President and he hasn't even arrived yet).

At that moment, another smaller passenger jet landed in the far end of the terminal. Soon it taxied towards the terminal. The activity on the tarmac went into a frenzy. This was an unexpected treat for Kamthibi and Trish. He had always loved traditional Zambian dances. Trish looked in utter amazement to what was a spectacle to her. The young men dancers paired with the young women in lovely short leopard skin-coloured skirts and thin tops. The men leaped into the air and the young women gyrated in the most sexy and provocative way. This looked like the *chinga'nde* traditional Zambian dance from Southern Zambia. The older women wearing brightly- coloured *chitenje* clothes were more restrained and dignified in the way they danced. They were ululating. There were television and still camera people everywhere. The red carpet was rolled out as the taxing plane came to a stand still in front but closer to the terminal building.

"Kamthibi," Trish said excitedly. "I want a couple of those *chitenje* outfits. They look gorgeous."

"You mean to take home as souvenirs?"

"No, what do you mean souvenirs?" Trish replied impatiently, "I will wear them. I have always wanted to wear something very colourful at least once in my life."

The doors of the small plane opened. A short lone Zambian man walked out and waved. The small crowd waved and the dancers went into frenzy. He descended from the plane. At the foot of the stairs, the people waiting to welcome him were top government officials. The police officers and the military men saluted and there was a line through which the President slowly and deliberately walked, said something to each person and shook hands. The queue ended up at the dancers where he stood momentarily as the dancers went nuts dancing with maximum ecstasy. The President took something out of his pocket and gave it to one of the leading older women dancers. No doubt that was a *sowela*. This is the traditional way in which Zambians reward performers. You give them a small sum of money as appreciation. The dance group might have been organized by the local political party members to welcome the President returning from a foreign visit.

The President walked away from the dancers and immediately a TV microphone and other microphones were held in front of his face. He made a brief statement probably lasting two minutes and then he was escorted to the Presidential black Mercedes Benz waiting in the motorcade. The motorcade drove off led by a police car and several police motorcycles all with flashing blue and red lights. No doubt there were also loud police sirens although Kamthibi, Trish, and the passengers could not hear much. Towards the end of their wait, one of the back doors was cracked and the stewardesses and some passengers peered through to watch the entertaining and interesting events on the tarmac.

"Do you know what the time is?" Trish suddenly asked Kamthibi.

Kamthibi looked at Trish. He didn't say anything. Then he froze into a knowing smirk- smile and showed Trish his bare wrist.

"Ok, Ok," Trish responded, "we are not to worry about time to avoid frustration."

Passengers began to pour out of the jumbo jet, carefully walking down the slightly swaying stairs. Kamthibi took one step on the stairs and stopped for a few seconds to take a wide view of the blue sky and the pleasant warm air. He breathed in and felt the thrill and excitement of being back home sweep through him. There were airline and terminal personnel at the base of the stairs. They were talking Zambian Nyanja. That sounded so sweet. The passengers were walking in a slow single file towards the arrival lounge. When Kamthibi stepped from the last stair on to the ground, that's when it happened. Kamthibi couldn't resist it. He put his carry-on bag on the ground as Trish watched in utter amazement mixed with amusement. Kamthibi knelt down, put both his hands on his side and bent down and kissed the ground.

"Are you the new Zambian pope?" one of the Zambian airport officials quipped. There was laughter. A few Zambians shook hands with Kamthibi.

"Welcome home", some of the officials said, "happy Christmas. You must have been away from home for a long time."

"Yes, home sweet home. The land of honey and milk," Kamthibi replied. Some of the Zambian ground crew laughed again about the expression "land of honey and milk," "I have not been home since five years ago. I live abroad."

There was so much that was happening that was new to hear and see that Trish for a while was in a fog. She was beginning to see a new side to Kamthibi. But the incident where Kamthibi had just kissed the ground on his own home soil deeply touched her. She didn't know whether she would ever love her home country that much even if she had stayed away for five, ten or even twenty years. She admired Kamthibi for his apparent strong love of his home country. Her love for him was quickly being accentuated by his deep love of country. She admired the loyalty. She instinctively knew that such a man in love with a woman would probably be very loyal to her to the death. She glowed and the warmth spread inside her to know and to be in the company of such a man. She momentarily wondered why a woman, his Zambian wife, would ever let such a man go.

From the upper terrace and balcony of the airport terminal there was a crowd waiting for their guests. They screamed names and waved vigorously each time passenger and host recognized each other. Kamthibi and Trish were now walking from the tarmac to enter the airport arrival concourse and lounge.

"Hey, Mthibi!!" someone shouted excitedly walking from inside the arrival concourse, "welcome home!!"

"He-e-ey! Teketa!" Kamthibi shouted to his close high school friend, "How are you?"

They embraced. They locked and shook hands vigorously, swaying their locked hands many times over in utter jubilation.

"Did you break your hand in an Ali and Frazier incident?" Teketa laughed pointing to Kamthibi's small cast on his arm, which Kamthibi up to this point had gotten used to.

"No, no," Kamthibi replied joining in his friend's hearty laughter, "you know with our advanced age we can't perform the Ali shuffle. Oh, by the way," Kamthibi paused, "meet a good friend of mine, Trish Butler." He turned and gestured to Trish who had been standing by watching yet another cultural spectacle. She could barely understand what the two were saying. They were loud and excited. The Zambian accent was getting worse. But when they turned to her Zambians quickly switched and spoke somewhat clear straight English.

"My name is actually Patricia. But your friend Kamthibi calls me Trish. I am finding out you called him Mthibi. I have a lot to learn."

"Yes," Teketa responded, "during our boarding secondary school, we shortened his name to Mthibi Simbazako. By the way," Teketa said turning to his friend but loud enough for Trish to hear, "is this our new *mulamu*?" (Sister-in-law).

"Y-e-s and n-o-o," Kamthibi said hesitating and looking at Trish.

Teketa laughed out aloud and Kamthibi joined him as they locked hands again swaying them vigorously back and forth toward each other's bodies.

"Mthibi," Teketa said wiping his tears, "if you are in court being cross examined, you would be found guilty and sentenced to life imprisonment without parole. This is a "yes" or "no" question."

"Tris-sha, we always joke," Teketa turned to Trish and shook her hand again, "welcome to Zambia. My old beaten up car is outside. I can drop the two of you anywhere you want. Come on, I will help you through customs so long as you are not carrying guns, bombs and marijuana. Ooopps!" Teketa said under his breath, "I'm not supposed to joke about this."

When they arrived in the baggage claims area, Teketa disappeared.

"Who is he?" Trish excitedly asked, "You must be close buddies."

"I have known him since we were freshmen at Chizongwe Secondary School. He is the Air Zambia Aircraft maintenance engineer. Although he works here, I didn't know he would be right in the arrival concourse to meet us. This is a sweet coincidence. I am glad he is giving us a ride. I wouldn't have had a clue how much a taxi costs from here to anywhere in town. Prices here always change so drastically."

Kamthibi and Trish breezed through immigration after the Zambian immigration officials saw Trish's return air ticket. The customs had really improved since Kamthibi was last home. He remembered that last time there were long queues. Bags took forever to be brought from the plane. He remembered that virtually every passenger's bag was turned inside out. The officials at that time were poorly paid government employees. An "Airport Authority" which was an independent profit-making company now executed customs and other airport duties. They didn't even need Teketa's help to get through customs.

The employees were younger and more efficient. As a result, within minutes they had gone through customs and were outside the airport waiting for Teketa. They even changed some money from American dollars to Zambian kwacha at the rate of one US dollar to eight kwacha. This makes anyone with foreign money, especially American dollars, enjoy a cheaper and superior life style in Zambia. Teketa rushed to the parking lot and drove his car to the front curb of the terminal building where Kamthibi and Trish were waiting with their luggage. Kamthibi's Teketa still had the same car from six years before. It was small and decrepit. The small tyres were all bald. It had dents that should have been smoothed out years before. It was discoloured from the tropical sun's heat. Some light blue smoke spewed out of the muffler. The car's body chassis was so screwed up that when it drove, it looked like a crab walking sideways. Many of the cars they were to see on the road were to be in this unfortunate condition. Teketa put Kamthibi's suitcase in the small, very narrow back part of the car, which passed for a narrow trunk. Trish shared the narrow back seat with her large green backpack. Kamthibi sat in the front.

"Why don't we fill up at that petrol station before we leave," Kamthibi said leaning over pretending to glance at the tiny car's gas meter as they pulled away from the airport terminal curb.

Once they pulled up at the petrol pump, Teketa looked at Kamthibi once with an apprehensive look that asked how much the gas attendant should put in.

"Full tank," Kamthibi said reaching in his pocket for a big wand of kwacha currency notes he had just exchanged.

"It's great to have a friend who earns American dollars abroad," Teketa said, "thanks a lot Mthibi. I don't know when I last bought a full tank of gas. I can't afford it these days. The price of mealie-meal is going up again next month. Mealie-meal is what we cook our staple food with Trish" Teketa said turning to Trish. He further said that the full tank would shock his wife, Milika. They will not have to buy any petrol for a whole week and probably more.

"That's no problem", Kamthibi said as they drove out of the airport, "the full tank was eighty-eight kwacha but that's only ten dollars for me. A full tank for my car in the US is eighteen US dollars. I will do that any time for a friend."

"Eighty-eight Zambian kwacha is a month's pay for a lot of people these days," Teketa said, "you see Trish-a, life is very rough here," Teketa added trying to involve Trish in the back seat who had so much to absorb, "I am the Aircraft Maintenance Engineer for Air Zambia and I can't afford a new or descent car and let alone buying a full tank of petrol. Can you believe that?"

"I am so sorry," Trish said, not knowing what else to say.

She was enjoying the new scenery and she never knew Africans had so many different physical features. Everyone in Zambia she had seen so far was wearing Western good clothes. Elephants of course couldn't be near the airport. They would be run over. Were there any wild animals nearby? She wondered what Kamthibi would think of these thoughts. He had not said anything yet about the African wild animals. Where were they? There was green neatly manicured grass along the airport road. There were large bushes of bright purple flowers. The weather was gorgeous; blue sky with scattered floating white clouds with dark edges. There was a farm or ranch on the right with cows grazing. Cars passed and others zoomed by in the opposite direction on the two lane smoothly paved road. Many small and big trucks had passengers packed in the back. Some small trucks were carrying large piles of over size fresh green vegetables with some vegetables draping on the side. A lone passenger was dangerously perched on top. Kamthibi and Teketa were holding feverish conversation no doubt catching up on events and friends over the past five years. This was information overload for Trish. She loved it. She was in Africa.

"Trish," Kamthibi turned around to look at her, "Teketa might drop us off at Crystal Rose Motel nearby if we can get a room. You can take a shower. The cost there should be a modest thirty to fifty dollars per night. The big luxurious tourist hotels downtown can cost from one hundred to three hundred per night. I thought we don't have that kind of money."

"That's all right Kamthibi," Trish replied feeling very apprehensive. That was the first time they would be alone in a room. That was not the way things should have worked out when people are romantically in love. 'The first time has to be special. Would he want to just do it?' she wondered.

At the junction of the International Airport Road and the Great East Road, Kamthibi mentioned to Trish that there used to be a nasty looking shanty compound right on the corner. It had ragged and dirty-looking sharks with walls built out of mud and roofing out of discarded scrap metal. The roofing was supported with rocks and old car tyres. It was embarrassing for the city, the government, and the people of Zambia. This was what people from abroad first saw as they drove to downtown Lusaka from the airport. A few years ago, the city government demolished the squalid shanty compound structures saying they were built illegally. They replaced the sharks with better-looking middle class medium-sized houses. The large billboards welcomed drivers to Lusaka the "Capital of Zambia" and the "Garden City."

They turned left towards the Crystal Rose Motel. They drove east on the Great East Road towards Chongwe for about six miles or about ten kilometres past several commercial farms when they came to the Crystal Rose Motel sign. There was a tall ten-foot wall that surrounded the motel. Outside the gate by the road, there was a makeshift market. Women, men, boys, and girls were selling fruit, candy, fritters, sugar, cooking oil, vegetables. The make shift markets were a common sight driving from the airport. Teketa turned right to the gated entrance and stopped at the gate. The security guard walked to the car and peered in and went back and raised the black long metal pole that served as a barrier.

Kamthibi was thankful that the Crystal Rose Motel was still in business. It had not changed much. It had an open large lawn, which was dotted with six to seven round grass thatched structures with tables and chairs in them. The structures, which are equivalent to *mphungu* in Kamthibi's language, were connected with different coloured light bulbs. The bar was at the far end of the lawn in an equally big grass-thatched structure. Near the check-in building was located a podium and a dancing stage whose floor was built of dark and light flat rocks held together by concrete. The bright purple flowers were blooming everywhere.

Kamthibi had strong memories of the place and the scenes. This was the place to be on a Saturday night as a young man in the nineteen seventies. The place used to be packed. You could only get here if you hitched a car ride. Immaculately-dressed and well-paid men parked their fiat cars and walked to the huts with their dates. These men were not always single. They sat in the thatched huts with gorgeous young women. They drank beer, laughed, danced, and the women drank Cinzano light champagne. Kamthibi's college friends had neither the money nor the car to afford, let alone enjoy such life styles that they could only dream of. Once they bummed a ride to the Crystal Rose Motel, they liked to dance to the hottest band at the time - the Afromods. If they were lucky, a guy who was a friend of a friend would buy them a beer. But Kamthibi and his college friends would dance together for whole evening holding on to their only beer bottles until they were as hot as tea as they often joked at that time. They sweated and had a great time. None of the girls, if asked, dared to ever dance with his friends. They were nonentities who didn't even have a car or money. In a strange way, many of the men and young women who led those apparent glamorous lifestyles were probably dead by now from the raging HIV and AIDS epidemic. Kamthibi felt good that he had enough money in his pocket now to buy a thousand beers and had a girl with whom he could dance all night.

They parked in front of the check-in office. Teketa and Kamthibi chatted about how the Crystal Rose Motel had been the place to be on Saturday nights during its hey days.

The young man at the check-in desk said they had plenty of rooms and they were fifty dollars per night, which was four hundred kwacha. They were assigned room thirty-two which was right in the middle of the group of buildings that looked like bungalows. There were a couple of tourist brochures on the check-in counter. There were a few of the Safari lodges, game parks, and white water rafting on the mighty Zambezi River, and the Mosi-o-Tunya or the Victoria Falls. But the one that caught Kamthibi's eye said: "A Guide to Zambian Etiquette." He grabbed it and noticed a logo he had not seen before. Kamthibi quickly glanced through the first sentences: "Greetings always start with a hand shake with the customary: 'How are you?' or 'How did you leave your family or how was your journey?' Kissing and hugging a Zambian in public, as a form of greeting, especially by a total stranger creates obvious embarrassment and awkwardness."

"This is great!" Kamthibi exclaimed. "Who wrote this and do you have any more copies?" He asked, flipping the brochure back to front and he looked at the back to find the authors and publisher.

"It's a new organization known as ZANOBA and we just run out of copies. We expect some on Monday when the manager goes into town," the young man replied. Kamthibi took the last copy and walked out with Teketa.

"Mthibi, you mean you never heard of ZANOBA?" Teketa asked.

"No, I live in the bush or small rural town in Illinois and have virtually no contact with anything about Zambia," Kamthibi explained to his friend as they got back into the car.

"It stands for Zambia Knowledge Bank. They just want to document Zambian culture. This is their very first brochure, which has been very hot among tourists and other foreigners. You should have been able to get a copy on Air Zambia. They probably ran out," Teketa said, as they drove to the front of room thirty-two. They unloaded the luggage and Teketa helped carry Trish's large green backpack into the motel room.

"I will leave you two so that you can rest," Teketa said as he was about to walk out, "but I will pick you up at eighteen hours which is six p.m. in Trish's Irish time. We will eat a proper Zambian dinner. My wife will be happy to see both of you."

"Thank you for the ride, Teketa," Trish said, "I am looking forward to meeting your wife and kids. How many kids do you have?"

"We could only afford three but had the fourth one by accident," Teketa laughed, "We can't afford any more children these days with the high cost of living."

"I am in Zambia in Africa!" Trish yelled as soon as Kamthibi closed the door. She playfully yelled and flung herself on her back on the double bed flicking off her shoes to the floor, "I am so excited but tired. Who cares? I am with the most loving, wonderful man in the world." She was in her blue jeans long pants and jacket. She flung her long hair backwards onto the pillow and removed her earrings and placed them on the mantle on the side of the bed.

Kamthibi smiled and removed his jacket and tossed it on a chair and also flung himself on the bed almost on top of Trish. They locked into a momentary kiss when there was a sharp knock on the door. Kamthibi jumped up and so did Trish and both quickly straightened themselves. Kamthibi opened the door. It was Teketa.

"Trish forgot this in the back seat. Fortunately I noticed it just after the gate." It was Trish's fanny pack. "I will see both of you later." Kamthibi closed the door and looked at Trish for a long time.

"I was very relaxed in his car. It's your friend, right?" Trish tried to explain and rationalize, "besides, the back seat was so small the fanny pack was uncomfortable on my waist. So I removed and placed it down beside me. What's the big deal?"

"Trish, this is serious. You had all your money in there, over two thousand US dollars." Kamthibi sat down on the bed holding and shaking his head, "this time we are very lucky. If this was a taxi, you would be flying back to Ireland now because there would be no spending money."

"Ok, Ok, Gosh Kamthibi," Trish said belligerently, "so I screwed up. I am an Irish village bumpkin who is unsophisticated. So what? I am learning. This is all new to me. Just tell me what to do. Should I put it in my underpants, inside my private parts or should I be more graphic, or maybe in my bra so my chest will barge out?"

"Your private parts would make the money unusable", Kamthibi smiled as Trish seemed to be searching for what to say next. The corner of her mouth twisted and then she couldn't resist it. The floodgates were open. She broke into laughter. They both laughed so hysterically they collapsed on the bed.

"Can you imagine," paused Trish, "me taking the money to the bank and the teller saying this money smells funny?"

They both continued to laugh hysterically rocking the bed, slapping it, and flopping around on it.

"Then," Kamthibi paused wiping tears from his eyes, "the teller would ask where you got the money from. You would reply "England" and you would be lying." They both resumed laughing hysterically.

"Ok, Kamthibi," Trish finally said exhausted, "we are having our first fight. And if this is how the fights are going to be, everything will be all right. Oh, my." Trish breathed out a big sigh, "Now where were we? What I did was pretty stupid. What should I do?"

"First, the fanny pack is the last place I would put large sums of money in", Kamthibi explained "the two rules my dad and mom taught me when I was young travelling by myself to boarding school was to spread your money and second have it on your body all the time. Never remove your fanny pack from your waist for any reason. We were talking small sums of money like two dollars. But the principle is the same. Put some of it in traveller's checks in your bag, put small amounts of cash everywhere including your underpants or bra. Besides if someone is going to steal your money from your bra, socks, or underwear, it doesn't matter because you might be already dead or passed out. That was my parents' logic. It worked for me."

"Ok, I will be more careful and will use some of the advice. I am glad this happened under this circumstance. Maybe it's God communicating to us."

There was another knock on the door.

"I hope I didn't forget my huge back pack in your friend's car this time because it's right here?" Trish quipped pointing to the bag.

"The cleaning person forgot to put towels," it was the young man from the check-in desk. He handed Kamthibi some towels.

"Thank you," Kamthibi said, "what's your name?" he asked in Nyanja..

"I am Freedom Musumali, Sir."

"Thank you, Mr. Musumali," Kamthibi shut the door.

"His name is "Freedom"?" Trish asked with surprise.

"Such names are not unusual among us Zambians."

"Are we friends again?" Trish coyly walked over to Kamthibi and put her hands around his neck. Kamthibi held Trish around her waist. They kissed for so long that Kamthibi's temperature was already too high. The anticipation was killing him. But he hated to be too impatient. Trish pulled back and looked suddenly restrained.

"What's wrong?" Kamthibi whispered.

"I'm just so happy, I don't want to blow it. I want to make you happy. I know you want sex," Trish was drifting into a fog verging on verbal diarrhoea.

"Please," Kamthibi grabbed her by the arm, "just tell me. Is it your period?"

"No, no," Trish replied.

"You have a headache?"

"Now don't be funny. I wouldn't be caught using that line if I didn't want sex with you."

"Don't break my heart by saying you just want to be friends or love me just like a brother."

"No, No, No. That's not it," Trish said waving her palm down.

"Then, what is it, Trish?" Kamthibi was getting angry and impatient and grabbed her arm.

"Look, you are right to be angry. I can't talk about it right now," Trish said running her hand through her long hair several times, "I promise I will tell you tonight."

Kamthibi had learned over the years that you don't force a woman to say something she doesn't want to. Women sometimes have deadly secrets, which can kill or severely injure an impatient or very curious man. He loved Trish enough to wait. Besides, the day was so exciting he was not about to ruin it by forcing conversation that Trish had said she was not yet ready for.

"While you are taking a shower and changing," Kamthibi said, "I will walk to the gate of the motel and check things out. I have not talked Nyanja for a long time."

He held Trish around her waist again and gave her a quick kiss on the lips. She lovingly caressed her hand around his forehead down along the side of his face, near his eye, cheek, and up to his chin and she gave him another quick kiss on the lips. Trish walked into the bathroom and closed the door. There was a scream and the door flew open.

"There is something walking on the floor! It ran into the corner under the toilet."

Kamthibi knocked on the toilet bowl with a shoe and a lizard wiggled out from under.

"That's a harmless lizard," Kamthibi said, "You never saw a lizard in Gandy?"

"No," Trish replied shaking her head, "thanks, Kamthibi you are my hero."

Kamthibi flicked the lizard along the floor with his shoe out of the bathroom and out through the front door.

"Since I was at Tamanda Primary School, we learned during nature study that these lizards are actually man's friend. They eat flies that spread germs to our food. But we have no flies in our modern in-door plumbing. While I am at it, I might as well slay this spider."

There was a house spider in the corner of the toilet, which he smashed with the sole of the shoe. He disposed of the offending vermin in the trashcan.

Kamthibi slowly walked to the motel gate flicking and kicking some small pebbles along the way. He was still so pumped up about being back home. Since it was a late December afternoon, rain could be expected any time. The dark clouds were gathering. Kamthibi greeted the security guard and chit-chatted with him in Nyanja for a while. He told the security guard how he missed speaking in Nyanja when he lives abroad in America. He was an expert in seed technology and has a wife and three kids. Was the white woman he was with the kids' mother? Kamthibi knew that it was a mistake to talk about his wife and kids. But the man had mentioned his wife and family. It was only fair. But this is Zambia where people are not too obsessed with secrecy or privacy, as people in the West prefer to call it. I might just marry two wives -one here in Zambia and another in America; a *munthu* or black wife here at home and a white one in America.

"What do you think?"

The security guard laughed heartily. Kamthibi knew he was providing scintillating gossip for Crystal Rose Motel and the man's social circles. But he did not care. This was home where people were more forgiving and understanding of genuine human dilemmas.

The Nyanja they were using is a perfect language for urban multicultural communication with a mixture of classic Nyanja words, town Zezulu words from urban South Africa and English which has been *Nyanjarised* and Zambianised, not necessarily her Majesty the Queen's English. Kamthibi talked to the children and the women who were selling various products including mangoes. How he missed mangoes. He bought one and devoured it right way. He knew he was taking a risk eating a fresh fruit that is unwashed and sold by the open road exposed to flies. He couldn't wait to eat the free fresh mangoes straight from a tree in the village. He would not dare get one for Trish because she could end up in the emergency room, not with her condition. Kamthibi would be content to just narrate to her his adventures at the motel gate minus the possibility of his engaging in polygamy. Trish took a nice, long, warm bath in the big bath tab although she would have preferred a shower. She changed and put on fresh clean clothes. She wore a casual dress, which would be worn in spring in Ireland. She was saving her sneakers for when she would do a lot of walking in the city or when they travel to the village. She lay down on the bed covering half of her lower body with the bed spread. She wondered why it was taking Kamthibi so long. He won't have enough time to take a bath and change before his friend comes to pick them up. Maybe that's why he put his wrist watch away. 'Maybe time truly does not matter in Africa after all,' she thought. Trish switched on the small am/fm radio that was nailed to the side of the bed such that she could not move it. She tuned through several stations until she found a station in which they spoke English. She was surprised that they played so much contemporary Western pop music. They played more variety than the radio stations in Belfast or anything near or around Gandy. Trish dosed off.

Kamthibi tried to open the door but it was locked. Fortunately, he had taken the spare key with him because he knew Trish would probably be sleeping. She needed the rest. He unlocked the door and as quietly as he could took a bath and changed. He lay down on the bed beside Trish, who looked so serene in her sleep. He noticed that her prescription pill bottles were on the bedside table. She must have just taken the second dose of the day on an empty stomach. She was supposed to take the medication with food. But he did not want to wake her up. Maybe he could take a nap before they went to his friend Teketa's house. He slowly and carefully lay down on the bed beside her.

"Oh, you are back," Trish said. "I had locked the door. I didn't want any more lizards wondering in looking for flies."

Trish lifted her head and laid it on Kamthibi's shoulder as he put his arm around her. She snuggled and put her leg on top of him. This was pure torture and pleasure at the same time for Kamthibi. But he tried for once to ignore his natural and most urgent urges again.

There was a loud knock on the door.

"Just a minute!" Kamthibi yelled as he jumped up from the bed to go and open the door. "This must be Teketa. Are you ready to go?"

"Not really," Trish replied as she slowly stood up from the bed wringing her hands, "I am so nervous. I don't know how to behave at a Zambian home."

"Just be you," Kamthibi reassured her, "go with the flow. You will be all right. They are just my friends."

The three of them walked to the car. They turned left at the gate onto the Great East Road which was a two-lane paved highway. They drove west, back toward downtown Lusaka, although they would not be going anywhere closer to downtown Lusaka. After the International Airport Road, there were big houses with tall concrete wall fences on the left. On the right was a big tall water tank that is visible for miles around the city. On the right side of the road were all the medium and small houses bunched close together. They did not have fences around them. This was the beginning of the Chelstone Township. People were walking everywhere up and down the road and the streets. Teketa clicked the right blinker on just in time to turn right. The car sputtered and chocked as he shifted gears rapidly but very carefully as if afraid that any false move could disintegrate the rickety, small, aged car. The slightly blue smoke was evident from the muffler when Kamthibi glanced back periodically.

"Oh, my wife did not have tomatoes," Teketa said, "so she asked me to get some from the Chelstone Market."

They stopped at a large structure enclosed in a worn out, red mud brick wall. There were piles of bags of charcoal outside, men banging and fixing metal containers, a make shift car garage, and a tyre-mending place. People were milling around conducting business or just hanging out. There was loud music from inside the wall. It seemed some commerce had spilled to the outside of the wall. There was trash piled up high across from the wall. Teketa parked the car alongside two other cars and told Trish and Kamthibi to wait in the car while he quickly ran inside the market to buy some tomatoes.

At first nothing happened. Then within seconds several barefoot boys in dirty, torn patched shorts and shirts hustled over.

"Madam! Madam!" one of them yelled, "Nice cheap wrist watch, necklace, earring. Only fifteen or ten kwacha! Dollar also ok!"

Several of the boys waved their wares in a competitive fashion to Trish at the back window of the car. The boys were hawking a variety of items such as wrist watches, necklaces, ties, earrings, bangles, batteries, small elephant wooden carvings - all kinds of trinkets.

"What should I do?" Trish asked.

"Just ignore them. They are very pesky. You notice they are not coming to my window. If you are *Muzungu* they know you have a lot of money to buy anything."

A man came to Kamthibi's side of the car. He rolled down the window.

"Do you want your spare tyre mended? We can do it in ten minutes for five kwacha. Do you want your car washed? I have some boys who can quickly do it for you for five kwacha."

"No," Kamthibi replied as politely as he could, "*tiyenda manje manje tiyembekezela binangu mkati bagula* tomato." (We are about to go. We are waiting for someone who is buying tomatoes inside the market.) "*Imwe, bafana!* (You kids)," Kamthibi said in Nyanja through the window, "*Yendani uyu muzungu safuna kugula.*" (Go away. This white woman does not want to buy anything.) Some of the small swarm of boys reluctantly wandered away. Others simply stood at a distance maybe waiting for the next car.

"Oh, that was wrong," Kamthibi laughed aloud and turned to Trish in the back seat. "I should have said "*Dona*" instead of "*Muzungu*." "*Muzungu*" is white man and "*Dona*" is white woman. That's the way the terms evolved back in the days of British colonialism."

"Whatever, Kamthibi," Trish chuckled. She could care less.

"Well, just a minor detail," Kamthibi remarked.

Shortly, Teketa returned with the tomatoes wrapped in old newspapers.

"Don't be surprised if dinner or *nshima* is late this evening. We are late buying the ingredients for the relish or *ndiyo*."

"Trish!" Teketa said excitedly, "in fact in the village, a meal can take many hours to cook. Children have to chase the chicken. Its feathers have to be plucked and the village chicken takes hours of boiling before you can eat it. Peanuts have to be shelled and ground. You are lucky we are in the city where we pick up frozen tasteless chicken from the supermarket." They all laughed.

Teketa and Milika's home was located in Kaunda Square Stage II, just down the road from Chelstone on the Great East Road. Teketa did not pay rent for the house. This was government policy for all employees of public or parastatal companies. It was a beautiful new two-story house owned by Air Zambia. This was a new upscale neighbourhood. The rest of the Kaunda Square neighbourhood just across the street had smaller plain houses squeezed close together, built of concrete blocks. Since the financing of the homes was done by individuals with small loans from internationally-financed urban housing loans, many houses were in various states of completion and often neglect. Some houses, for example, had glass windows but several of them would have wooden or sack windows. The houses lacked the trimmings of a well-built modern upscale home.

The car pulled up to a huge, tall, opaque black metal gate. A muffled weak car horn, no doubt due to a weak battery, brought someone who swung the gate open from inside. You could not see the house from the street because of the massive tall concrete wall that surrounded it. You could only see the roof.

"Why are there so many high walls around large houses?" Trish asked.

"Oh, if you don't have a concrete wall," Teketa replied laughing, "while you are fast asleep and snoring at night, thieves will steal and clean out everything from your house - car, fridge, TV, stereo, plates. Last week," Teketa continued as he got out of the car to command his furiously barking dog to shut up, "three houses down, a car and curtains were stolen. That's an everyday story."

"Trish," Kamthibi said excitedly as he opened his car door, "when we lived in Lusaka, we had an Irish neighbour four doors down. He was single and in his late twenties. When he first moved in he said he liked to be free and did not like the idea of even the short wall around his house. He didn't want to feel like he was behind a prison wall. Only a month later after twelve attempted burglaries on his house at night, he put razor sharp wire above the wall around his house, big pad locks, welded stronger burglar bars on his window and installed an expensive alarm system in his house. Apparently the burglars had practically camped outside his house every nightfall because he could see them at night standing and lurking around bushes waiting for him to go to bed so that they could try to break in."

It was getting dark and beginning to sprinkle. Teketa told his son Filimoni to close the gate and lock it. The front porch light came on, switched on by someone from inside who was anticipating their arrival. The front door opened.

"Welcome home *awise* Phyera," (the father of Phyera) Milika, Teketa's wife said smiling, "and our visitor. I heard that she is our new *mulamu* (sister-in-law)."

Kamthibi and Teketa laughed nervously. Trish did not laugh. Kamthibi wondered whether Trish remembered the joke from the morning at the airport. Even if she remembered the conversation, she might not have recognized *"mulamu"* as the Zambian word for sister-in-law.

Milika was about five feet nine inches tall, and just a little shorter than her husband. She was slightly stockier for a Zambian from having four children, piped water, a rich diet, and a car. She had dark hair supplemented by long braids that were draped to her shoulders. She had a brown skin complexion with bright lovely straight teeth, which sparkled when she smiled. Her face looked sweaty and greasy no doubt from the kitchen heat. She had wrapped a faded traditional *chitenje* cloth around the lower half of her body. She was wiping her wet hands on the *chitenje* cloth she was wearing, which was a sign that she had been interrupted cooking in the kitchen.

The front door opened into the living room. They all sat down on two sets of thick but sinking cushy-soft luxurious couches. The television was on to the only channel in Zambia. No one was paying attention to it throughout the guests' stay.

There were lovely framed photographs of the couple and their children hung on the living room walls. There was another beautifully-framed picture on the adjacent living room wall. The large glass decorative cupboard displayed mementos from Britain, thin sets of wine glasses, mugs with golden etchings. The home had all the trappings of a middle class home whose occupants were world travelled and sophisticated.

Firm Zambian traditional formal greeting handshakes were exchanged between Milika, Trish, and Kamthibi. Each child politely shook the guests' hands and walked away shyly. Even the eighteen-month old toddler mimicked her older siblings and first shook Trish's hand but then lost interest in the game on the long way to the second guest on the couch. Everyone laughed and urged the little one to go on and greet uncle Kamthibi next.

Teketa formally introduced his wife and children to Trish. The kids were told, "This is Aunt Trish visiting from Ireland. And you remember Uncle Kamthibi or Simbazako. You remember how our oldest first born could say Uncle "Simbazako" when he was small? He ended up saying *"Ako Zako."* " They all laughed except Trish.

Milika promptly disappeared to the kitchen and brought back some soft drinks, glasses, small plates, and a large plate of cookies all on a tray.

"We thought you might snack on this while I prepare *nshima,*" Milika said, "Filimoni, come and serve the visitors."

Filimoni, who looked thirteen years old, poured the soft drinks into the glasses and placed each drink on the coaster on the small coffee table next to each person. He did the same with the small plates of cookies or biscuits as they are called in Zambia. The young kids peeked at Trish and ran stampeding and thumping excitedly to the kitchen giggling and yelling, *"Muzungu! Muzungu."*

"Imwe namwe (you kids)" Kamthibi overheard Milika in the kitchen telling her kids. *"Muzungu, Muzungu wakuti. Ni Aunt Trish aba."* (White man, white man, stop that. She is Aunt Trish.)

The kids instantly stopped their game, and instead chanted "Aunt Trish! Aunt Trish!" several times.

Kamthibi and Teketa caught up on Zambian politics, the ups and downs and exploits of the national soccer team -which soccer club was top in the league. They talked about who of their secondary school classmates had tragically died of the HIV and AIDS epidemic. They discussed the worsening of the economy and the perpetual stories of crime and especially burglaries at night in homes in Lusaka. The special crack armed police robbery squad that patrolled at night had achieved some quiet in some neighbourhood. Not all was bad. They discussed how their respective parents were doing in the villages in their old age. Kamthibi sensed that this was not the right time to bring up his relationship with Trish and the ups and downs and often worsening marriage with his wife in the US. He anticipated that at some point his friend's wife, Milika, would bring it up and rebuke Kamthibi about Trish. Milika and Nora had been good friends when Kamthibi and Nora lived in Lusaka when he worked at the Ministry of Agriculture as the country's number two top seed technology specialist.

Zambian families are very fluid as they always have an assortment of household relatives. Kamthibi saw at least two other young older girls who were not Teketa's children. For one thing, they were much too old to be the couple's children. One of them was a live in nanny who watched the couple's eighteen-month-old when both were at work. The other girl was a niece from Milika's extended family who was living with them for a while because both the girl's parents had died in a road accident. The young girl who was the nanny watched the toddler as her principle responsibility. She dropped out of school in Grade 6. Her parents lived in Kalikiliki shanty compound. The older woman, who was the house servant, took care of such chores as cooking, sweeping, washing laundry, and ironing. Her name was Mrs Jere. Her husband was a labourer in a building construction company.

Milika had been surreptitiously checking on Trish. Trish was quiet, staring at the TV, with her hands crossed on her bosom and clearly looking bored.

"Since the men are catching up on sports and politics, come and join us in the kitchen," Milika announced glancing in the direction of Teketa and Kamthibi who were engrossed in their conversation. She smiled, beckoning to Trish.

"Thank you," Trish replied as she walked into the kitchen, "I almost asked but did not want to intrude."

Trish stood up, stalked, and gingerly walked into the kitchen. Kamthibi and Teketa smiled as they heard the kids scream and giggle even louder as they came dashing into the living room and even overshot into the dining area table. It was the kind of giddy scream, reflecting sheer excitement kids show when the "monster" suddenly catches up with them in the common tease-and- run-away-from-monster game. The toddler finally seemed to figure out how to play the game too, and staggered in slow motion out of the kitchen holding his loose pants; landed on the bottom several times and got up. The commotion was threatening to reach fever pitch. Teketa barked at them to sit down, stop running around, and quit making noise.

"Sorry," Milika responded. "I just wasn't sure you would feel free away from Kamthibi. This is our humble kitchen."

"It looks very much like my kitchen at home. This one is even bigger. Is there anything I can do? I need to do something to help."

"You can chop the onion and the tomatoes on that cutting board," Milika pointed to the cutting board by the kitchen sink, "the nanny will help with chopping the rape greens."

"Milika, you are so lucky that you can work and get so much help in the kitchen and a nanny for your baby," Trish said.

"Well, life is a little easier because you can pay the nanny and another house servant for very little. But that's the only way many people get jobs in the city if they have little education, are poor, or come from the villages in the rural areas. There are also a lot of female relatives in most homes who can help in the kitchen."

"I wish I had that type of help when I was raising my two children and working at the same time."

"You mean you only have two children?" Milika asked

"Yes."

Milika chatted with Trish as she gave orders, fried some of the relish meats, added cooking oil, and spices and in between told the noisy children to go to the living room to play with daddy and Uncle Ako Zako. When the children went to the living room playing noisily and interrupting the men's conversations, Teketa put the toddler on his lap and after a while told them to go to the kitchen to see mummy.

Three pots of red kidney beans, chicken, and *kapenta* were cooking. Delicious smells wafted from the kitchen and tortured Kamthibi who had not eaten any Zambian food in almost five years. Trish never showed up once again in the living room. The conversation was too interesting in the kitchen as she kept busy being put to work helping out. Kamthibi was relieved that Trish was probably learning a lot about Zambian culture this way before they headed to the village.

Finally, the forerunner of the main meal was evident. The nanny set the dining room table putting plate mats all around. She brought clean water in a large basin. She put on each plate mat, a small plate slightly bigger than an average saucer. Four steaming serving bowls each containing chicken, *kapenta* (anchovies), rape or collard greens, and red kidney beans were placed on the table. Finally, Milika brought in a large serving of the white steaming hot *nshima* and placed it right in the dead centre of the table. Trish brought in a pitcher of drinking water with ice in it and drinking glasses on a tray.

"*Awisi* Phyera *bwerani ku thebo*," (Father of Pyera come to the dinner table) Milika said in Nyanja standing on the edge of the living room. This was like sweet music to Kamthibi's ear because of all the anticipation and being back home.

"*Amake* Filimoni, (mother of Filimoni)", Kamthibi said to Milika, "this is a big feast. In the United States, I miss *rape* and *kapenta*. Even red beans are not cooked the same way they are cooked here."

"Maggy", Milika called.

"*Ma!*" answered one of the girls from the kitchen

"*Mudye nawo bana* especially *uyu mung'ono. Ngati abvuta umulete kuno nizamdyesa,*" Milika yelled instructions towards the kitchen. (Please eat with the children. Especially feed the toddler. If she gives you trouble bring her here. I will feed her).

Teketa and Milika sat on the opposite ends of the long table. Trish and Kamthibi sat on one side and their oldest boy, Filimoni, sat on the other side of the table near his mother.

"Did everything go ok in the kitchen," Kamthibi whispered to Trish so softly that he was inaudible to the rest of the people at the table.

"Yes," Trish whispered nodding her head rapidly several times.

Kamthibi first lifted and passed the large basin of water to Teketa to wash his hands first as the head of the household. But he deferred to Kamthibi saying that Kamthibi and Trish should have the honour of washing their hands first as guests. After Kamthibi and Trish had done, the water was next passed to Teketa. Milika and Filimoni washed their hands last in that order.

"May the Lord bless the food we are about to eat, Amen," Teketa said a short prayer. Kamthibi remembered that that was exactly the same short prayer they heard in the dining room before meals during five years at Chizongwe Secondary Boarding School more than twenty years earlier.

"Trish, are you going to manage to eat with your hands?" Teketa asked as the bowls of relish were being passed around.

"Do you want to try?" Kamthibi asked too.

"Of course, I will try," Trish replied, "I want to try to learn some Zambian culture."

"The *nshima* is very hot," Milika warned, "we will get a knife and fork for you just in case. Maggy, would you please bring a knife and fork." The girl promptly popped out of the kitchen and brought the knife and fork and placed them by Trish.

"Thank you," Trish said to the young girl.

Hot *nshima* needs some getting used to eating with bare hands. Predictably, Trish squirmed, and aaahhhed!! And ooopppssed!! And dropped the small lump of her first *nshima* like a hot piece of amber, which it might as well have been. She quickly licked the tips of her fingers each time she dropped it again and again. She instinctively used both hands to help, which is against custom. You always only use one hand when eating *nshima* except for young children who are learning how to eat food properly anyway in the first place. Everyone at the table was light-hearted about Trish's predicament. Kamthibi made some small lumps of *nshima* like Zambians normally do for a young child. Then he placed a number of these on Trish's plate telling her to wait until they cooled down.

Trish refused to use the knife and fork. Teketa and Milika tried to persuade her repeatedly but to no avail. In between casual conversation, Kamthibi devoured the *nshima,* gracefully relishing the moment. He alternated between eating *nshima* with the *kapenta* and rape or collard greens. He mixed red beans with its thick gravy with chicken and its characteristic bright-yellow gravy created by cooking fresh ripe tomatoes with a touch of mild curry powder. Kamthibi took one bite of the chicken and paused with a grin.

"*Amake* Filimoni," Kamthibi directed his comments to Milika, "this chicken is not from the supermarket."

"I knew you would say that," Milika giggled with her mouth closed as she chewed the food, "I went to the market in Chelstone and got a live chicken. How could I feed a supermarket chicken to a traditional Zambian who has been away abroad? Ah, with its plastic tastelessness?"

The conversation kept shifting from pure English when someone felt Trish had to be included to Nyanja. Trish didn't seem to mind, as she was clearly preoccupied with the novel tastes and delicious smells of the food and navigating the *nshima* balls from her hand to the delicious gravy. She enjoyed the *nshima* at the end as it had cooled down somewhat. Her patience and persistence had certainly paid off. She ate a serving of each dish and about three large servings of *nshima*. Both Kamthibi and Trish must have been starving. Kamthibi had anticipated the Zambian meal since they flew out of London's Heathrow International Airport. Because the Zambian *nshima* meal is so filling, there is never a need for desert. But, as they all chatted in the comfortable living room after the meal, Kamthibi slowly drank two of the Zambian Mosi bottled beer. Trish drank a cup of black tea and declined anything else.

"Why don't you try just one Zambian Mosi beer?" asked Milika, "I know from when my husband and I lived in Britain that the Irish have good beer."

"Well, I don't know whether I should talk about this."

"What is the reason?" Milika asked, "feel free. I am sure we would understand."

"Since I was diagnosed with early lung cancer," Trish explained slowly. "I stopped both the drinking and the heavy smoking cold turkey."

"I am sorry," Milika said, "maybe I should not have asked."

"No, no it's all right. It's in its early stages. The doctor said I might beat it." Trish continued, as everyone was quiet expecting to hear more. "It's amazing what a threat to one's life can do to deeply entrenched life-long addictions. It has given me an amazingly deeper craving and appreciation of life, and has created an intense focus on strengthening and cherishing the simple human actions. Something simple like eating *nshima* with new friends. Every action and reaction now had a special meaning for me. It is not a joke because every bite of delicious food could be my last one. Every beautiful sunrise or sunset could be the last one. Every laugh and smile could be the last one. My every breath could be the last one. I don't feel like I am going to die now though," Trish smiled.

Although to a certain extent Kamthibi felt perhaps the same things Trish felt, her feelings were punctuated by a possible finality - death. Kamthibi could live on perhaps forever anguished and tormented by the torturous memories of a lost love. But he still would be living on. Trish did not have that option; not as far as she knew. There was a long silence.

"How did you get the cast on your arm?" Teketa finally asked clearly wanting to move the attention from Trish. It was like having an elephant in the living room and no one willing to mention it. Maybe they had been waiting for Kamthibi to volunteer the information.

"I fell from a bar stool and sprained my arm."

Everyone laughed very loud with Teketa laughing the loudest.

"Just like a Zambian," Teketa interjected, "drank too much and fell off the bar stool. That is very, very funny Mthibi. I have never heard of this one before." Teketa and Milika were wiping tears from their eyes because they were laughing so hard.

"No, this is the truth," Kamthibi protested, "maybe I will start from the beginning. I met Trish on the Internet in one of the chat rooms," Kamthibi began as he put his arm around her shoulders as they sat and sank next to each other on the cushy couch. Teketa and Milika were clearly intrigued by this piece of unusual information. The few educated and world savvy Zambians had heard of this exciting but sometime dangerous new trend in the West -love and romance in chat rooms. Most Zambians have only occasionally heard of rumours about the wonders of the Internet and chat rooms since too few people had computers, let alone afford the luxury of spending hours in chat rooms. It was fascinating for Milika and Teketa to meet two people in their home, one of whom is their close Zambian friend, who had actually fallen in love through this modern fascinating medium that Americans and other Westerners apparently have in every home and office, something that Zambians might never catch up with. It is still a taxing expense for Zambians to afford a pen and paper and a postage stamp to write and mail a letter.

"We fell in love and talked on the phone for hours," Kamthibi continued, "after three months, I decided to go and meet this woman, not in London or some big city like Dublin, but in her small village of Gandy in Northern Ireland just north of the town of Belfast. That was probably stupid and dangerous." Kamthibi paused for effect. The last statement no doubt only reinforced what Kamthibi knew Milika and Teketa and anyone with a sane mind would conclude.

"But here is where things got really dangerous. I was drinking at the cocktail lounge of the hotel I was staying in. I was celebrating the fact that I was to meet my lover, Trish, the following morning. I apparently slipped on the bar stool, and on my way down caught my arm in the side stool support and sustained a bad sprain but thank God not a fracture."

"How did that happen?" asked Teketa with scepticism that said that he smelled a mouse, "how and why do you get drunk in a place with all those strange whites around? Are there any blacks or Africans in Belfast?"

"I never saw any on the streets," Trish interjected, "but then I didn't live in Belfast."

"I suspect someone dropped the rape drug or something in my beer when I was not looking," Kamthibi resumed, "because that was only my second or maybe third beer. You knew me as a Zambian who used to drink like a fish in water. How could I get so drunk on just two beers? Anyway, I was taken to the Belfast hospital unconscious and admitted overnight."

Teketa whistled, shook his head and made the cricket sound with his mouth indicating how in grave danger Kamthibi had been.

"The following morning, I woke up to remember that I was to meet my lover, Trish, that morning at 10:30 am on a road north of Belfast. Nurse Agnes, who was very understanding and sympathetic to my situation, smuggled me out of the hospital and got a taxi. Meanwhile, someone planted prescription drugs under my hospital bed pillow. This was immediately reported to the police. It sounds like a Hollywood movie script. But it really happened. Love can make you do crazy things sometimes. That's how I got this small cast on my arm. I should take it off in a couple of days because it has healed so fast as the doctor had predicted."

"I know the rumours of this scandal are all over my small village by now. But I don't care. Life is short," Trish remarked shrugging her shoulders, "I feel sorry for my mother. She has to endure all of this." She was quiet for a while.

"Tell them about the police and why they arrested you," Trish suddenly nudged.

"No," Kamthibi protested saying that it was getting late, "I think it's too dangerous and embarrassing. Our hosts may chase us out of their house."

"What arrest?" Teketa asked in a perked up voice, "You mean you were arrested?"

"Yes,"

"For what?" Teketa asked as everyone else paid closer attention.

"Someone was trying to frame me with drugs at the hospital. They put bottles of morphine in my bed covers and the pillow. So the police car followed me all the way toward Trish's little village and arrested me and took me to the Belfast Police Station."

"This is dangerous," Teketa whistled, "who was framing you?"

"Trish's husband."

"Eh! Eh! Eh!" Teketa exclaimed placing his open palm on his mouth.

"Ma! Ma! Ma!" Milika said as she clapped her hands expressing shock.

"Her husband followed us to London Heathrow Airport," Kamthibi disclosed another intriguing detail. "I had to hide Trish in my big winter coat I was wearing. You can ask her."

"Yes," Trish added. "I was scared and surprised. We are on separation now."

"*Yaba,*" Teketa said, "her husband could follow you to Zambia. After all she is still his wife. Be careful. We have four flights from London every week. Trish's husband could be in Lusaka." Teketa tried to make light of the situation as they laughed.

Trish and Kamthibi looked at each other as if someone had stumbled into something both of them had thought about but were too afraid to say. This had crossed their minds but each of them did not want to ruin their plane ride to Zambia discussing worrisome things. But was it a distinctive possibility?

"Trish, can Richard follow us to here?" asked Kamthibi.

"I honestly don't know. He has a dangerous side especially when he drinks. I hate to think of it. Let's not ruin the evening."

By late that evening, the rain had subsided but was still drizzling. This was very characteristic of December rains when the crops and other vegetation begin to grow in leaps and bounds. A big meal of *nshima* makes one very tired. Trish and Kamthibi were even more tired as they had had a long day.

Trish thanked Milika a lot saying she had learned or at least seen how the Zambian meal of *nshima* is cooked. As Trish and Teketa were walking to the car, Milika stood on the dry porch away from the rain as she held the now tired and cranky toddler in her hands.

"Sorry about the awkward situation with Trish," Kamthibi hastily apologized in a low tone in Nyanja. "Nora and I have had a lot of serious problems in our marriage. We even went to a marriage counsellor for nearly a year. I don't know whether things will ever work out between us again. But I love this woman, Trish."

"That's why you Zambian men are really strange," Milika rebuked Kamthibi in a low hasty tone, "that's the way you African men are, when you see a *muzungu* woman, you damp your African wives." Kamthibi cringed.

"No, no," Kamthibi protested, "that's not how things are. I can't explain it. It's just love."

"We have known both you and Nora for a long time. If you divorce, she and your children will suffer. I am a mature woman though and I understand some of this although I don't necessarily agree with it. No wonder you are so in love with Trish. She is wonderful and said wonderful things about you. Few whites would behave the way she behaved this evening. Eating hot *nshima* and such." Both laughed nervously. They bid each other good night shaking hands. Kamthibi rushed to the car.

The rain sprinkled harder and only one head lamp was working on the car. Teketa's small car sputtered it's way to the Crystal Rose Motel. It was a miracle that both windshield wipers were working at all, let alone so furiously. Once they drove past the gate entrance into the motel grounds, the place was surprisingly still alive. The parking lot was full and all the little thatched round huts were filled with patrons. People were jaunting from hut to the bar and the dancing terrace. Some women were carrying their shoes in their hands and they held on to their long dresses while walking or jaunting across the obviously rain-saturated lawn. People were dancing on the terrace patio to loud dj music. The red, green, and yellow light bulbs which hung on long string cords between and around the hut structures, were flashing on and off on the entire lawn. It was a party atmosphere.

"Although I am not very worried, *mwamuna wake ni mambala* (Her husband maybe a dangerous crook)," Kamthibi said to Teketa quickly in a low English-Nyanja so that Trish did not hear anything. *"Angabwere kuno nakutipaya.* Check *ma passport ku* airport Air Zambia *yocokera ku* Heathrow *pa zina la mu* Irish Richard Butler. *Ngati mwamuona muni uze.* (He could come to Zambia and kill both of us. Check passports for Air Zambia arrivals from Heathrow for an Irishman Richard Butler. If you see him, alert me.) Teketa laughed through his nose nervously. Trish did not suspect anything since she had heard so much English-Nyanja conversation already.

Trish and Kamthibi thanked Teketa for the great evening and the food. Trish held on to Kamthibi's hand as the two jaunted toward their dry bungalow motel room. Once inside, Trish did not even kick off her shoes at the door as she would normally do. But instead headed for the bathroom. This worried Kamthibi. Maybe the new Zambian food did not sit right with her. Maybe it was the fresh water *kapenta*. Kamthibi remembered his first night out of Zambia in a hotel room in London many years ago as a young student going abroad for his Masters. He had eaten shrimp by accident. He spent half an hour vomiting, sweating, and feeling deathly ill in the bathroom of his hotel room that night. New food could do that to you. But the Irish surely eat a lot of sea fish. *Kapenta* would not bother their stomachs. But Trish had the strong cancer medications too. All these worrisome thoughts went through Kamthibi's mind as he stood waiting anxiously. He couldn't hear anything. He drew near and put his ear on the bathroom door. He still couldn't hear anything. He was sure she had fainted.

"Are you okay in there?" Kamthibi asked anxiously, knocking softly on the door.

"Yes," was the muffled reply from inside as the faucet water ran for a short while. When the door opened, Kamthibi was stunned at what he saw a few feet in front of him. His jaw dropped to the floor.

Trish was wearing a beautiful long, soft, red silk-smooth negligee; her slender arms stretched out but being slowly brought down to her side. Her face had a bright glow but she also had a nervous and uncertain look. Two thin barely visible strings supporting her negligee hung delicately over her shoulders. The front top of the negligee barely covered only the last third of her firm breasts whose nipples protruded in the most provocative way. Her soft, long brown hair, which had a touch of graceful silver to it, hung on her shoulders and onto her bosom as if begging to be fondled and moved to the back of her head. She looked nervous as she took half a step closer to Kamthibi. He could smell her soft sensuous perfume. To say that Kamthibi was mesmerized would be an understatement. Kamthibi thought this could only have happened in a movie. He never had this scene in mind in a thousand fantasies and dreams.

Kamthibi slowly stretched his shaking and trembling hand like a chameleon as if anticipating more shock than absolute pleasure. His hand finally touched her gingerly as if testing dangerous waters. He slid his hand slowly around her delicate waist. The feel of the silk negligee was so smooth that his hand instinctively caressed and squeezed her up and down to her soft bun. Trish gasped. She moaned once but stopped. He drew her to him so that their warm bodies touched and consumed each other. His other hand slowly reached for and gently caressed her breast nipple with his fingertips. Her nipple stiffened. He buried his nose into the deep cavity of her cleavage and let out a tiny helpless moan. Kamthibi was beginning to crawl into a land in which few men have entered in their entire lives.

"Precious", Kamthibi half whispered and moaned, "You are the most gorgeous woman in the world. Is this what you wanted to tell me?"

He was surprised that she still had a serious and nervous look on her face with her arms loosely around his shoulders. She was not doing anything more to accelerate things. She led Kamthibi to the bed and gestured for him to sit down. She sat on his lap and wrapped her arms around his strong neck. She could feel the enormous rock-hard shaft throbbing between his legs.

"As you can tell Kamthibi," Trish whispered in the feminine soft but firm voice looking at him. The dance music from the motel lawn was softly penetrating the room. The flashing bulb lights of different colours were visible through the thin cotton curtains. "I am confused right now and torn," continued Trish, "I have never done this entire negligee thing before. But I have been dreaming of doing this for a man I love since I was young. I never got a chance until this moment. I love you so deeply like I have never loved a man before. But I just came from a very abusive marriage. Sometimes you don't see what is bad in your life until you are out of it or you look back. For more than twenty years, my husband used to come home late at night, drunk, and force himself on me. For more than twenty years, I never felt sexy, romantic, warm inside or any of that. I want to give myself to you. God, I have never wanted to please a man so bad." Trish cupped Kamthibi's chin in her hand.

"I want to please you for showing me love and tenderness. But I still don't feel anything inside me from being so numb for so long. Everything happened so quickly when I met you in Gandy on that dirt road. Kamthibi, I need to thaw. Give me time. I am sorry. No man should have to go through what you are going through now." Trish wept and tears dribbled down her cheeks onto her delicate negligee, "if you want to leave me and dump me now, I will understand. But I want to be with you."

She wept some more and rapidly heaved her bosom up and down holding on to Kamthibi drenching his neck and shoulders with tears as she clung on to him like a frightened toddler.

"No, I won't leave you," Kamthibi said reflectively with his chin resting down on his clenched hand, holding Trish tightly while rubbing her back, up and down in long slow strokes, "I would be an absolute fool to lose you now, after what we have been through already. I have never felt the way I do with you in my whole life. My wife dragged my heart through the mud over many years. Then her affair exposed me to such pain that brought me to my knees. I bawled like a baby curled on the bathroom floor. In spite of all the bad things she did to me, there is just one thing that I still feel very awful about."

"What was it?" Trish asked surprised sitting up erect.

"It was.. well…when my wife and I were arguing in the bedroom. I had just found out she was having the affair…I just wish I could take it back because I am not like that."

"What was it? Is it something you said?"

"No, no, everybody says dumb things when they have a verbal fight."

"You hit her?"

"It was a slap…" Kamthibi quickly said.

Trish suddenly stood up.

"I'm not like that I swear Trish," Kamthibi pleaded tenderly pulling Trish back to the bed, "I just lost it. I had never been in that situation before in our entire marriage. It scared me. I don't want to ever do that to a woman. I hope you believe me."

"You don't seem like that type of guy, Kamthibi," Trish said, "I believe you because you did not have to tell me. This shows you are a good man with a strong conscience. But you are only human."

"I know you have cancer. But I will wait even if it takes a hundred years. You ignite something in me that I never knew I had. I want to protect you. I want to totally submit to you in passionate love. I am having too much fun for the first time in my life, Trish." Kamthibi held her chin, looked into her twinkling eyes and kissed her briefly. "You don't know how lucky we are to be in such deep explosive love and be such perfect soul mates." Trish wiped tears from Kamthibi's eyes.

"The cancer medication also has not helped things either," Trish said sighing with frustration as she stood up again.

"Why?"

"Some of the side effects are sexual. The first day I met you on the road in Gandy, I was so sexually charged all day for the first time in my life. I was floating on a cloud. Then I began to take the cancer medication a few days later, my desire just went down. I would like to feel like that again toward you. I hope it's soon because even I can't wait."

CHAPTER TEN

"*Odi! Odi!*" those were the words Zambians say aloud when knocking on someone's door when visiting or announcing their arrival at someone's house.

Kamthibi could not get up to answer the door. The knocking and "*Odi! Odi*" went on persistently and incessantly. In frustration, Kamthibi thrashed his head to wake himself up to answer the door. He opened his eyes to realize it wasn't a dream. He was lying in bed with a white woman he momentarily did not recognize. She was asleep on his bare hairy chest in a motel room in Zambia. He heard the knock again. The sleep fog cleared from his head. The knocking at the door with the "*Odi! Odi!*" female voice was certainly in Zambia. He could hear the thin characteristic song of the *tye tye* bird through the window. Maybe that was his wife Nora knocking. She had followed him back to Zambia. For a split second, Kamthibi panicked. But in the next split second, everything became clear. Kamthibi was topless and wearing boxer shorts only. He instinctively reached for his bathrobe and quickly slipped it on while shouting.

"Just a minute!" Kamthibi flew to the door, hastily twisted the key, and opened it.

"Sorry Sir," the cleaning woman wearing a blue apron apologized. "I wanted to clean the room. Sorry to wake you up. I didn't think anybody was still inside. I will clean your room later maybe after I finish doing the next one."

"What time is it? Have you been knocking for a long time?"

"It's twelve hours and I wasn't knocking for a long time. There are some people like the room over there where I had to knock all day and they didn't wake up. They were on a honey moon." The woman smiled. Kamthibi was still too sleepy to smile let alone laugh.

"Is breakfast still being served?" Kamthibi asked without thinking, "No, I mean lunch."

"Lunch is up to fourteen hours," the attendant replied walking away with her brooms, mops, clean bed sheets, and towels. Kamthibi closed the door and removed his bathrobe.

"Who was that woman at the door," Trish asked turning over in bed still half asleep. "Were you trying to make moves on her since I can't understand Nyanja?"

"That's the cleaning lady, Madam," Kamthibi said feigning sarcasm and pretending to tag covers off Trish. She held on to the blanket laughing and tagging it until Kamthibi let go. He quickly reached for his pants and whipped out a twenty kwacha note from the pocket. He stretched it, stared at it, and sniffed at it several times in a mocking way.

"Where is this money from?" Kamthibi said. They both laughed heartily again. Since the previous day's incident when Trish had forgotten her fanny pack full of cash in the back seat of Teketa's car, this was going to be an intimate secret joke only the two of them would understand. That was the magic of intimacy; secret meanings of words and actions. They continued to laugh each time their eyes met. It was so good to wake up to tears of laughter.

"Kamthibi, stop that!" Trish feigned being fed up and threw one of the pillows at him. Kamthibi snatched the pillow and put the money away in his pants pockets.

"By the way, that cleaning lady was cute," Kamthibi joked as he walked to the bathroom. "My God," he yelled suddenly, "I didn't realize this. We must have slept for more than twelve hours."

Trish and Kamthibi decided they would take it easy that day. They had such a hectic, but exciting previous day. They wished they were physically young again. They speculated that they could have joined in the drinking and the dancing at the motel up to the wee hours of the morning the previous night; exhausted or not. Today they could have gone on a whirlwind tour of downtown Lusaka although there wasn't much to see downtown. But they were both in their mid-forties. They were excited about each other and life. But they had their physical limits, which they could disobey at great risk.

They could only go on for so long on the fuel of excitement like they had most of the previous day, the first day together in Africa and in Zambia. Just being together felt so sweet. It was a special day they would cherish and remember for the rest of their lives.

For the first time, they ate a meal at the Crystal Rose Motel. The dining was modest and the menu very basic -three to five items with minimal variety. As they walked to the dining room, they noticed that the only TV in the whole place was in the main motel lounge area. Kamthibi predictably ate *nshima* with chicken. Although Trish complained that she was still full from her very first Zambian big meal the previous night, she ate an egg sandwich with tea and a few lumps of *nshima* from Kamthibi's plate. They played a game in which Trish tried to distract Kamthibi and then quickly steal a lump of his *nshima* while he pretended to look away.

Introductions were beginning to get culturally awkward. Kamthibi got into conversation with waiters, cleaners, and some of the motel staff. When a man and woman share a bedroom or a bed together, Zambians assume they are married. This assumption is indeed in accordance with tradition and customary expectation. So when Kamthibi introduced Trish as just "Trish", many of the staff already referred to her as "Mrs Simbazako", the "Mrs" or "your wife". Kamthibi could get away with introducing her as "Trish Butler" or as "my close friend" as he had done when he first introduced Trish to his friend Teketa at the airport. But this was not going to wash in the rural area, especially at Kamthibi's home village. People who live by tradition want things to be spelt out in black and white. Grey areas and uncertainty in matters of love between a man and a woman are very few or unheard of. What was he going to say during the *malonje* custom in the village? After all, what sane man and woman would travel together all the way from Britain, to the City of Lusaka, and spend days and nights in the same room and share the same bed and still be "separate" or "just close friends"? Trish and Kamthibi talked about this briefly over lunch. Trish said she did not mind what she was called so long it wasn't something insulting or derogatory. She realized cultures are different. After lunch, they decided they would take a walk along the Great East Road.

As they came strolling out of the gate to walk east along the road, the make shift market vendors began to shout at them.

"Madam! Madam! Boss! Boss!" they each called, "we have cold soft drinks, tarino, fanta, and sprite. We have biscuits, vegetables, and buns with sweet jam, fresh mangoes, and mango juice. All very cheap!!"

One of the young boy vendors ran holding a bottle of soft drink to Kamthibi and Trish, "Look, Madam, boss!" he said stretching his hand and the drink towards them, "feel, and feel. It's even cold!"

Kamthibi and Trish both touched the drink with the backs of their hands and indeed it was cold.

"Let's get a drink," Trish said to Kamthibi, "we might need it on our walk."

"Trish, these vendors know the psychology of a woman," Kamthibi laughed. The boy smiled at his victory. 'This sale would probably afford his family a meal tonight,' Kamthibi thought. "You are playing right into their hands. Next time they will try to sell you Alaska as the Americans would say."

They bought two drinks from the vendor and took them on their stroll. Kamthibi squeezed them into two of his blue jeans coat pockets.

"People here are freer," Trish said, "they are in the open more. This type of make shift market would never happen at home."

"It would be called unsanitary and a public health hazard," Kamthibi agreed, "but that's the price you pay either way, Trish. If you follow science, you sacrifice some of your freedom. If you follow freedom like these vendors, you risk sacrificing your life."

It was a sunny-warm blue sky and a little humid with patches of dark clouds slowly drifting across the sky. There were grey clouds in the far horizon in the west with occasional streaks of lightening accompanied by the rumblings of distant thunder. There was a tropical storm somewhere west of Lusaka.

Because of walking in the sun for the two days they were in Zambia, Kamthibi noticed that Trish's white skin was turning slightly red around her neck and face. They were already sweating. After walking for a few hundred yards, they discovered that it was very uncomfortable to walk without a shoulder or sidewalk. The fast-moving trucks and other large vehicles kept zooming by sending waves of blowing wind in their wake which forced Trish to have to hold her cotton skirt down each time a vehicle went by. She kept removing her hair from her face. Instead of turning around to return to the motel, Kamthibi suggested they walk up one of the numerous foot paths that always crisscross and connect villages and other dwellings in the country side in Zambia.

They took one of the paths and were promptly swallowed into the plush green grass, thick shrubs, trees, and other vegetation as they slowly walked on the path with Kamthibi in front. Then Trish looked on the ground and noticed something for the first time that perplexed her.

"Kamthibi!" she called, stopped, and looked on the ground again her curious eyes darting back and forth in the middle of the path. "I swear I have never seen so many different insects and bugs crawling around in one place in my whole life. It reminds me of when I would look through one of those nature encyclopedias in our school library when I was a kid."

There were a zillion insects and ants hissing and others screeching. Some big and small ants were crawling on the ground. Crickets and grasshoppers were flying and escaping away from the path making a din of noise everywhere. Colourful yellow, red, orange, and black birds sung their panic cries and curiously flapped their wings and landed a safe distance on the lush green short trees, grass, and shrubs around them. All the time, the birds kept their eyes and attention riveted on Kamthibi and Trish, as if the two were suspicious intruders and at worst predators up to no good. This was the rude truth the birds must have learnt from experience because most rural protein-starved Zambians always try to kill the birds to eat with their *nshima* meals. Several large *chipungu* birds, a type of eagle, were flying high and coasting in a circle.

Two birds whipped above their heads like jet fighters. They synchronized and choreographed their swift, sharp moves swiftly navigating around and over the trees. The two light grey *njiba* or wild pigeon birds pulled up and slowed down with their characteristic song echoing for miles, as they perched on top of a tall tree eyeing Kamthibi and Trish.

"What is this?" Trish asked excitedly pointing to the large bright red ant walking on the brown smooth path amongst the numerous black ants of various sizes.

"I don't know their English name," Kamthibi answered, "but in Tumbuka we call them *kaleza* which means, "lightening" because they are so red. They appear only during this period of the rainy season. Then you don't see them again until the following rainy season."

"If I had gotten a college education," Trish said. "I would have wanted to study something about nature. I have always been interested in nature. You know; wild animals, insects, bugs. If only I had been born maybe in a bigger city and maybe had not gotten pregnant in high school, who knows." Trish paused for a while.

"You can't always wish something had been different in your life," Kamthibi said holding her hand, "I used to think that way, too. But you just end up torturing yourself. Just learn to accept what you have."

"I know," Trish remarked, "but I can't help it. This is just too exciting. I bet many of these insects have dangerous stings and can kill you."

"It's funny how I have a PhD in seed technology, but I can only tell you everything you want to know about weevils and other insects that destroy crops but not much about wild ones," Kamthibi remarked throwing up his arms, "but I can tell you something from my knowledge growing up in the village. Come," he pulled Trish by the hand.

Kamthibi was so excited to truly share a piece of his childhood with someone whom he loved and cared for a great deal. They walked a few yards and he would explain what a particular ant or insect's Tumbuka name was and its habits. Then Trish yelled when she saw a huge swarm of the big black *sisinya* ants that were crossing the path in wide slow creeping straight rows. Kamthibi said *sisinya* ants stung him several times during his childhood in the village when he would be herding goats in the bush. His foot would swell for a couple of days and then would heal. Then Kamthibi pointed to a large black hard-shelled *chandondo* ant. He took a small piece of twig and flicked it over to show Trish something. The ant just froze as if it was dead. Kamthibi then told Trish this is how this particular ant escaped from its predators; just by pretending to be dead when attacked and also it's hard shell prevents other predators from devouring him or her. She laughed when he suggested they check the ant's pants so see if it was a girl or a boy.

Occasionally someone on a bike came through the path. Kamthibi and Trish got out of the way by standing in the bushes on the edge of the path. If it was someone walking, the person said *"Zikomo"* which means, "Hello there, I am passing." This is a Zambian way strangers and people in general acknowledge each other when their paths cross. Kamthibi made sure to say; *"Yeo"* which means, "I acknowledge you" as a courteous and friendly response. Although they must have thought it unusual that a white woman and man were walking on a path in the bush, they must have thought anything is possible in the vicinity of the Lusaka metropolis. After all, there were so many whites on commercial farms and homes around Lusaka. In the village areas where they would be visiting soon, such an encounter would need detailed *malonje*. This bothered Kamthibi slightly but he did not want to dwell on it. They would cross the bridge once they got there.

"Trish, come here I want to show you a very special ant," Kamthibi hastily said beckoning after Trish.

"What, what, Kamthibi," Trish said, "after all we have seen, can there be any more special ants?"

"Here," Kamthibi pointed to the ground as he picked up another thin twig to use as a pointer, "this is the infamous *sungununu* ant. It is tiny and roams the village bare ground. It stings sometimes in bad places of the body. I will tell you about the *sungununu*. Let's sit down under that tree and have our drink."

Kamthibi waded through the grass with Trish following him, away from the path, up to the base of the large *msekese* (laughter) tree. He flattened the grass around the base of the tree. He looked for a log and dragged it to the base of the tree. But Trish could not sit on the rough log bark with her thin cotton skirt she was wearing. Kamthibi took off his jeans jacket, placed the soft drinks down, and placed the jeans coat on the rough log for them to sit on together. Trish smiled, thanking Kamthibi saying what a sweet guy he was. He opened the soft drink tops with his strong white teeth. Since they were sitting down, they could not be seen from the path as the grass swallowed them. As they sipped their drink in the shade of the long leaves of the tree, Kamthibi told his story of the *sungununu* ant.

"Men elders in the village wear shorts because long pants are expensive and besides, they are too hot to wear most of the time," Kamthibi began, "One day a man was sitting with many others and it is believed it was in mixed company. Without the man's knowledge, the tiny *sungununu* ant had surreptitiously crawled through his shorts all the way to the most tender and most sensitive spot of his private parts. In the middle of his speaking, the *sungununu* ant stung him. He is said to have gasped, squirmed, and grimaced but could not directly touch the part of his anatomy that was being offended to maintain his dignity and for fear of public embarrassment. He contemplated dashing into the nearest house to investigate but that was his in-law's. He opted to rush to the nearest tall shrub on the edge of the village behind which he immediately hid and removed the rude tiny *sungununu* ant which he is said to have angrily crushed and ground into powder between his fingers. Shortly the man resumed his seat at the gathering, smiling but still sweating from the secret ordeal that probably only village men know."

Kamthibi laughed and Trish giggled nervously throughout the funny story.

"Kamthibi, were you ever stung by one?" Trish asked with a mischievous smile, "You know, in your private part?"

"Well, I must have although I can't remember. It was such a long time ago. Fortunately, *sungununus* neither kill nor harm people's reproductive organs. It's painful when they sting but they only make a small round welt which usually disappears in a matter of hours. But there is a poem that every young Tumbuka girl and woman memorizes about the *sungununu* ant. I remember it from memory from my childhood. It goes like this. I will first recite the poem in *Tumbuka* and then I will recite the English translation." Kamthibi began

Kuluma kwa Sungununu

Miyezi yinandi ya chihanya

Zuba cifundizi

Dongo na fubvu pacalo

Bvula yawa puuuu

Maji ghakwenda

Kunjila pasi posweka

Kununkhila kwa bvula ya kwamba

The Bridge

Tudoyo tunandi
Twayamba kwendakwenda
Tukwenda pasi, kuduka, nakwimba
Tudoko tudoko na vikulu
Tubinkha, tobilibila, tuswesi, tutuba
Twamitundu yiwemi yinandi
Sisinya zupanga ciwawa

Ka sungununu kadoko kabinkha
Kakwenda pasi pa muzi
Kopenja woluma
Mwanakazi wali na musi na thuli
Wayika mwana pasi walije thebela
Mwana wakusebela
Mwana walila gwaaa
Mwana waonkha sono sono
Wolila vici?

Anyina babeka
Pokhalila pa mwana
Wasanga kotupa
Kanyerere kafipa kadoko
Ka sungununu kaluma mwana

The Sting of the Sungununu

Six months of searing
Dry heat
Dry brown dusty earth
Rains finally pour in torrents
Brown water rapidly filling
Meandering through

Gaping crevices of parched earth
The sweet smell of the first rains

Trillion insects suddenly
Burst into dizzying activity
Crawling, singing, hissing, flying
On the ground and in sky
Hissing and buzzing
Tiny, small, and large
Black, green, red, white insects
All lovely colours in between
Lone, pairs, many and numerous
Hissing herds of the sisinya

The tiny black sungununu
One of them
Roams the village dirt
Alone
In search of food victims

Pestle and mortar pounding
Mother wearily places
Bare bottomed baby on the ground
Baby babbles playing mouthing
The soil that is everywhere
Baby suddenly shrieks in gasps
Cries in sudden bursts
Baby just breast-fed mother wonders
What could be the matter?

Mother inspects carefully
Baby's bare bottom

Locates a tinny bump
The tell-tale sign
Of the secret sting of the
Tiny black Sungununu *ant*

After the poem, Kamthibi and Trish put their arms around each other's waists and sat quietly. The silence of lovers was pregnant with emotion. In that sacred moment, each was soaked in their own feelings and thoughts. Kamthibi played with the top of the soft drink placing it on and off the bottle. Trish absent-mindedly swatted flying gnats from around her face. She rubbed her legs to keep ants and other creatures from crawling up her leg. She didn't want another experience of the man in the village. Kamthibi was thinking 'why should this moment end?' He wished he could bottle it away and re-experience it later again. But that would be futile. Nothing in life is ever lived exactly the same way again. Life experience had already taught him that. They both instinctively stood up. They held each other locked in an intimate embrace for a long time. Kamthibi leaned against the *musekesi* tree as they kissed.

"Let's go," Trish finally said pulling Kamthibi's hand, "the ants and flies are chewing my legs."

They somberly walked back to the main road. By the time they walked back to the motel, the sun was setting and sending its long amber rays across the tall wall on to the bright purple flowers along the lawn. The tips of the green trees were the only parts getting the soft sunrays just like long-necked giraffes are the only ones that eat the sweet tender blossoms of the tall African acacia trees.

CHAPTER ELEVEN

That evening after dinner, Trish and Kamthibi talked and argued as they discussed plans for their travel to the village. Nkhorongo village was located more than five hundred gruelling road miles in the far corner of the Eastern Province of Zambia in the remote and tiny Lundazi District in Chief Magodi's area. They together debated the possible risks and the enormous personal rewards of the trip. They agreed that Trish's cancer was not going to get in the way of this rare lifetime experience for both of them together. However, they had to make an allowance if her illness suddenly worsened. The trip would deepen their love; she would really know the genuine Zambia and he would revisit his home and socially reconnect but with a heightened appreciation of his village roots.

Trish was determined to experience what she continued to characterize as the true Africa of her secret and wildest dreams since she was a little child growing up at first in the working class streets of Belfast. In a round about way, Kamthibi made it known to Trish that evening that this would not be a tourist guided picnic during which the tour bus can simply leave when the tourists are bored of staring at the African natives in exotic unclothed state or wearing bright-coloured clothes or grass skirts. Kamthibi suddenly sat in quiet contemplation as he blankly stared into the open space.

"What's wrong?" Trish asked anxiously.

"Nothing," he replied.

"Clearly there is something bothering you," Trish said tenderly as she grabbed his hand and lovingly caressed it between her small hands, "each time the topic of going to your village has come up, I see a certain tenseness in your face. If we are going to do this, we have to trust each other. I am afraid too. I don't want to go there and enjoy myself at your expense. If that's the case, I would rather not go."

"No, no," Kamthibi protested, "it's not that I don't want you to come with me."

"Then what is it?" she tagged and shook his hand insistently, "I am a big girl. I can handle it. I want to know. I'm curious."

"I have to be frank. I am feeling conflicted like I have never been before. I think of my children a lot, wondering how they are doing," Kamthibi began, "I think I should tell you this because it would not be fair for you to come to the village and not be aware of some of the potential trouble. In my Tumbuka village culture, my responsibility to my marriage, to Nora and my kids, are to be always top priority. According to tradition, I might not hear direct criticism from my parents. But I will certainly hear it from my grandparents and especially the *nkhoswe* from Nora's village."

"Who is the *n-kh-o…*?"

"The *n-kho-swe*," Kamthibi enunciated the word slowly for Trish's benefit, "he is the person who is traditionally appointed to look into serious grievances in a marriage."

"What is likely to happen then with this person?"

"They have the power to call a *mphala* of a meeting of elders to discuss the marriage grievance. My showing up with another woman at the village without Nora and the kids is obviously enough to convene a *mphala*."

"I could have used that in my marriage to Richard," Trish said, "through all the abuse, I had always felt so helpless as there was no one I could turn to. It's funny that I think of him sometimes."

"But you know what Trish?" Kamthibi said, "I am not surprised you think of him. That independence in Western marriage is sweet when the going is good. Part of me says I should enjoy and deserve my romantic love with you. After all, I am not the one who slept with someone outside my marriage to Nora. But part of me says I should respect *mwambo* or tradition, my family and the people in the village. To just show up with you without any explanation will cause trouble, although I don't know how serious. I feel guilty and anxious."

"I shouldn't go then?"

"No, that's not what I am saying," Kamthibi paused for a while, "I don't think anyone will harm you. But my eldest sister is something else."

"What about her?"

"Neliya has always been a pain in the behind, to use an American expression."

"Why?"

"She is always speaking her mind on all matters. And she does it openly. For your sake, I don't want any hostile scenes while we are in the village. I wouldn't have mentioned her if we were not going to the village. She openly criticizes everyone whenever she thinks they are wrong. She does not mince words either. She is loud, crude, and always too opinionated."

"Well, maybe you should go alone."

"No, no of course not", Kamthibi said, "Don't be silly. She will obviously not like you and me being together. If she only spoke Tumbuka I wouldn't worry about it. But she is a school teacher and can speak English."

"Kamthibi, be honest. Is there going to be a brawl with your sister trying to kill me?"

"No, no, she wouldn't do that. She never crosses that line. She is not that type. She is just one of those crazy nutcase that every family has. When I was young she used to tease me so badly sometimes that my grandparents would intervene."

"If she is a black sheep of the family, everyone has one of those. I will just ignore her."

"I will be there to protect you," Kamthibi held Trish around her shoulders and squeezed her.

"Well, it's good you told me," Trish kissed Kamthibi, "that's why you are such a great guy. I feel better now. I should have met you just after my high school."

They agreed that her early cancer diagnosis should not be told willy-nilly to everyone. People tend to react differently, often negatively, when they learn someone has a terminal illness. However, they had to inform close special relatives, one close friend, and if necessary the British Embassy in case Trish needed medical evacuation at some point. It would be irresponsible, selfish, and inconsiderate of others if they were to completely conceal or keep it as a secret or act like the cancer did not exist at all. They agreed that achieving happiness and one's fondest dreams is never risk-free.

Kamthibi and Trish were bound to the motel premises and their room that evening as they wished they had a car. Although Kamthibi wished they could visit and see a couple of family friends and former neighbours from the past in several parts of the city of Lusaka, it was not going to be possible, at least not that night. It would be difficult to visit even Teketa and Milika. As luck would have it, as Trish and Kamthibi were lamenting their situation, Teketa and Milika visited with their small toddler Maureen.

Milika and Trish talked about what Trish would need in the village -clothing and sanitary items. They joked about what type of exotic foods she would expect; perhaps more exclusive *nshima* and relishes she would never have seen or heard of in her life. Milika was born and grew up in the city. Her father was a high-ranking government bureaucrat until he retired into restaurant business. Although she had visited her home village now and then, maybe three times, her impressions of the village life tended to be alarmist. This tended to be the case among urban educated Zambians. Kamthibi could never understand this.

There had been street demonstrations downtown Lusaka that day. News reports said two police officers were injured and two stores owned by businessmen of Asian origin were looted. The Asian businessmen are what Zambians call *Ba Mwenye*. But the use of the term '*mwenye*' on the news would be considered rude or inappropriate. Otherwise the city was quiet. According to Teketa, the government had raised the price of mealie-meal for cooking the *nshima* staple meal. Urban people feel more squeezed as unemployment is as high as twenty per cent. Price controls created shortages of bread, cooking oil, sugar, butter, mealie-meal, and detergent. The main University Teaching Hospital did not have medicine or nearly enough doctors. Crime in the city was so bad, especially at night. The pickpockets were so fierce that white tourists did not dare visit downtown as they became obvious targets. The black market for exchanging American dollars and other foreign money was so intense at Katondo Street in downtown Lusaka. The President and other top politicians, and the few rich never experienced the sting of these shortages and economic problems. 'If they are aware of the problems, then they are not doing enough' was the conclusion most citizens reached. Indeed many continued to amass wealth and travel abroad to London for shopping and others to South Africa for medical treatment. Teketa was telling Kamthibi some of these things to confirm that since his friend had immigrated to the United States, nothing had improved in the country. They were both in a frenzy of loud heated passionate discussion of Zambian politics. But because Teketa and Kamthibi had both grown up in the village in their early childhoods, they settled and agreed on one thing: rural dwellers still had an advantage as they grew their own food.

The government was subsiding the cost of housing, education and food to keep the urban people happy. They debated the wisdom of such continued government policy in the light that everything now was deteriorating. It seemed like the leaders in government were always inept whether in Zambia, Uganda, Nigeria, or anywhere in African countries. New faces or even military coup d'etats would probably not change anything. This is one of the reasons why Kamthibi had emigrated to the United States with his family. Discussing and confronting economic and political issues and quality of life in his home country never failed to make Kamthibi feel angry. Such political discussions always inflamed him since they made him feel both angry and frustrated about conditions never improving in his country. It was a topic that he would rather not discuss because it was always so futile, depressing, and sometimes robbed him of sleep, Kamthibi confessed to his friend. Zambians seem to always blame capitalism, American imperialism, Westerners, or foreigners for all their economic ills. "Although some of the blame might be justified, where did we lose the ability to look inward and take responsibility for some of our bad actions?" Kamthibi rhetorically asked his friend Teketa.

In this emotional cloud, it was always difficult for him to appreciate some of the many positive changes and achievements that had taken place in the country since the early days when it gained political independence from British colonialism. Kamthibi was only ten years old at the time and this is close to thirty years later. He was one of perhaps millions of early beneficiaries of the development policies and programmes of the newly- independent young Zambian government. He attended five years of secondary school, obtained a Bachelors Degree at the newly-built University of Zambia over four years, and obtained his Ph Degree in the United States over five years all on Zambian government scholarship.

Teketa and Milika left just in time, for Kamthibi was getting hot under the collar. He wondered what Trish thought since the British also colonized Northern Ireland or Ulster. Trish was beginning to learn something new about her man. He got very intense and angry when discussing politics or maybe injustice. But she would never have known this side of him at least this soon.

Kamthibi and Trish waited until the very last minute so that they did not ruin the evening and the visit. Trish gave Kamthibi an eye signal and nodded once.

"There is something Trish wanted to tell you," Kamthibi said to Teketa and Milika as they were standing up to head to the door. They sat back down, "she did not get a chance to tell you the other night."

"We did not want to spoil the dinner or the evening," Trish said in a surprisingly confident voice. "I have early stages of lung cancer."

"Ohhhhh!!!! We are sorry," Milika responded in a shocked voice.

Teketa and Milika were quiet for a while as they were no doubt trying to absorb this shocking new reality.

"When was it diagnosed," Teketa asked finally and broke the silence.

Trish explained with as much detail as she could. She talked about the medication she brought with her prescribed by her family doctor when she had left Ireland. She talked about being tired at times especially in the evening. She couldn't walk as far and sometimes lost appetite.

"Are you sure you are ok?" Milika asked with concern, "maybe you shouldn't go to the village. The tiny hospital in Lundazi may not even have medicine for you or even X-ray film. Even our major big University Teaching Hospital in Lusaka runs out of just basic equipment and medicine. You can stay here with us until Kamthibi comes back from the village."

"Thanks Milika," Trish shook her head and smiled, "I have come this far. I must go to the village; with my man." Trish proudly smiled and stood up and put her arm around Kamthibi's waist who was standing with his arms crossed on his chest.

Teketa and Milika did not understand. Trish had to go with Kamthibi. She wanted to live a full life. After all, these might be her last days. After Teketa and Milika had left, they both felt relieved. At least in Zambia two friends now knew. It went better than they had expected. Trish wrote a letter to her mother telling her she was having a good time. She was staying at a place known as the Crystal Rose Motel on the outskirts of the capital city of Lusaka. She was to travel for maybe one or two days to sight-see the country. She was doing all right and enjoying Africa. She told her mother not to worry or reply since she didn't know if she would be at the same address when she returned to the city. Life is always fluid and often unpredictable here. But she was enjoying every minute of it. She thanked her again for lending her the money for the trip. Trish was careful to give her mother the minimum information. She didn't want to be deceptive but why disclose details that would worry her mother unnecessarily?

CHAPTER TWELVE

"You, Madam, for the first time are going on a guided tour of the beautiful and bustling City of Lusaka today!" Kamthibi yelled as he hugged Trish before they walked out of the motel room. He playfully swayed Trish from side to side in his arms several times and gave her a quick kiss on the lips.

"I am so excited, Kamthibi," Trish said as they stepped out and Kamthibi turned the key to lock the door behind them, "I want to mail the letter at the Post Office. I want to buy a couple of *chitenje* cloths to wear in the village. Maybe a head dress too. What do I say in Lusaka street language if I want to buy something from someone at the market?"

"It's called Lusaka Nyanja."

"Yes,"

"You say, "*nizi ngati*" or you can just say: "how much is this?" Everyone knows basic English."

"No, I don't want to speak English," Trish protested laughing, "I want to try the local language."

"I am not promising anything. This is the *Simbazako* tour of the city personalized for my sweetie." Kamthibi said as he briefly put his arm around Trish's shoulders and squeezed her to him.

They walked to the motel gate entrance to hitch for any ride into town. The exception were the huge packed trucks, with passengers dangerously perched on top of some merchandise, which looked like it was ready to tip over because it had been piled very high. This was early in the cloudy morning and most public buses were packed literally to the roof. People were hanging out of the doors of the buses that spewed out thick black diesel smoke. Shortly, a sparkling brand new Mazda sedan drove out of the gate from under the raised big metal barrier and stopped a few yards from where Trish and Kamthibi were standing. The driver was wearing a suit and a tie. He leaned over to roll down the passenger's window.

"Are you going into town? I can give you a ride up to the airport road," he said.

Trish and Kamthibi got into the luxurious car. Kamthibi was on the passenger front seat and Trish got into the back seat. As they pulled off into the road, the man shook hands with Kamthibi and Trish.

"My name is Sandford Mvula," he introduced himself, "I am the manager of Crystal Rose Motel."

"Oh, ya," Kamthibi said, "I saw you walk into the motel lobby from a distance. I didn't know you are the manager. I am Kamthibi Simbazako and I live in the States." Kamthibi glanced at Trish in the back seat.

"I am Trish. Tricia Butler," she introduced herself, "I am visiting Zambia from Ireland."

"Welcome," Mvula said, "are you the Simbazako who used to be at the Ministry of Agriculture Seed Division?"

"Yes", Kamthibi answered.

"I have heard of you. You are the Dr Simbazako, one of the first Zambians to get a Ph. D degree in Seed Technology. I am glad to meet you," he enthusiastically shook Kamthibi's hand again. Sandford Mvula said he had gone to the University of Zambia probably much later that Kamthibi's time. He had been to the UK to train in Hotel Management. He had not yet visited the United States. He hoped they were having a good stay at the Motel. He would be more than willing to help should they report any problems to him. He dropped Trish and Kamthibi at the junction to the airport. Kamthibi and Trish walked for a mile to the big Chelstone Township water tank where there was a local bus station.

"Those going to town! Going to city centre! *Ku town! Ku town ! Tiyeni apa!"* (Those who are going to town get in!) The drivers of the small local buses were screaming at the top of their lungs.

There were three twenty-passenger mini-buses all waiting to fill up with passengers before they could go into town. As a result each one of the drivers dashed to them saying, "Madam! Madam! Boss! Boss! Come into my bus! It would be leaving for town any minute now or as soon as we fill up." Trish and Kamthibi got into one of the buses and waited for maybe half an hour before they left. The mini bus was half full because that was not peak time. Just before work at eight in the morning or just after work at five in the evening when it was virtually impossible to get on a local bus. No wonder people drove their rickety cars to the ground.

As soon as they left, Kamthibi began to explain what the various landmarks and buildings were. He was loud enough so that the passengers, the conductor, and the driver caught on to what was happening.

"These are the farm fields on the left for the Natural Resources Development College with a nice orchard of mango, orange, and guava trees. On the right is the Kaunda Square Stage Two residential area. Teketa and Milika's house where we came the other night is the third one on the first block. On the right is Munali Secondary School, the oldest boys' secondary school built by the British during the colonial days way back in the 1940s. Many of Zambia's first political leaders including President Kaunda got their education here."

Trish absolved all she saw and was impressed by the vast expanse and sprawling city and they were not even downtown yet.

"On the left is the University of Zambia and its beautiful grounds. This is probably the best-looking place in Lusaka and it's not because I went to school there for four years. On the right is Kalundu with its large expensive houses. Here is the Mulungushi Conference Centre. On the hill there is Zambia's magnificent National Assembly or Parliament building. The top part of the roof is decorated with copper, Zambia's major export, and glitters in bright lights at night."

"I can see that we have educated people and a European tourist," the young driver said, "We will charge you people more than the normal fare."

The whole mini-bus broke out into spontaneous laughter. People who had missed the joke asked what had been said.

"What did he say? What did he say?" Trish asked Kamthibi.

"*Baba mwati bwanji?*" (What did you say sir?), Kamthibi asked the driver aloud in Nyanja laughing and feigning that he had not heard what he had said.

"You the educated older people with white tourists should pay more for the ride," the drive said again paraphrasing, "we only get money to feed hand to mouth. You know there were demonstrations in town yesterday because the government had raised the price of mealie-meal. The price of petrol was raised only two months ago. Money is now becoming a problem. *Tizafa na njala*, boss." (We will die of hunger).

"*Bwana, kuti ninali nandalama maningi sembe niyendesa ka* brand new Mazda, *osati kukwera ka* mini bus," Kamthibi replied. (If I had a lot of money I would be riding my own brand new Mazda car and not riding a public mini bus).

"*Koma, ni zowona. Tiseka cabe ba* boss," the driver said as a last comment. (That's true, sir. I am just joking).

Kamthibi really loved the exchange. If there was something he was always proud about his fellow Zambians, it was their sense of humour. They can make you laugh at anything any time. The warmth and friendliness is infectious. Kamthibi could always see the vulnerability of the people in this in how slave traders, European colonizers, missionaries, and other foreigners might have taken advantage of this goodness of heart two hundred years earlier in those first encounters between Africans, Europeans, and Arabs. They misinterpreted this simplicity and love of other human beings as naive, childlikeness, lack of sophistication, or at worst being primitive and uncivilized. 'Couldn't one argue that these people are actually more civilized?' Kamthibi asked no one in particular in his mind.

Kamthibi and Trish were dropped off at the north-end of Lusaka's busiest, most famous and well-known road -Cairo Road and began to walk south along it. It is the head quarters of banks, major store chains, famous supermarket chains, music stores, commercial offices, tourist and travel agents, the main Post Office, expensive clothing stores, fast food restaurants, famous bars, the Lusaka Hotel, Embassy offices. Thousands of Africans, some of whom are men and young beautiful women and a sprinkling of whites and people of other skin colours walked or traded on it, including vendors and other street hustlers. Kamthibi had known Lusaka from the time when much of the space between buildings was empty grass; when he could stroll casually into a snack bar, get an ice cream cone, and play the jukebox. Now every piece of real estate had been used up over the previous thirty years. Kamthibi didn't think Cairo Road was a place where you could relax any more. It was too crowded with queues virtually everywhere when you wanted to do anything. He made this known to Trish. Maybe he was being old-fashioned. But he couldn't help it. This was all a new experience to Trish and she loved all of it.

The vendors, the colourful clothes, the sounds, languages she couldn't understand - she had never seen so many black people driving virtually all the cars on the streets, and the spectacular sky scrapers for an African city. Nothing close to what she had ever seen in Belfast. There was so much more life on the street here. She got the impression that life could never be boring being on these streets.

They mailed the letter at the Post Office. Kamthibi mailed a post card to his friend James in Manchester, Nurse Agnes at Belfast Hospital, and his kids in the US. Although he had serious differences with their mother, Kamthibi did not want his children to feel their father had abandoned them. He wanted them to know he loved them. The post cards would let them know that their dad was visiting back home in Zambia.

Kamthibi and Trish sat down and got a drink at a café adjacent to the Post Office. He said he wanted to take Trish to his favourite market -the Balamu African market. The open-air market there was meant for people with European styles -you could buy tomatoes, onions, cabbage, tulips, carrots, or vegetables associated with middle and upper class tastes. The Balamu market had all of these in addition to many exotic African traditional foods. Marketeers drove far to the outskirts of the city and collected these foods.

When they finally arrived at the market, Trish couldn't wait. She was like a kid who had been primed to enjoy Disney Land. But even more, what Trish saw made an immediate impression. This was a huge place with thousands of people conducting trade transactions. There were hundreds of stalls lined up with all kinds of merchandise. The women were wearing very bright colourful clothes. Young men were conducting make shift games of chance in the middle of a large curious crowd. There were stalls of fresh Kafue bream fish, live chickens, dried wild vegetables, cooked dried mice, dried caterpillars, dried *inswa* (flying ants). There were bags upon bags of charcoal piled up, beans, dried fish, cabbage, and piles of fresh mangos. Trish told Kamthibi excitedly that she could spend all day and not visit every part of the market. She said it was tempting for her to spend all day there just to feast on the new sights, sounds, voices, and languages. The marketeers were aggressive but in a friendly way. Trish heard them say the now familiar. "*Muzungu, Muzungu*, dona, dona, boss, boss, this is cheap," (white man, white woman, sir just buy this at a cheap price).

Kamthibi grabbed Trish's hand. She walked behind him as they navigated through the narrow market stalls that were jammed with merchandise. They were heading for the heart of the market. They arrived at a concrete rectangular structure with a metal roof but with several divisions of wooden tables and benches inside. There was some smoke and delicious smells of beef and chicken. It was hot as several open charcoal braziers had huge pots of *nshima*. Some *nshima* was boiling and strong sweating women were stirring huge pots. The women were competing for lunch customers and beckoning to Kamthibi and Trish to go to their table. The price was only four kwacha per serving. "What is the *Muzungu* going to eat?" they asked. They could fetch some bread and eggs and make a quick egg sandwich for her. That's what whites prefer. Kamthibi asked Trish about what she would eat. They were surprised and laughed when he responded in Nyanja that the *Muzungu* would eat *nshima*. Comments went around that many white Zambians who live in Lusaka now eat *nshima*. With that, Trish and Kamthibi ate *nshima* with many other customers. The *nshima* was still too hot for Trish and they didn't have time to wait. The lady borrowed a fork, rinsed it nicely and gave it to Trish to use. They thought it interesting that the *nshima* was too hot for her to eat with her bare hands.

After lunch, they went to buy three *chitenje* cloths for Trish and three *duku* or head-dresses. Kamthibi bought freshly-ground snuff tobacco, which he always bought for his mother from the Balamu market. She was often more excited about the tobacco than any of the presents he took to her. They also went to the main Balamu Chemist where they bought a few small supplies for their trip to the village; some painkillers and bug spray. It began to rain.

After they crossed the Libala Street from the shops next to Balamu market to get a taxi, Trish ducked behind Kamthibi like a scared dog cowering behind him. She was ashen white.

"What's wrong?" Kamthibi turned to face her.

"No, no, don't turn," she said in a hushed voice pointing toward a taxi, "it's him!"

"Who?" Kamthibi looked toward a white taxi that had just pulled up next to the curb about fifty yards in front of them.

"Richard! Oh, my God I don't know how he got here!"

"We have got to get away. Quick!"

Kamthibi grabbed Trish's hand and they dashed through the nearest entrance into the market. They ran and zigzagged between the vegetable stalls bumping into people as they parted perturbed at a strange sight of a Zambian dashing through tagging a white woman along. When the people who had sold them the *nshima* saw them, they shouted that they could serve Trish and Kamhtibi more *nshima* again. Some shouted asking if the couple were running away from *akawala* or muggers. Kamthibi headed to the deep part of the market that had numerous small clothing stalls enclosed in metal roofing. He approached one market seller and hastily slammed fifty thousand kwacha notes into his hand.

"*Mubiseni uyu muzungu. Nibwera manje manje kumutenga,*" Kamthibi said (Hide this white woman. I will come and get her soon.). Turning to her he said, "Trish, I am going to get a taxi and when the coast is clear I will come and get you."

"Ok," Trish replied out of breath and ducking into the stall behind the display racks of long dresses and heavy coats. 'Son of a bitch' she swore under her breath. How did he even get here at the market?'

After a while, Kamthibi burst in from a different direction. He slapped another forty thousand kwacha in the young man's hand.

"I will get this women's coat and scarf for this price," Kamthibi said grabbing the two items from the rack, "is that a good deal for you?"

"Yes, of course boss!" the young man said enthusiastically, "you can probably get two so that the lady can change. You don't want her wearing the same colour everyday, do you boss?"

"No, no, I don't need another one. But don't tell anyone who comes asking that there was a *muzungu* woman here. *Wamvera*?" (Do you understand?)

"Yes," replied the young man.

"Are you sure it was him you saw?" Kamthibi asked as he helped Trish put the long ankle length blue coat so that no one could see her skin from afar.

"Yes, of course. I have lived with the man for more than twenty years, remember?"

"I checked all over outside the market and didn't see any white man."

"This is a huge market. Maybe he is somewhere in here looking for me."

"I hope Teketa didn't blow it."

"What do you mean?"

"I didn't tell you this because I didn't want to worry you," Kamthibi said quickly, "I asked Teketa to check the incoming passport holders at the airport for a "Richard Butler" and to tell me if he saw him. Maybe Teketa came to our motel this morning to warn us and missed us. I will check with him on our way. We both know some old school mates who are now with Zambia Police."

By this time there was a crowd of onlookers of the spectacle of a white woman hiding. Some in the crowd said maybe both Trish and Kamthibi were spies. Arguments broke out. Kamthibi was sure the gossip of the sensational events would spread in the market like wild fire and at any time local political officials could detain them for questioning as suspicious people.

"Come on," Kamthibi said to Trish, "the taxi is waiting. You wait at the gate. When the coast is clear we will dash for the taxi. Once we are in, you lie low in the back seat."

They were back at Crystal Rose Motel within half an hour.

CHAPTER THIRTEEN

Teketa drove Kamthibi to the City Main Bus Terminal adjacent to Cairo Road but behind the Lusaka railway station. Indeed one of the immigration officers at the International Airport had seen Richard's passport and had immediately alerted Teketa. Teketa had rushed to Crystal Motel as soon as he could but Trish and Kamthibi had already left for downtown Lusaka and Balamu city market. Since Richard did not have any idea where Trish was going it was safer to leave immediately for Lundazi. Since a *muzungu* at a bus station is such a rare event, Trish could not go to the bus station with Kamthibi to catch the bus. There could be a risk that Richard could hear of it although Lusaka is a big city. Kamthibi and Trish had agreed that they did not want Richard to get wind about where she was going. Teketa agreed to keep an eye on Richard because people in Lusaka could tell the goings and comings of many foreigners, especially whites. The plan was for Teketa to buy two tickets and arrange for the bus driver to stop and pick up Trish who would be waiting by the side of the road at Crystal Motel in the dark that evening.

The Zambia Bus Company had a schedule that they generally followed but no one ever got upset if the bus was late or did not show up at all. Every evening there were up to three buses that left for Chipata. The aim was for passengers to travel all night on the two-lane mostly paved highway and to arrive early the next morning in the provincial headquarters town of Chipata in time to get on connecting buses to other towns including outlying areas such as Chadiza, Msoro, Jumbe, Lundazi, and even to the town of Mchinji over the international border into neighbouring Malawi. They would be lucky if they got on a bus that night.

Teketa and Kamthibi arrived to find the bus terminal jammed with Christmas holiday travellers. It was a vast open structure with a high silver corrugated metal roof. The bare red brick concrete surface had every inch occupied by a family, man or woman with their luggage. Some had beds and furniture clearly suggesting that they were making a major relocation. The new terminal still looked clean although it was so overcrowded that the Lusaka City Council simply could not keep up with picking up some of the trash frequently enough. The new toilet facilities were an improvement to the old decrepit place that had been left by the colonial system. For public facilities, the old place still had stinking open buckets of human waste that had to be picked up by night soil men at dawn. But this was barely six years ago before the newly-built place had been opened. Kamthibi wondered why it had taken the City Council so long.

Kamthibi carried his bag and Teketa carried Trish's large green backpack and they found a small spot in the large mainly sitting crowd where they put their bags down. Kamthibi went to the ticket window offices to find out about the buses to Chipata and Lundazi. There were long queues at the ticket window. For each destination that was open for ticket purchase, there were two separate queues -one for men and another for women. The tickets were then sold alternately. Kamthibi wished Trish had been there to stand in the women's line too because it looked so much shorter. But something funny was happening. The ticket window sold only about sixteen tickets; to eight men and eight women. But then both sixty-passenger buses got full and left. After walking around the crowded bus terminal, Teketa and Kamthibi found out that some tickets were being sold through the back door to the seller's relatives, friends, and friends of friends first. Some unemployed young men and pick pockets who regularly roamed the terminal in search of victims, lined up at the window for hours, bought a ticket for a departing bus and occupied a seat inside the bus. Once the bus was declared full, they would sell the ticket and seat to the desperate passengers who wanted to leave. It was getting late. Kamthibi had no way of going back to Crystal Rose Motel if they did not get on the very last bus to Chipata. Richard could find them. Who knows what would happen? Teketa was gone since he had to go to bed early to be at work the following morning.

A *mishanga* boy approached Kamthibi.

"*Muyenda kuti bamdala?*" he asked. (Where are you going old man?").

"To Chipata,"

"*Naona kuti mabasi yabili yamusiya. Nigulisa tiketi ya ku Chipata.*" (I have noticed that two buses have left you. I am selling a bus ticket to Chipata.)

"How do I know the ticket is real, ha?" Kamthibi asked, "I need two."

"*Mungachecking'e ku ticket office. Sining'amuname kabili nisebeza pano* everyday *bamdala.*" (You can check at the ticket office to see if it's authentic. I would never cheat you because I work here everyday).

The *mishanga* boy sold Kamthibi the two tickets for almost twice the price. It was worth the risk. What else could he do?

Kamthibi picked up the two bags to board the waiting bus,

The bus to Chipata was standing still under the huge corrugated metal structure of a roof. Ticket-holding passengers crowded and jostled in front of the door. This is where pick pocketing was likely to occur. Kamthibi shoved around to create a safe space for himself. Women who had already battled and boarded had arranged to have their babies passed to them through the bus window. Some women were pleading to have someone help them hoist their heavy bags on to the top rack of the bus. Some of the *mishanga* young men charged a fee just to help hoist the luggage barely a few feet up. Those with big items like heavy beds, bicycles, and furniture, only used the metal staircase loading dock leading to the roof of the bus.

There was a rumour circulating that one of the two buses that had left earlier in the evening had flipped over just after the airport in a freak accident. It had lost one of its back wheels. It was said that none of the passengers had serious injuries because the bus had apparently been moving at a slow speed.

Suddenly, the ignition of the old Italian-made Fiat bus was switched on and the driver pressed the gas pedal twice and held it down and loud for half a minute. The bus roared like a lion. The urgency the sound conveyed and the smell of combusting diesel fumes brought rich and exciting childhood memories to Kamthibi - the excitement of travel; of leaving home and family to a distant boarding school, going home for school holidays, or to a new unfamiliar destination.

"Quickly give me the small bag through the window!" were shouts from inside the bus and back and forth between the outside and the departing passengers inside. "Tell her to write me!" "Have a merry Christmas!" "Say hello to everyone in the village!" "Whatever you eat during Christmas in the village, bring me some!" "Driver wait! My wife took a child to use the bathroom, please wait!" "Tell him not to pay the rent until I come back!" "Tell grandmother I will be sending the children's school fees during the New Year!" The bus trembled and rattled as it idled for a while. Then the driver hit the gas pedal twice quickly again. There was another frenzy of loud messages again. Kamthibi remembered fondly that when he was in the sixth grade, after seeing the bus drivers drive and navigate the rough and bumpy rural dirt roads, he had wanted to become a bus driver when he grew up. There was a certain romance the Zambian drivers put into bus driving that would attract any young boy to the occupation.

It was raining so hard that torrents soon ran along the edge of the building. The mist of rain blew and twirled into the open space of the open bus shelter. During a break in the swirling wind, some of the crowd drew closer as they stood huddled together under the roof of the wide open structure as the wind continued to whip the mist from the rain in twirls through the station. The bus inched forward as the driver rapidly hit the accelerator and paused so many times. He hit the horn as the bus door closed. Kamthibi felt depressed about leaving Lusaka but was excited about going home to the village. He had already talked to the bus driver into stopping at the front gate of the Crystal Motel on their way out.

It was late at night. The Cairo Road streets looked quiet and deserted except for a few night owls trapped by the rain. The city streetlights looked hazy and out of focus through the misty bus windows and the heavy rain. The bus entered the Great East Road heading east, leaving the city centre behind and streetlights thinned out. Soon the bus was past Chelstone Township. As they neared the Crystal Rose Motel, Kamthibi stood up and walked in the isle to the front of the bus to look out for Trish. The bus stopped. A dark figure dashed out from the security guard booth of the gate and ran towards the bus. Kamthibi opened the bus door as the interior lights were switched on.

Trish caused quite a stir because she was not only white getting on a bus going to a rural area, but she was also wearing one of her spring Irish dresses as well as a Zambian *chitenje* with orange bright colours. She had liked it when they bought it at Balamu market. She wasn't wearing the headdress though. She would wear that once one of the women in the village taught her how to wear it. Besides she didn't want the scalp of her head to get hot and sweaty. Then her hair would get wet and nappy. There were looks of consternation among the passengers. There were chuckles, positive comments, and looks and stares from most passengers at this unusual scene -a white woman wearing an African clothing. Trish was getting used to the attention and learning to ignore it. Kamthibi was getting used to it too, but could not ignore it completely. Trish wanted to enjoy life and do the things she had wanted to do since she was a child. She had loved the TV programmes and magazines that showed African women wearing bright- coloured clothes. She had secretly wanted to wear these clothes throughout her life. They had so much more life than what she thought were the relatively dull-coloured and monotonous Irish or European clothes.

Trish joined Kamthibi. The bright lights of the International Airport receded into a dark black abyss like a space ship would disappear into the black hole of the far galaxies. The piercing lights of the bus' beams were like sharp laser knife slicing through thick darkness.

As the bus picked up speed, the roof leaked in some spots and a small glass pane was missing on one of the windows three seats in front of Trish and Kamthibi. People volunteered coats to help each other out. They were now tearing through the three hundred and seventy –two miles to Chipata. The driver hummed as he pressed the accelerator in a rhythmic manner. Hardly a soul spoke in the bus except for the humming. 'A lovely song was behind the humming,' Kamthibi thought. The mountains of the Muchinga escarpment were still at least two hours away as the driver never shifted gears and the bus maintained a constant speed. This also showed that the old Fiat bus was in good condition for the five hundred-mile journey. The wipers on the surprisingly small windshield with a metal divider in between swiped feverishly as the rain picked up and then slowed down in intensity. The rain caused a sudden fading swishing sound mixed with the sound of the bus engine and the lone humming of the driver. Occasionally on this narrow road, the twinkling head lights from an oncoming car momentarily lit the inside of the otherwise dark bus and whipped by like a powerful rocket into the opposite direction flashing its blinding bright beams.

Kamthibi and Trish said little to each other as Trish removed her *chitenje* cloth and used it to cover both of them. Trish snuggled against Kamthibi and laid her head on his shoulder. Kamthibi leaned against the window and closed his eyes to try to sleep after the tiring and anxious moment at the bus station trying to get tickets.

After a while, Kamthibi sensed that they were approaching the steep mountains of the Muchinga escarpment along the Luangwa River Valley. This is the continuation of the geological wonder of the Great East African Rift Valley that starts from Northern Uganda through Kenya, Tanzania, and eastern Zambia all the way to Zimbabwe and South Africa. The bus slowed down as the driver shifted gears many times until it strained, moaned, and jerked forward slowly. When Kamthibi peered through the window into the pitch black African darkness outside, he could see the vague outline of the mountains along the road against occasional light of bright lightening, as the bus crawled along; speeding downhill and slowing down to a crawl going up steep meandering inclines. . There were dangerous sharp bends, too. The driver had to be really awake and alert.

It stopped raining. The bus slowed down and stopped. They had arrived at the Luangwa Bridge. Passengers woke up to peer outside. A baby whined and cried in the back of the bus. A foul smell of human defecation filled the bus. The baby had apparently soiled its diaper. There were cries everywhere for the driver to let the mother out and clean the baby. Some yelled that passengers were going to choke to death if something wasn't done immediately. People held their breath and others pinched their noses. The younger passengers thought this was all so funny as they mimicked adults and held their noses, while all the time giggling. The driver yelled for everyone to open the windows. He said this would not be straightened out until after the bridge because there was still strict protocol prohibiting passengers mingling around the bridge. Kamthibi opened his window. The fresh but warm and humid air of the Luangwa Valley wafted into the bus.

The smaller Luangwa Bridge just down the river below had been blown up during the African struggle against Portuguese colonialism in neighbouring Mozambique. The Frelimo (Front for the Liberation of Mozambique) African guerrilla freedom fighters were conducting armed struggle to kick out the Portuguese who had colonized the country for perhaps more than two hundred years. Since independent Zambia supported the African struggle in Mozambique, Zimbabwe and South Africa, and sometimes the Frelimo guerrillas sneaked into Zambia to seek refuge, the Portuguese saboteurs blew up the bridge to hurt and disrupt

Zambia. At that same bridge, a couple decades earlier, a bus company of Zambia fully loaded bus travelling from Chipata to Lusaka, was blown up by a bomb lobbed into it by a white Portuguese saboteur who had pretended to be a hitch hiker. Twelve passengers had died and dozens injured. Four of the dead passengers were school girls from St. Monica's Secondary School. At that time, Zambian soldiers armed to the teeth were stationed at the expensive newly-built massive bridge to strictly monitor all passengers and traffic crossing the bridge night and day. The soldiers boarded the buses. Requiring all passengers to disembark, for a strict checking of identity was mandatory. Foreigners, especially whites, and anyone without Zambian nationality identities were all more scrutinized and if necessary interrogated and detained. At that time, Kamthibi would not have dared to bring Trish along because the soldiers would have looked at her and Kamthibi suspiciously. But now, more than twenty-five years later, the lone soldier casually walked to the driver's side of the window, said hello to the driver, and waved the bus to cross the bridge. The regulation said that only one vehicle could cross the massive suspension bridge at a time. The vehicle had to travel at no more than fifteen miles per hour.

Shortly after the bridge, the driver pulled the bus over. The woman and her baby came out of the bus to have the baby's diaper changed and cleaned. Passengers walked out of the bus to use the bush open-air bathroom by the side of the road. The drivers switched with the one who had been sleeping on the front seat now taking over the driving.

After a while, passengers were settling down to fall asleep. The bus slowed down and Kamthibi was saying 'what now again' under his breath and sat up. Through the bright lights of the windshield, he could read the huge bright yellow reflecting sign in black letters: "DETOUR." The bus took a slow right and the bumps and rattling of the bus was suddenly deafening. Some parts of the Great East Road were not yet paved. This detour was made while the main road was being paved.

The bus picked up speed but suddenly slowed down for a bad bump. The driver and the passengers were tossed up and down. On sharp corners, the bus leaned to one side as if tipping over, scaring passengers.

"Hey!!! Tell the driver he will kill us!" one frightened passenger yelled, "tell him to slo…." Before the passenger could finish the sentence, the bus came to a sharp corner as it leaned to one side once more, and hit a big bump that sent passengers springing almost all the way to the roof and then brought down again like bags full of peanuts. The driver meanwhile turned the steering wheel rapidly from side to side to negotiate for better spots in the rough and bumpy make shift road. When he slowed down over the bumps, the bus the passengers were engaged in a slow dance in which their bodies swayed gently from side to side and then rode over the bumps gently up, down, back and forth.

"This is nasty," Trish said.

"Yes," Kamthibi agreed, "I wonder how long this is going to go on." He told Trish that this wasn't new for him since he had travelled on worse and rougher roads since early childhood.

Everyone woke up. The driver might have been in need of company since he instantly began to speak to the passengers. He said the horrible bumps were a blessing in disguise since he was afraid he would fall asleep if he did not have anyone to talk to.

"I will never be able to make it to my home village with such a rough driver," one woman complained to another in the seat behind Kamthibi and Trish, "my parents have never seen me since nineteen sixty. They haven't seen all my children. I would like to experience village Christmas again."

The passengers who had been asleep began to speak to one another. They explained where they were going and where they came from. After a while, the bus was back on the paved road again. At dawn they arrived at Kacholola bus stop and the driver pulled over. He explained that they should all have a one-hour rest and that they would resume the bus ride after that. At that, the driver turned the ignition off and pushed his seat back to take a nap. Some passengers went out to relieve their aching bladders. Kamthibi and Trish welcomed some quiet sleep.

The ignition suddenly was turned on and the bus trembled as it idled. The driver waited and asked aloud if everyone was in and he hit the horn several times and the bus took off. It was now clearly dusk and passengers could see the landscape outside. It was lush green all around with small hills and tall mountains along the road. Clouds were perched but slowly moving on top of the mountains. People were walking along the road with hoes on their shoulders heading to their fields. Some people were already bent over in their fields hoeing and tilling their gardens. Some paused, smiled, and waved as the bus went by. Kamthibi thought this was a beautiful and inspiring early morning sight of the elegance of nature and people going about their normal important business of life.

He was afraid Trish was missing all of that. He turned to her. She was still asleep with her head rested on his shoulder. The *chitenje* cloth had slid down. A button must have popped out of her shirt during her sleep because at his angle, half her breast was exposed. Kamthibi looked and shook her with his shoulder while he stared at her bosom with a mischievous smirk and grin frozen on his face. Trish opened her eyes, which caught his looking down further than her neck. She pulled up her *chitenje* cloth and covered her bosom while playfully hitting Kamthibi on his shoulder with her small fist several times.

"You naughty boy," she chuckled and smiled, "what are you looking at?"

Kamthibi drew Trish's attention to the beautiful hills and the mountains, the people working in the fields, and especially the ripe red and yellow delicious mango fruit all over the numerous mango trees, dotted all over garden fields and around village huts. Kamthibi salivated at the thought of eating and devouring juicy fresh delicious mangoes with some of the sweet juice dripping down to the ground.

As the sun rose from the bright red glow in the horizon, Kamthibi and Trish saw more and more congregation of village huts along the road. There were people riding alone on bicycles, and sometimes two and three to a bicycle. Goats, chickens, pigs, and cows roamed the edge of the two-lane road, which by now was the paved side again. Kamthibi and Trish rode the bus all day as passengers who had reached their destination dropped off and others got on.

When the bus stopped, men, women, young boys, and girls rushed along the side of the bus to display for sale baskets of ripe fruit like mangoes, bananas, and guavas. Some were selling deep oil fried fritters, scones, and buns with or without margarine spread on them already. At Nyimba bus stop, everyone got out of the bus to purchase and eat *nshima*, which was served with chicken. There were many small roadside restaurants, market stalls and grocery stores. Nyimba had a police station, two Indian-owned shops and a small airstrip.

The Eastern Province had many villages but also long miles of virgin fertile forest. Trish realized as the bus drove on and on, that this was the part of Africa that any book or television documentary could never truly reflect; the real Africa of vast open spaces where time seems to be somewhat still frozen. By the end of the trip, a million eyes must have stared at Trish because she was such a rare but famous exotic human -a *Muzungu* to be in the same rugged looking bus with the rural village Africa. What a spectacle and miracle! For the white person not to demand privilege? She would demand to ride a brand new car with an African driver to boot just as in the colonial days or even now. Kamthibi must have equally explained a million times that Trish was from Britain and was visiting with him to experience Zambia and life in the village. Nobody had ever heard anything about Ireland.

Was Kamthibi her servant or maybe working for her? Some asked. Kamthibi laughed and explained in a somewhat oblique way that he and Trish were very close friends and knew and understood each other just as we do among each other as Africans among ourselves. There was sceptical laughter punctuated by an incredulous clap of the hands. How could an African and a white person understand each other? Some said this was obviously marriage. They were sure the two would soon get married because it means she truly understands our culture and our important African traditions. Some said if she was married, how could a husband allow his wife to go this far with another man? Kamthibi thought how over the years European superiority complex and colonial subjugation in Zambia, Africa, apartheid in South Africa, and subjugation of Native Americans makes it possible for these otherwise great African human beings to be perpetually sceptical, suspicious, and assume the worst arrogance for all white people's human intentions. Kamthibi thought maybe these painful human episodes would all end but maybe not in his generation or even lifetime.

Most passengers who got on looked curiously or just absorbed the whole experience of sitting next to or being in the same bus with these two - a white European woman and an African Zambian man who spoke their language, so they would be able to later tell friends and relatives when they arrived at their destinations in the villages.

They crossed many small and large bridges, over flooded rivers and streams rushing with red-mud water: Nyimba, Lupande, Msipazi, Katete, Msandile, Lunkhwakwa, Molozi, and Rukuzye. After bouncing over the last one hundred and fifty miles, the bus finally crossed the Lundazi River and entered the small remote town of Lundazi just before sunset. The town had grown over the previous ten years. It had six Indian-owned retail shops, a small district hospital, a secondary school, a one-room police post with a small minimum-security prison, a post office and a few government buildings. It had a small grass airstrip that only the country's President used once in a very long while. The tiny bus station was deserted for the day. The Zambia Bus Company office was only about half a mile walk on the dirt street to the famous Lundazi Castle Hotel.

Kamthibi and Trish carried their bags with Kamthibi carrying his on his shoulder. The Castle Hotel was nestled between and underneath the big, tall, and smooth hundred-foot blue gum trees. There was a river and a dam of blue water behind it. The streaks of the long rays of the sunset made the castle red brick walls glow even more red and beautiful.

The Bridge

"This must be the best hidden secret in the whole of Zambia and maybe Africa," Trish remarked as she removed the large green backpack from her shoulders and plopped it down. She gawked at the castle hotel before her, mesmerized. Kamthibi placed his suitcase down and put his arm around her shoulders.

"It is a sight from ancient England, Scotland, or Wales," Trish finally said after a long silence, "this is amazing, and beautiful and surprising to be in this remote area of Africa."

The Lundazi Castle Hotel was built in the 1930s as a rest station for British colonial administration bureaucrats, and other officers. It was built of red bricks, with cylindrical rooms fitted with narrow spiral stairways leading to the upper second floor of the perfectly round castle hotel rooms. Some of the tiny windows dotting the side of the castle were triangular in shape. The designs and shapes along the top edge of the roof were those of the shape and beauty of the queen's and king's crown. The roofing tiles were replaced with corrugated metal roofing in the 1970s. Trish couldn't believe she was going to spend a night in it -with Kamthibi. 'It was all so romantic and unreal,' so she thought.

The rooms were immaculately clean with smooth and glittering red wax floors. The twin beds had mosquito nets hung over each one. The dining room at the back of the hotel was overlooking the Lundazi River and the dam with the blue waters. The dinner menu was rice, beef stew, vegetable-beef soup, coleslaw, coffee and tea, bread or cake. The Castle Hotel staff literally baked the bread themselves and slaughtered and cooked the chickens from scratch. There was a chicken coup on the side of the motel and Kamthibi had seen a bag of baking flower and a number of raw baking ingredients and big baking ovens in their kitchen.

Trish was very exhausted and achy all over from the bumps and pounding on the bus. After a warm bath and dinner, she took a painkiller and the third, and last, daily dose of her cancer medication. She warmly hugged and kissed Kamthibi good night. She crawled into her bed under her mosquito net. Trish said she would have loved this as a kid. It looked like one's very own private playhouse. Kamthibi replied that he understood because he used to love to sleep in one when he was a kid. As a child, it just looked so cosy and protected from the big bad biting mosquitoes, and hyenas, and leopards, and any marauding monster. They both slept early, so they could get up early, as Kamthibi's village was still twenty miles north of Lundazi town.

It would be more accurate to say that Kamthibi and Trish slept like logs rather than babies because neither of them could remember stirring during the night. It was a good thing they had nets over their beds because without them, the malaria-infested mosquitoes would have feasted mercilessly on their deadtired bodies. Nothing would have deterred the mosquitoes.

Kamthibi chatted proudly in Tumbuka with the hotel staff. They were not sure who he was until he explained that he was grandson of Headman Simbazako of Nkhorongo Village in Chief Magodi's area. Predictably the conversation of sudden familiarity ensued. They, of course, knew where the village was and also that Headman Wizaso Simbazako had a very educated son working in America. Kamthibi collected some information about transportation and what was available at the Indian shops, to plot his next plan of action.

Kamthibi walked to the Indian or *Mwenye* owned shops and purchased a brand new bicycle. He asked and negotiated with the Indian shop owner if he could drive him, the newly-purchased bicycle, and another passenger, in his pickup truck to Boyole Primary School. This would, of course, be for a fee not in kwacha but in foreign currency or American dollars. Ayub Patel, the middle-aged Indian shop owner, ironically declined the offer of American dollars. He said he would have no use for them because he wouldn't be able to use or cash them anywhere in the small remote rural town.

Mr. Ayub Patel, a veteran and fourth generation Indian shopkeeper in the town, said buying the brand new bicycle from his store was enough for Kamthibi to deserve what amounted to a merchandise delivery trip to Boyole School. He added that it was a risk for him to venture into remote parts of the district during the rainy season because of dangers of being stuck somewhere because of flash floods and washed-out bridges. But Mr. Patel commented, in his broken Tumbuka that Asian traders use with their Tumbuka customers that the roads over most streams were still passable. Besides, he knew Headman Nkhorongo, the long retired schoolteacher, as he had lots of business with him over the years.

After putting the new bicycle in the back of the pick up truck, Patel drove to the Lundazi Castle Hotel to pick up Trish and the luggage. They drove to Boyole Primary School on the Chama-Lundazi dirt road. Kamthibi sat in the front cabin with Patel with Trish in the middle. Along the way, they picked up passengers who were not going beyond Boyole School.

They arrived at Boyole Primary School during early afternoon. Mr Patel apologized that he wished he would drive them all the way to Nkhorongo village especially with the European lady who probably had not walked much in her life.

"You know our friends in these advanced countries drive everywhere from when they are babies," Mr Patel said in Tumbuka, "they even drive from the house to the mailbox. They drive to the restaurant window to get food. I understand they even drive from the living room to the kitchen, from the living room to the dining room, from the bedroom to the toilet," Mr *Patel* chuckled at his own joke. Kamthibi wondered where he picked up that one. He had never heard it before.

Kamthibi resisted a smile of collusion and replied that he understood and knew there was no road, and had to cross three creeks and a stream before reaching his home village. He had walked the distance everyday as a child when he went to his first grade at Boyole School. Mr Patel wished the two well, shook their hands, turned around and drove back to Lundazi.

Kamthibi let out a big loud sigh of relief. He put his arm around Trish's waist and Trish reciprocated as she placed her hand on Kamthibi's back and drew closer to him until their bodies touched.

"See all this valley below us along the Lundazi River," Kamthibi said proudly stretching his arm out and pointing with his forefinger, "from the left horizon in the east over the knoll, all the way to the far west, is our Nkhorongo village land, originally settled by Headman Simbazako, my Grandfather."

"Oh, it's a beautiful valley, Kamthibi."

"Sometimes I imagine that my grandfather probably stood at this very spot or some other high elevation and looked at the land and the view and thought it beautiful," Kamthibi continued, "then he went back over this way to the east and got some of his Ngoni tribe relatives to come and settle in this undisturbed virgin land here. I know all these different fields along both sides of the river as belonging to my father and mother's clan. We used to swim in the river as boys and then eat peanuts or sweet melons from any of the fields because the gardens belonged to our aunts, grandfathers, uncles, and other relatives. As a kid it felt like living in heaven on earth. And then there was walking to school. It was so much fun." Kamthibi paused, stared into empty space, and gazed into the far horizon again as if he was trying to reclaim the sweet bygone memories. "Let's get ready for the last leg of our journey," he abruptly said and snapped out of the reverie.

Kamthibi went into the bush and got some fibre from the *Chiyombo* tree. He took out a pillow from his suitcase and tied it around the long bicycle pipe that stretches between the saddle and handle bars. He used two long thin strips of rubber sliced from an old car rubber tube to tie his suitcase and Trish's large backpack firmly on the bicycle's rear carrier. Kamthibi pumped and added some more pressure to the tyres. He struck each tyre across with his stretched out forefinger. On both tyres, there was the characteristic high pitch "ting!" This is the sound that was the characteristic sound you want to hear from a well-pumped bicycle tyre.

"Trish," Kamthibi announced after he pulled the bicycle to an upright position away from the tree it was leaning against when all of this was being done, "you will sit on this bar,"

Kamthibi patted the pillow which was around the bar pipe, "with your legs crossed to one side well away from the front wheel and the rotating pedal, and your hands holding lightly onto this single pipe between the handle bars."

"Yes, I remember seeing hundreds of people on roads riding bikes like this. Lovely, I will be sitting between your arms," interjected Trish trying to make light of her anxiety at this new experience, "but I didn't think I would be doing it. Is it safe and comfortable?"

"It is either this or walking all the way to the village," said Kamthibi, trying as much as possible to make light of Trish's anxiety.

The first mile riding on the narrow bush footpath to Nkhorongo village was smooth with Trish yelling that she was getting the hang of it. Kamthibi knew he could easily reclaim his boyhood well-horned skills of riding a loaded bicycle through thousands of paths by day and many times at night on moonless nights. However, the path gradually headed down slope leading to the first of the three creeks. The footpath was dangerously eroded by rain such that there were thin strips of the path left in the middle with deep dangerous galleys on either side. As they approached the first eroded bad strip on the edge of the path, Kamthibi applied brakes to slow down the heavy bicycle. He planned to navigate along the left edge, but Trish was nervously and unconsciously guessing along the right edge. She instinctively steered and leaned the handlebars in that direction. A brief struggle ensued with driver steering to the left and passenger to the right as both screamed to stop steering it in the wrong direction. It was too late as the heavily laden bike dangerously swung and zigzagged back and forth, criss-crossing the path from left bush to right bush several times. The front wheel bumped into a galley and Kamthibi tried to apply brakes. The bicycle careened off and headed dangerously into the bush. Kamthibi stretched out his right leg to try to break their fall. Trish screamed. They barely missed a tree before the bicycle fell and they landed and ended up in some weeds, grass, and a thick shrub. Trish landed on her bottom sitting up. Her butt would be slightly sore the following morning. She sustained a long thin scratch from the bottom of her neck to just below her ear lobe from a sharp, thin, dry twig. Fortunately, Kamthibi only scraped his knee and there was a green stain on the knee of his pants. He wondered what would have happened if he had landed on his still healing arm. Other than this, both escaped the incident with no serious injuries.

"I am sorry Kamthibi, it was my fault," Trish said as she brushed herself off and carefully looked and inspected her arms, elbows, and legs for more scratches.

"No, Trish, it was my fault," Kamthibi responded pointing to his chest, "I should have warned you to fight the instinct to steer the handle bars too. When as a child you ride in front for the first time as a passenger, your dad tells you not to ever try to steer the handlebars too. 'Otherwise we will crash' dad usually warns. It's a learned passenger skill. I almost mentioned it before the ride. I didn't want to make you more nervous. I don't know how much difference it would have made anyway."

As Kamthibi retrieved the heavy bicycle with luggage still bound on the carrier and intact, Trish began to laugh hysterically at the thought of how the accident had happened with both of them fighting each other, steering in opposite directions. Kamthibi joined in the laughter.

"What are we going to do now?" Trish asked as she wiped her tears and continued to pat the thin scratch on her neck with a tissue to wipe any lingering blood residues.

"'That was so funny," was Kamthibi's initial response, "I think I will push the bike along and we can just walk the rest of the way. We have already covered a third of the distance."

"I totally agree. This is too dangerous for an inexperienced Irish girl. We are lucky neither one of us got seriously hurt."

Each time they met people they would stop and exchange greetings. Kamthibi would then identify himself as Headman

The Bridge

Simbazako's son visiting from America. And the woman with him was his British workmate. There was no point explaining complex details about Trish to total strangers or maybe some of them claimed to be distant relatives. Kamthibi did not doubt their claims, as clan links are very strong between all the villages. But he had never lived in the village long enough as an adult to appreciate all the intricate nuances of a complex network of kinship, relatives stretching back sometimes to the 1870s many generations back. But Malonje was going to pose a challenge in the village with Trish being with him.

They walked and crossed the three creeks, including the largest one of the three, the Denkhule. They all had three large logs laid across them from bank to bank serving as a bridge. Crossing them meant carefully balancing the two wheels of the bicycle along one log and walking and pushing the bicycle along carefully.

CHAPTER FOURTEEN

Because of the nature of the quick and quite abrupt decision to visit his home village because of the circumstances in Ireland and London, Kamthibi could not have possibly informed his father, mother, brothers and sisters about his coming, let alone with a woman companion. After all, there were no telephones, faxes, electricity, let alone e-mail in the village. If Kamthibi had decided to send an advance letter it probably would have arrived long after they had come and gone. Now the moment was almost there. He felt a little apprehensive. How would everyone react? He trusted and loved his family. They wouldn't humiliate him and run him and Trish out of the village. But if his crazy older sister Neliya was there by any chance, she was the unpredictable one. That would be uncharacteristic of most of his relatives except his first-born oldest sister. The whole thing had happened so quickly. Kamthibi kept repeating as if to dissuade himself of the fear of the possibility and creeping doubt that he may have screwed up and badly miscalculated in his decision to take Trish to the village without telling anyone in advance.

So it is that Kamthibi and Trish walked in that mid-afternoon in the bright African sun through the small path to the village pushing the bicycle that carried their luggage along. They were drenched in sweat. They had walked five miles from the main road at Boyole School. Their feet were killing them, throbbing, and roasting in their hot sweaty gym shoes. This was now their last hundred yards. Two dogs began to bark; usually the sign that strangers are approaching the village. They could have been in a scene in a movie. As they emerged out of the tall grass, the fascinating scene of the village was before them: two rows of round mud huts and bigger mud rectangular thatched houses stretched into the distance to the far end of the village. The village was like a secret hidden at the end of a mysterious bush trail. Children, presumably nieces and nephews, stood frozen still staring at Kamthibi and Trish. Kamthibi spotted his mother near the small kitchen hut holding a pot from which she had just discarded some dirty water. A mob of chickens immediately scrambled to quickly gabble the wet morsels of food. For a few split seconds, his mother looked at him and then Trish and her jaw dropped in utter surprise at what she was seeing.

"Children!" she quickly composed herself and yelled,"Why are you just standing there staring at your uncle? Come on, help your uncle with the bike and their luggage. They are not dancing. The guests have walked a long way in the hot sun. Misozi! Will you please get chairs for the guests to sit on. Hurry before they sit in the dirt and ruin their clean clothes."

Kamthibi couldn't help but smile. That was his vintage mother. It was as though he was ten years old again. The children sheepishly hustled over to watch while the older, stronger boys relieved Kamthibi of the bicycle and untied the luggage and took both into his parents' house. As Kamthibi wiped his sweaty brow waiting for the chairs, he and Trish saw the goats bleating with young in tow while wondering about the village grounds, chickens with their chicks in tow, roosters chasing hens, pigeons singing in their coup, the mud houses, the *nkhokwe* food storage containers, a grass bathing shelter, the smell of goat dung, and smoke, from open cooking fires. All the sights and sounds of his childhood village reconnected him to the primordial comfort such memories evoke. Kamthibi breathed a big sigh of relief as he gave the first chair to Trish and then he plopped down on the second one. The chairs were old and creaky. His mother grabbed a reed mat and laid it down next to him. Then she walked toward Kamthibi and half crouching and curtsying, she shook hands in the characteristic Zambian customary way of greeting. She then shook Trish's hand and paused.

"I can see your guest must be a quick learner. She seems to already know how to shake hands and greet in the Zambian way," Kamthibi's mother chuckled. She sat down on the mat with her legs stretched out but crossed one on top of the other. She was barefoot like most village people are. She was wearing an old faded *chitenje* cloth over a dress whose top was half in shreds from heavy use and obvious wear and tear. Her small hands felt rough and tough from hard physical work. In spite of her obvious ageing since the last time Kamthibi had seen her, her voice still had a melodic lively touch to it and her verbal wit and humour were undiminished.

"Her name is Trisha Butler. Her family name of *chiwongo* is Butler," Kamthibi said sensing that his mother was searching for a way to address her during the traditional greeting.

"*Monile anya Batala. Muli wuli?*" (Greetings lady Butler. How are you?) Kamthibi's mother laughed knowing that she had butchered the pronunciation of the English name and that she couldn't possibly pronounce any English words because she had never been to school in her life, having been born in the late 1920s.

"*Nili makola k-w-a-li n-a-mwe,*" the four Tumbuka words came out of Trish's mouth slowly in a jerky way. I am all right and how are you). On her insistence, Kamthibi had coached her on rote, memorizing the four greeting words in Tumbuka during the previous few days in readiness for the trip.

Kamthibi's mother broke out with hearty laughter so did the children and other adults who were slowly congregating as word went around that Headman Simbazako's son who lived in America had just arrived with a *muzungu* woman.

"She says, "*Nili makola!*" (I am all right) so you must have taught her so that she is able to talk to your illiterate mother," Kamthibi's mother was beside herself with laughter and amusement, "that was very considerate of you my son.... Mister

Simbazako," she began addressing Kamthibi in the Tumbuka way of addressing to show respect. She suddenly took on a sombre and more serious tone of voice, "Tell us, how are you?"

Kamthibi briefly told his mother about his safe plane trip from Chicago in America to London in England, and then to Lusaka; how they spent a few days in Lusaka and visited with Teketa's family. Kamthibi's mother remembered Teketa, her son's secondary school friend, whom he had brought home to visit one weekend from school. He told her how he and Trish caught a bus in Lusaka and travelled all night through the five hundred miles and were dropped off at *Boyole* Primary School that afternoon by Ayub Patel and how they walked the five miles to the village.

"Mother," Kamthibi said in Tumbuka, "although I walk, eat, and work where I live in America, I always think of all of you here in the village. I don't sleep. My heart is always with all of you here in the village. I have come here for two reasons: I want to spend Christmas with you but also to show my friend here, Trish, where I come from. My children, your grandchildren, Phyera the girl and her two younger brothers Mabvuto and Mangani are all alright. Their mother, my wife Nora, is physically all right. But we have had some serious problems in the marriage lately. I am not sure the marriage can survive. We are at each other's throats everyday. These are the things we will talk about later."

"Oh!!!" Kamthibi's mother shook her head, "I knew something or visitors were coming. I have not only had strange dreams lately, but today everybody else in the village is gone, but I kept just being pinned around the house finding one small thing to do after another."

"Mother, my *malonje* is very important and serious," Kamthibi emphasized. *Malonje* is a very important Tumbuka custom during which a guest gives a good systematic account about the purpose of the visit and in what condition the guest left their home or family. The host then also takes turns explaining the condition of affairs in the family.

"You are right," Kamthibi's mother concurred, "something this important should wait until your father, brothers, and aunts come back in the evening. I don't know why everybody had to go somewhere this afternoon."

Kamthibi's mother said she was happy they were visiting for Christmas but consoled him briefly about his marriage, saying life and marriages were like twins as both had difficult ups and downs. She stood up and left to begin preparing supper.

Kamthibi knew that Trish was lost because she could not understand any of what was being said. All of it was so complex that it could not be explained briefly even into just a few sentences. So he tried to give her a quick overview to catch up on just some of what was going on.

Kamthibi deliberately told the bit about his facing marital problems to his mother so that indirectly she would put one and one together and she would conclude that Kamthibi's relationship with Trish was not just an innocent or platonic one. Since they had had no interest or ample opportunity for disclosing each other's marital details, Kamthibi wanted to tell Trish that Nora's family, came from Basiti village six miles away towards the west. Nora was a city girl. Her parents having moved from the village when Nora was barely a few years old. She had visited her village only a few times in her whole life. She was not very steeped in the traditional Tumbuka culture. Signs were that she hated, had some contempt, and was suspicious of the traditional customs like most urban Zambians, especially those that are educated. However, when two Africans get married, the two families also marry. That's why there were some deep attachments between the Simbazako family at Nkhorongo and Nora's clan at Basiti Village.

"What is your mother's name?" Trish asked.

"Her name is Faginess NyaNthula," Kamthibi replied, "but this is not the whole answer. Among the Tumbuka, women traditionally never use their husband's name. There is no Mrs Simbazako or Mrs Fitzgerald. They use their maiden last name or a name of their choice. The term "Nya" is a prefix that means adult female or a sign of respect. So my mother is *aNyaNthula*."

"So I would be *aNya*Butler,"

"Exactly."

The children, who were Kamthibi's nephews and nieces, sat around the guests giggling as Kamthibi made small talk with them. What grade were they in and did they know how to read and write. Who was their teacher? They were on school holiday that's why they were at home on a weekday. Shortly, Kamthibi's mother called the children and told them to chase and catch the black rooster. Kamthibi knew supper was probably three hours away because the chicken was going to be caught, slaughtered, de-feathered, and cooked for at least an hour. Village chickens are very hard. But they are very tasty and have a rich flavour.

Trish and Kamthibi were served mangoes and roasted peanuts which filled them up until dinner which was later that evening. As according to custom, continuous streams of extended family relatives from Kamthibi's village, his mother's village only two miles away, well-wishers, and other villagers trekked to greet them the rest of the afternoon.

A big bon-fire was made in front of the house to keep mosquitoes away. Dinner was like in old times. Kamthibi's two younger brothers, now in their mid-thirties, supervised the bringing of the wooden table outside into the moonlight. Kamthibi's father, his brothers, and several pre-adolescent and adolescent boys ate with the men. Kamthibi's mother, Trish, her daughters -in-law, female relatives, all the young girls, and children ate near the hut kitchen within talking distance. Trish was given a separate serving so that she ate with Misozi, Kamthibi's tenth grade niece. The small dinner talk and the big delicious meal with chicken reminded Kamthibi of his meals on the plane whenever he flew. In comparison to the tiny stale meals served on the plane, this was a large feast. Kamthibi joked that if they were to serve our *nshima* to every passenger on the plane, it would be so big and heavy that the plane would not be able to take off the ground. Everybody had a hearty laugh.

As dinner drew to a close, Kamthibi's father, Wisazo, reminded everyone to put away the plates quickly so that they could conduct *malonje* for Kamthibi and Trish. Soon everyone sat around the fire with Kamthibi's father sitting on Kamthibi's left and his mother on the far right. Trish was sitting next to Kamthibi. The flickering flames of the fire created a red glow on everyone's face.

Malonje is a very special Tumbuka custom in which the guest explains not only the purpose of the visit but all the possible systematic details so that the hosts or relatives have a full account of whatever is going on in the hosts' life and that of the family. As a child, Kamthibi had sat through so many *malonje* of his older sisters angrily returning from their marriages because they had quarrelled with their husbands or because of some other persistent problems. This time Kamthibi was the narrator of the *malonje*. He had to word everything very carefully. It is quite a demanding task requiring tremendous verbal skill and tact.

Kamthibi's father, in his usual calm, deliberate voice, said he and Kamthibi's mother and virtually everyone else in the village were taken by complete surprise by his trip especially bringing a *muzungu* woman whom no one had heard about before. There had been no letter or any signal about Kamthibi and Trish's coming. Why did they make such a sudden journey?

"Although I have come to spend Christmas with you my family," Kamthibi cleared his throat, "I cannot lie to you because I am a grown, mature man. I brought Trish so that she can see you and appreciate where I come from. My wife Nora and I have had serious problems. I found out she was sleeping with another man and she just doesn't listen to me anymore. She has become a different woman. Maybe I have also changed. But what breaks my heart and makes me really sad, is my three children. What will happen to them? My wife and I are no longer happy. We have tried everything to fix the marriage. This is why I have brought Trish," Kamthibi nodded in Trish's direction, "I love her very much. Although she is *muzungu*, we understand and care about each other. She has been eating *nshima* as you saw tonight. I am not getting any younger. I want to be happy in the few days, perhaps years that God has given me for the rest of my life."

There was a long pause and all the family members quietly reflected this piece of hot news. Trish could sense something was happening or being said about her. It must be positive since no one was throwing rocks at her - at least not yet.

"What you say makes sense," finally Kamthibi's father said slowly. "Among the Tumbuka, we say that sometimes a man finds a woman who makes him happy far away from his village, from another tribe. In your modern types of jobs and life, you need a woman who is going to support you day and night. Your mother did that for me when I worked as a teacher. What your wife Nora is doing is dangerous. But there is one problem here - the marriage between you and Nora is still intact as far as we and everyone knows. Her clan and family have not been informed that the two of you are facing marital problems. Nora's family is likely to send the *nkhoswe* to me as soon as they learn of this situation. They are likely to call a village *mphala* (village court of elders) because of you, my son, being with another woman when you have not declared your intensions to divorce or become polygamous. You never informed anyone about your problems. You will hear about this from your maternal grandparents, too. They are likely to show up to talk with you. You know polygamy is allowed in our culture. They might demand their *lobola* or bride price back and cause all sorts of problems for all of us here in the village."

"Yes, I know that," answered Kamthibi, "but I am not asking to be polygamous."

"Yes, I know", Kamthibi's father said, "the reason I am saying all of this is that you should explain to the lady that you will sleep in separate houses the few days you are here. I don't want to be sued and taken to the *mphala* by the Nkhata's clan. This way if they take me to court, I can simply say, while they were here, they never spent a night in one bed."

Kamthibi could not disagree. He and Trish did not want to cause problems for the entire family. So he would explain the situation to Trish later that evening. She would sleep in the *nthanganeni* which is a hut for unmarried young women and girls. There was only Kamthibi's niece who went to Lundazi Secondary School and two other younger girls.

Afterwards, everybody joined in free flow spontaneous conversation. They ate more peanuts and mangoes. The younger kids were cautioned not to eat any more mangoes as they might wet their beds. They talked about the weather, what all the different siblings were doing; what grades Kamthibi's children were in and how everyone, especially the younger nieces and nephews, wished Kamthibi had come with them to visit everyone and play with other children in the village.

"We have been terribly distracted by the guests and *malonje*," Kamthibi's mother said, "the *Kulimizgha* annual ceremony is tomorrow. Every woman in our clan cooked three huge clay pots of beer, *mthibi* and *zinduku* traditional sweet brews."

"Guess what?" Kamthibi turned to Trish excitedly as he clapped his hands rapidly several times and said in English, "great timing! The annual *Kulimizgha* ceremony of the Simbazako clan is tomorrow. I am so excited. I have not been to one, since oh, more than twenty years ago."

"What is it about?" Trish asked surprised at the sudden excitement in Kamthibi's voice.

"I hate to spoil it for you," replied Kamthibi, "all I can say is that there are lots of people, beer, sweet traditional brews, and it's perfect for you to wear your *chitenje* cloth. Can you dance, balance a calabash on your head, and walk?"

"Y-e-s, a little bit, and it depends on the type of dance," Trish replied hesitantly smiling and obviously joking.

Kamthibi resumed conversation in Tumbuka with his mother, father, brothers, and other relatives. When conversations were in Nyanja, Trish could pick up some words that were either in English or derived from English. But now she could not understand a word of what was being said in Tumbuka. She would rely on Kamthibi to sometimes quickly interpret some important pieces. It would be unfair to expect him to interpret every single piece of conversation, Trish thought, because Kamthibi had the right to enjoy this obviously rare time with his family in the village. Sometimes Trish wished she was Cinderella and could simply click her fingers or click her heels and she would be able to speak or maybe just understand Tumbuka. Kamthibi and everyone else seemed to be having a ball around the bright ambers of the bon-fire in an African night.

As everyone was clearing things away and saying good night, Kamthibi had a short opportunity to explain to Trish the sleeping arrangements. He grabbed Trish's hand and they walked some distance in the bright moonlight and stood under a tree that was located almost half way between the two huts. The one hut was the *nthanganeni* the other hut was the *mphala* where all young single unmarried men and boys sleep. Kamthibi told Trish that they didn't have much time since everyone was sleeping early in readiness for the *Kulimizgha* ceremony early the next day. Since he was still married to Nora, Trish and Kamthibi sleeping in one hut, would create social upheaval after they left. Nora's family would likely take Kamthibi's father to court for breaching marital customs and protocol. Kamthibi hastily said they would talk about the details later. He hoped Trish understood.

"I understand completely Kamthibi," Trish replied as they held hands under the tree. The moonlight was making funny white patches where it penetrated the openings between tree leaves and branches, "I wouldn't want to do anything to cause problems in your family if I can help it. I will miss snuggling and talking to you though tonight."

"I miss more than snuggling," Kamthibi said as they hugged and held each other and kissed.

"Don't say that," Trish quipped, "that makes me feel bad."

With that, Kamthibi and Trish walked over to the *nthanganeni* to set up the sleeping arrangements. Once inside the hut, Kamthibi lit up one of the candles they had brought from Lusaka. He climbed on a stool and tied the mosquito net string on one of the tree rafters on the grass hut roof. His nieces brought a reed mat and laid it down under the net. Trish got a sleeping bag and a small pillow from her backpack and laid it on top of the mat. The mosquito net was then tacked under the mat creating some good, comfortable, and safe sleeping space for her. She took out a small double AA battery flashlight. Misozi could speak slow formal English. If Trish needed anything, she had to just ask Misozi. Kamthibi told the girls: if a hyena came at night and was knocking at the door, "just scream and I will bring my American machine gun and that hyena won't know what hit it." The girls laughed and giggled and thought all of this was so funny especially from their American uncle. "If Trish needs to use the bathroom during the middle of the night, take her to the outhouse as she has a flashlight." The nieces roared on the floor with laughter again especially that a *muzungu* would use an outhouse. Trish sensed there was something naughty and funny Kamthibi was saying to the girls, but couldn't tell what. She asked and Kamthibi kept saying nothing while laughing. Trish and Kamthibi stepped out of the *nthanganeni* and kissed good night. The moon was even brighter.

Once inside the hut and in his covers, Kamthibi was too excited to sleep. He kept tossing. His nephews were all asleep. He knew the moonlight was still bright outside. He lit the candle on the floor, stepped outside and closed the small door behind him. He sat down and began to think. 'Why am I drawn to this remote African village so often? Why am I in this place in Lundazi, in this village many times? Why do I think of this place so often? The bus journey from Lusaka to the remote Lundazi district is no piece of cake. It is over five hundred miles away on a two-lane road that was paved more than twenty-five to thirty years ago. It's challenging to drive or ride on a bus as the road is badly damaged in many places. Why don't I forget this place and enjoy my life in the United States which has so much food, cable TV, medicine, automobiles, cell phones, computer communication, best schools in the world for one's children, and where one can generally expect to live to be in the eighties? After all, the cost and hassle of travelling to this remote place I call my home village are overwhelming. But the ten thousand mile flight from the US and the five hundred mile bus journey to this home village has a special place in my heart. Every desolate-looking village hut, rural shopping centre, the endless farm fields, the wilderness, and thousands of mango trees all hold special meanings for me. Oh, so many pleasant memories and the excitement of travel away from my childhood familiar village. That first bus ride was so exciting.'

Kamthibi was suddenly vividly aware that he was sitting on the front of the small hut along the narrow edge known as *chiwundo*, by the thin closed wooden door. The yellow glow of the candlelight was visible along the edge of the rectangular doorframe. The bright half moon was sparkling just above his forehead in the western side of the star-studded sky. The moonlight created mesmerizing shapes out of the village huts and the trees. It was serene and calm except for the soft chirps of crickets. The serenity of the place was intoxicating. Kamthibi felt this was heaven on earth. This was another night in his home village. He was savouring every moment like a death row inmate who had been given just an hour to enjoy total freedom before execution.

This is the place where his mom and dad's house is literally less than eighty yards away from his hut. His brother and his two wives' houses are sixty yards away. His other brother and his wife and their children are less than twenty yards away. Roosters, chickens, and the cacophonous sounds of birds wake him up in the early morning at dawn after a full eight hours of refreshing sleep. The air he breathes in the morning is fresh and crisp. When he wakes up and opens the front door of his hut, he can see all these people he loves at a glance. They greet each other every morning. Kamthibi walks a hundred yards to his mother's house to wish her and his dad good morning or them to his hut some mornings. He was overwhelmed when he realized how much he missed this precious human intimacy. He wiped his tears.

Indeed if ever there was such a place that was close to being heaven on earth, it must be Simbazako Village. The village grass-roofed houses are perched on a small elevation in a gorgeous valley ensuring the capturing of cool breezes. The sun shines in the clear, cloudless blue sky everyday. His small beautiful hut that had been built for him, the size of the modest living room of my American house, has a well-manicured dirt yard. His brother's wives collected the dirt paints of light, red, and black stripes from the tiny creek nearby. In the days to come, as he would sit relaxing in the shade in his small structure known as *mphungu* enjoying the bright sunshine and the cool breeze, he would begin to understand something ancient. He could appreciate why the British and other Westerners always grabbed these lands by force and often displaced and killed the native Africans.

This is the place where the many acres of fertile land, where most of the food is grown, is literally four feet behind his hut. The land produces abundant corn, kidney beans, sweet potatoes, pumpkins, peanuts, cotton, peas, and cassava. There are numerous mango fruit trees and other succulent tropical fruit like guavas, bananas and paws-paws during the appropriate seasons.

His five, seven, and nine-year-old nephews and nieces roam long distances around the village fields and bushes, walking three miles to school, playing with incredible freedom within the security of all adults in the six villages knowing and protecting all the children. He appreciated this security and the innocence the children enjoy because he grew up here at Simbazako as a child in the village.

But all this security and tranquillity was under severe threat of being undone because of the AIDS pandemic and other modern forces. Kamthibi had followed the AIDS epidemic since the 1980s. From the stories he had heard so far, he had come to a now alarming and predictable observation: too many men and women had died and are dying of AIDS. Unfortunately for the vast majority of the world, the answer will not be as easy as just seeking HIV/AIDS prevention or a vaccine. No doubt this will and would help. Kamthibi placed his head between his hands and his elbows on his knees. He shook his head slowly and thought: 'There is something that is much more fundamental that had happened over the last thirty to forty years that will have to be acknowledged if the AIDS epidemic will be halted in these villages and perhaps cities - this is the near total breakdown of most of the moral and family rules that traditionally kept a lid on the emergence and spreading out of serious and virulent diseases and epidemics such as AIDS and others'.

Another thought randomly occurred to Kamthibi. He now came to understand why when Americans and other foreigners truly lived in Africa for a while, something always draws them back to the continent. He had often heard people refer to it as a "bug." The gorgeous serene night sight was just such a "bug." Kamthibi stood up and went inside the hut and to bed. His mind was finally tired enough for him to sleep.

After the first rooster had crowed at dawn, Kamthibi heard steps and women's voices. It was *aNyaNthula*, his brothers' wives, and other women getting ready for the *Kulimizgha* ceremony. Kamthibi contemplated waking up. There was nothing really much for men to do. Since Trish was in the *nthanganeni* hut, would she also wake up and join her fellow women in the preparation? Would they tell her to go back to sleep? 'She probably needed all the rest and sleep after all that walking the previous day,' Kamthibi thought.

Kulimizgha involved the women of the clan cooking and brewing huge quantities of traditional beer, and *mthibi* and *zinduku* sweet traditional non-alcoholic drinks. They are brewed from corn or maize and finger millet grains. On a designated day, men, women, and young people from many surrounding villages gather at the field or garden of the individual clan member who is sponsoring the event. The large crowds of people hoe and till the whole big field in a matter of a couple of hours. This would be the same amount of work that would have taken the individual person or family weeks to accomplish hence resulting into loss of crops to weeds. After the work is completed, all the people gather, drink, eat and get merry. The aim of the *Kulimizgha* ceremony is really to pool communal labour so that one person or family doesn't spend weeks working on their field. It's a time and effort saving ritual. But there is more to it. The same ceremony is repeated in as many fields as people request and organize.

Kamthibi woke up and got out of his sleeping bag and dressed. He used the outhouse. Since all the women were gone, he asked his young nephew to get him water in a basin from his mother's house. He brushed his teeth and washed his face. He joined his two brothers and other men as they all headed to Headman Simbazako, Kamthibi's father's field, for the *Kulimizgha* ceremony.

There was already a huge crowd of men and women gathered along one edge of the field. They were standing abreast in a long single line. One half of the line was men and the other women. The field was overgrown with weeds almost drowning the corn, pumpkins, peas, and other crops. The crowd would together weed and make ridges where peanuts were later to be planted. This is tedious and back-breaking work that takes individuals and families weeks and sometimes months to do.

Since women were lined up in the far half of the line along the field, Kamthibi could barely spot Trish. She was wearing a colourful Zambian dress complete with a *chitenje* wrap around. She would wear the headdress or *duku* later. She had blended in so well, it warmed Kamthibi's heart but in a scary way. He momentarily had a panicked feeling as though he had lost her. He wanted to talk to her but he had to follow custom and protocol. His mother, grandmothers, distant aunts, elderly women from Nora's and many other villages were there. These are the women who are known in Tumbuka as *nchembere* and are revered in the village as custodians of custom and virtue. Kamthibi could not walk straight to the large group of women and simply stand and say: "Hey Trish! How are you this morning?" This would be looked at as being arrogant, rude, or just being disrespectful.

Kamthibi excused himself from his brothers and other men. He carefully walked along the edge of the field but behind the line of women. He parted the grass as he walked. He had to walk with dignity, poise, and respect - walking behind instead of in front - some of the shrubs between him and women as if he was afraid they would see him. The women were busy greeting each other, talking, and laughing. When Kamthibi was within earshot of Trish, he called and beckoned to one of the young boys nearby.

"Would you please ask your *muzungu* aunt to come here," he told the boy, "tell her, uncle Kamthibi would like to talk to her."

The boy did a double take and looked confused and perplexed for a while as if asking 'how can a white woman be my auntie at the same time?' He walked over to Trish and Kamthibi noticed him point back to his direction twice.

Kamthibi crouched by the small shrub in the grass. His head was clearly visible from where the women were standing and some sitting. He thought Trish seemed to have a seventh sense with people or was it that Kamthibi's nieces and sisters-in-law had already taught her a thing or two overnight about how to conduct herself as a woman? Instead of rushing and galloping over, Trish walked slowly and deliberately to where Kamthibi was crouched in the customary Tumbuka male traditional style. She first knelt down on the grass in her beautiful colourful *chitenje* wrap just about two yards from Kamthibi. Then she sat down with both her legs together to one side like Zambian women do.

"You are pulling my heart strings," Kamthibi said smiling, "honey, you look fabulous."

"This is a first," Trish said smiling coyly, "why are you calling me honey for the first time?"

"Listen, we don't have time," Kamthibi said hastily holding Trish's hand between his hands, "who taught you to sit like that?"

"Your niece and other women taught me last night and this morning. I got up at dawn. You wouldn't believe how fresh and crisp the air felt that early. You missed out."

"Shhhh!!!!!" Kamthibi said placing his forefinger on his lips when Trish wanted to say some more. He squinted and corked his ear trying to concentrate. He was overhearing several women in a conversation he was not supposed to be hearing. But the women must have forgotten that voices tend to carry in the quiet bush.

"This man Kamthibi Simbazako has great poise and dignity. Look at the way he summoned her and sat down in a dignified way. Most educated men would not act this way. Their noses are always bent and in the air. But Kamthibi has many degrees. Even this *muzungu* woman, what's her name? Ti-ri-shi? She is also learning. No doubt from him. Look at the way she walked to him. But word has it that Nora doesn't want him any more. What a shame? You mean our Nora *Nkhata* of Basiti village? If Kamthibi lived here in the village, he would marry five wives. Easily. I would be the fifth wife." There was loud laughter in unison from the women like all Zambian women and girls learn to laugh together. Then someone said, "Women love a man who has dignity and self-respect."

Even if he were to tell all of this to Trish, Kamthibi wasn't sure he would tell the bit about five wives. There were so many voices and tall grass, he couldn't tell who was saying what. But the conversation he had overheard warmed his heart. He would share some of it with Trish later at an appropriate time.

"Listen," Kamthibi resumed.

"What are they saying?" Trish asked anxiously.

"Nothing, I couldn't tell. Something about the brew looks good. A compliment to my mother's beer brewing skills, I guess," Kamthibi told a white lie, "I might not see you. You look beautiful. Take a break and sit in the shade if it gets too hot for you. Send a child if you need me or send Misozi."

"Your niece, sister-in-laws, and these women will take care of me. Actually, I feel better than I have felt in a long time. So don't worry." Trish smiled.

"I feel like kissing you but I will settle for holding hands." Kamthibi said holding Trish's hands.

After a few seconds, Kamthibi and Trish bid each other goodbye. He slowly walked to where the men were standing, as the *Kulimizgha* was to start any time. All the women and the men stood in a straight line with hoes in their hands. The women were already ululating like excited songbirds heightening the crowd's feelings of anticipation, expectation, and excitement as they were all poised to commune in something very important.

A woman in a high-pitched voice that people swore could be heard six villages away led the first of a series of *Kulimizgha* hoeing songs.

Woman Leader: *Ameri!!! Ameri Mwe!!!!* (twice)
(Mary!!!! Mary!!!!)

Crowd: *Ameri, Ameri Nawo!!!!!* (twice)
(Mary, Mary I called her!!!)

Crowd: *Namcema kanai kose*
(I called her four times)

Some in the Crowd: *Hole Weee!!!!*

Crowd: *Ameri !! Ameri Nawo!!!!*
(Mary, I called her!!)

The Tumbuka traditional *fwemba* dance song was transformed into a hoeing and *Kulimizgha* farming song. The song says a young man is having a romantic escapade with a young woman called Mary. As lovers do, they arrange to meet. He goes to meet her for the early evening romantic liaison. He stands outside her *nthanganeni* hut and calls her name four times: "Mary, Mary, Mary, Mary." She never comes out to meet him knowing that her father was still awake just in the house next to the *nthanganeni* hut.

When they responded to the song, the crowd and Kamthibi raised their hoes at once and struck the earth at *"Namcema,"* *"Kanai,"* *"Kose"* *"Ameri!"* *"Ameri!"* *"Nawo!!."* This was a total of six strokes with the hoe, turning the soil over in a rhythmic fashion.

The feelings were electric and transcending. Kamthibi had never felt that before. His heart was throbbing in his rib cage at a constant pace. He was sweating profusely. The repetitive motion of singing, raising his hoe in synchrony with a thousand other hoes over and over again, was intoxicating. He felt so alive. He couldn't compare it to any other feelings he had ever had. He expected to hoe for a short time and then rest since his arm was still weak and not a hundred percent healed. Besides, people with soft town desk jobs have soft hands, so is the common saying in the village. Kamthibi's hands did not even have one callous yet. He expected to get blisters. Everyone, including Trish, was sweating profusely. But he was surprised how he kept up the rhythm and especially the hard physical work.

After what seemed like a surprisingly short time, a third of the huge field was hoed. Then there was a mandatory pause between songs so that people could rest. Some women paused longer to breast feed their babies freely in full view of everyone. The ululating by the women never stopped. The atmosphere was festive. The feeling, according to Kamthibi, was that of floating on cloud nine.

Another song was started. When it finished, there was another even longer pause. The last song, which would for sure see the completion of the hoeing and tilling of the entire field, started.

    Woman Leader: *Nili na njara, Njara ya sima!!!* (twice)
        (I have hunger for nshima!!!)

    Crowd: *Nkhupenja sima, Yituba mbee notofuka*
        (I want nshima, white and soft)

    Woman Leader: *Nili na njara, Njara ya sima!!!* (twice)
        (I have hunger for nshima!!!)

Crowd: *Nageza maoko, Natema nthozi yiwemi*
(I have washed hands, I have cut a good lump of nshima)

Woman Leader: *Nili na njara, Njara ya sima!!!* (twice)
(I have hunger for nshima!!!)

Crowd: *Nakonya makora, Nakubwita mu msuzi*
(I have moulded the nshima and dipped it into the gravy)

Woman Leader: *Nili na njara, Njara ya sima!!!* (twice)
(I have hunger for nshima!!!)

Crowd: *Wuli ceeeee, Wa nyama ya nkhuku*
(The gravy is bright red from chicken meat)

The song was perfect for *Kulimizgha* because it depicted someone hungry, wanting *nshima* with delicious chicken. No wonder the crowd sang it ecstatically. The crop the crowd was toiling for was for growing maize that was going to be used to cook the *nshima*. Eating *nshima* with chicken is the ultimate experience in a Zambian cuisine.

As the crowd finished hoeing and were on the opposite end of the huge completed field, the people continued singing as they proceeded in a single file away from the field into the bush with hoes still on their shoulders. They stopped occasionally to lightly stomp their feet on the ground to mimic the strokes of the hoeing rhythm. The ululating this time had subsided.

The men and women noisily divided themselves into small separate groups that sat down in circles a good distance from each other. Each group sat on the green grass under the shady canopy of several trees. This activity was punctuated by an occasional louder call of mothers asking their young babysitters to bring the baby for breast-feeding. Some women walked around with their sweating babies visibly sucking on their breasts, which looked like small black watermelons. Kamthibi was scouring the groups of women in the far end between the trees when his brother tapped him on the shoulder and pointed to the group of women just nearby. Trish was among them. Kamthibi was relieved that somehow she had survived the long ordeal of many hours of physical labour in the hot sun. Now he could at least see her.

Suddenly, the loud conversations and laughter faded down. There was drumming that was coming from a distance behind the woods and maybe even from another neighbouring village. But within minutes, it got closer. Soon, one could hear the sound of the sharp *mapili mapili* percussion and then the heavy booming rhythmic sound of the *Muganda* drum. The drumming was coming from just behind the bushes and then in quite dramatic fashion, twenty-one young girls and women emerged from the woods standing abreast in a single line. They were wearing short colourful *chitenje* skirts with a top that was wrapped around their upper bosom to cover their breasts. They had shiny-smooth, dark-ebony, and chocolate brown skins. They were bare-foot and each balanced on their heads, a glistening calabash with a white plate covering it. The girls looked beautiful and elegant. They all walked, taking one synchronized step forward at a time, following the deep rhythm of the big lead drum. There was spontaneous cheering and chanting from the crowd. Someone led the last of the *Kulimizgha* songs in which everyone joined in the singing once again, this time using his or her feet to mimic the hoeing strokes. The ululating from the women became hysterical. It was an experience words could not describe. Kamthibi just felt so lucky to be alive. The two young men who were drumming were just behind the girls.

The girls all knelt down with the calabashes still balanced on their heads. Older ululating women then walked over in a very theatrical way and each unloaded the calabash from the girls' heads. The drumming got less loud.

"*Moba! Moba!* (Beer! Beer!)," several women yelled as they held the calabashes that had beer in them.

"*Kuno! Kuno!* (Here! Here!)" The group to which the beer was designated yelled back, still singing while raising their hands, and chanting.

The women took the calabashes of beer to the groups. There were similar shouts of *"mthibi!"* and *"zinduku!"* which were the two non-alcoholic drinks. The calabashes containing these drinks were then taken to the respective groups. Men's groups had more beer calabashes than women's. Some of the older young children had their own calabashes of the non-alcoholic drinks. At one point, Kamthibi and Trish's eyes met and they smiled. Kamthibi could see the sparkle in Trish's eyes.

Soon, everyone had settled down and were drinking and laughing, enjoying the fruit of the day's labour. One young man stood and had an exaggerated stagger and slurred speech. He shouted enough for several groups near him to hear what he said. He said he wanted his sister. He didn't know whether she was alive or not. People at first wondered what the ranting of the drunken man would lead to. But he couldn't have been already so drunk because everyone was barely through the first calabash.

"Some get excited over women," the man continued, "some even marry white women without following our custom -our Tumbuka custom!" The man was pointing to his chest and looking in the direction of the group of men Kamthibi was sitting with. As the drunken man was being led away, his last words were telling: "We the Nkhata clan, from Basiti village, will take you to court. See you in court!"

"This man was obviously planted," Kamthibi's brother whispered as he elbowed Kamthibi, "that's a common practice when people have a grievance they feel unable to talk to you about it directly. They will drink a sip of beer and pretend they are drunk and say things they would not say directly. It's a dirty tactic. But people always do it. Don't worry about it. The Simbazako clan will handle it."

There was a buzz about the drunken man at the end of the *Kulimizgha* ceremony as people dispersed and walked back to their villages. This piece of a hot incident would provide folder for wild rumour and juicy gossip. Nora's relatives could immediately convene a *mphala* of elders of the village. His sister

Neliya had not showed up yet. Kamthibi was thankful that Trish did not understand Tumbuka. But what if someone had translated it to her? He walked to the village with the men and Trish with the women.

CHAPTER FIFTEEN

At the end of that long *Kulimizgha* festive day, everyone in Nkhorongo village was happy but exhausted. The evening after dinner, conversation and buzz in the entire village was about what the planted drunken man had said. It was as if there was an elephant in the room and finally someone had said something about it. Some said Kamthibi might have already divorced his wife of twenty years. Others speculated and were convinced he would not divorce the wife with whom he already had three children. Instead, Kamthibi was so African he would defy European custom and become polygamous and marry both the white woman and the African woman. After all, they argued, he grew up in that same village and had seen nothing wrong with some of his uncles and grandparents marrying several wives.

Meanwhile, the Simbazako clan was not worried because they believed them, or at least Kamthibi's father, had acted wisely and had covered all the bases. Indeed, all they had to say in the *mphala* hearing if convened is that Kamthibi and Trish had never shared a hut, let alone a bed at night during their stay in the village. The young men and women who spent nights with the two in their separate *nthanganeni* and *mphala* huts could bear testimony to that fact

So much had happened that day that Trish wished she and Kamthibi could be alone for a moment just to share and talk about the excitements of the day. She had enjoyed herself so much. She was unfamiliar with how to properly handle the hoe. She had tried her best. She was beginning to get frustrated because she couldn't understand the language. She yearned for coherent fluid conversation with an adult English speaker, just for once. She missed her home and relatives in Ireland. There were certain things she had heard she was curious and burning to ask Kamthibi about. With all that was going on, Trish had forgotten and skipped some doses of the cancer medication. She had felt some chills and a slight temperature the previous night. But that could have been nothing, though she wanted to alert and touch base with Kamthibi about some of this.

Trish and Kamthibi had been taking their meals separately according to custom. On Trish's insistence, they were served dinner together just for once. A young nephew brought into the *mphala* hut a covered plate of *nshima* and a covered plate of *ndiwo* or relish. He carried them decked one of top of the other and then placed them down in the middle of the small hut. The young boy came back with a small basin of clean water and then two cups of drinking water. A reed mat was placed just beside the *nshima* for Kamthibi and Trish to sit on. The boy walked out so the guests could eat. Kamthibi asked Trish to wash her hands. He was taking his time washing his hands when he overheard the loud voice of his mother outside.

"*Iwe nawe unamphuvya!!*" (You clearly don't take instructions very well!), Kamthibi's mother was rebuking the nephew, "*nanguti upeleke izi dende kwa balendu osati zila. Hamba katole!!! Yendeska!*" (I had told you to take this relish to the guests and not what you took. Go and get it back!! Hurry up!)

At that same moment, Trish uncovered the plate and she let out a blood-screeching scream that could be heard throughout the village. Everybody outside froze. The young boy was standing at the door with another identical pair of covered plates with his jaw to the floor and eyes as big as a saucer.

"What!! What!" Kamthibi instinctively held Trish tightly in his arms.

"Dead…. dead …mouse in the plate!" Trish gasped jerking both arms and hands up and down pointing at the plate, hyperventilating. She kicked her feet rapidly up and down in a child-like tantrum while covering her face with both hands. She quickly dragged herself on her bottom to the edge of the wall of the hut. She covered her knees with her skirt holding it down to her knees and put her chin on her knees.

"Oh, that's *mbewa* (mice), the traditional *Tumbuka* delicacy", Kamthibi said as he covered the plate back and grabbed it and gave it to the boy. Kamthibi walked out to see what was happening. His mother and all the women who were preparing the meals were sombre. Kamthibi smiled. They all smiled. The kids giggled.

"Well, it was a mistake", a*NyaNthula* explained, "I had told your little nephew to take this *ndiwo* to the guests. But instead he took the wrong covered plates. I hope our guest is ok."

"Don't worry mother, I understand."

Kamthibi went back into the hut and held and consoled Trish who was still shaken, facing the wall with her back still to the offending *nshima*.

"I told you that I can eat all the exotic vegetables but I can't stand even just seeing a mouse," Trish said, "I'm sorry. I know this is your culture."

"It was just an honest mix up," Kamthibi said rubbing her arm, "you probably would have liked eating it."

"What?"

"I am just teasing. The brittle dry tail is the most delicious," Kamthibi smiled as Trish glared at him.

"You must be enjoying this, Kamthibi," Trish said, "I just made a fool of myself. Everybody now thinks I am this hysterical, wimpy, *muzungu* woman."

"Let's come and eat," Kamthibi tagged her arm.

"No, I don't even feel like eating now," Trish feigned pouting, "I will not eat until I leave this lousy village."

"You want the Irish government to come and rescue you or maybe Amnesty International?"

After a while, they ate the delicious *nshima* meal with chicken and green vegetables cooked with freshly made peanut powder.

Kamthibi was predictably emotionally distracted and mentally preoccupied. He only visited the village about every five years. He was trying to juggle too many balls in the air and as a result some of them were dropping. He was spreading himself thin. He was trying to hangout with his mother as he truly cherished and loved her precious company. He felt lucky to have such a mother. He was talking to his brothers and father, together and separately, to just catch up on their personal lives and families. Kamthibi was also worried keeping an eye on Trish so that she was comfortable enough. Ordinarily, couples share their day's experiences at bed time. But since they were sleeping in separate huts, he wished he could spend more time with her. He told his nephews and nieces to work hard in school to get a good education. He joked with them.

That festival night, Kamthibi and Trish briefly met under the tree that was half way between their huts to quickly exchange good night kisses and I love yous. As they were walking away from each other for the night, Kamthibi turned around.

"Oh," he said almost as an afterthought "my mother's family at Bapechi village have given us a goat for Christmas, not to keep as a pet but to eat."

"Oh, I see," Trish responded in an obviously terse way. Kamthibi was surprised that she did not laugh at the joke.

"So, I will be going to Chipewa village early tomorrow with my brothers to pick up the goat. My mother thought it might be a good thing for me to visit with her family a little."

"Ok, see you", Trish replied and went off.

Kamthibi shrugged his shoulders and went off to his *mphala* hut to go to bed. He was too exhausted to think.

As she lay in her sleeping bag in the complete darkness under the mosquito net that night, Trish couldn't understand why she was getting angry with Kamthibi. Her anger built up all day the following day. She went with Kamthibi's brothers' wives and did some of her laundry at the creek, including Kamthibi's. Kamthibi went with his brothers to pick up the hapless goat and were back by noon. But to Trish, Kamthibi might as well have gone to planet Mars and stayed there for a zillion light years. Why was he having so much fun when she was angry, frustrated, not feeling well and she had had no coherent conversations in what seemed like years? If she was in her village in Gandy, she could have called up her mother or gone out to lunch with her friends or her daughter Jill.

It was quite dark that evening when Trish and Kamthibi walked toward each other alone under the tree. It was still dark as the moon was coming out later that night. They exchanged tense "His!" and Kamthibi could sense something was wrong.

"Why are you avoiding me?" she asked placing her hands on her hips with her elbows sticking out. Trish couldn't wait to launch into Kamthibi.

"What are you talking about?" Kamthibi asked surprised, thinking something was wrong, though he had not expected this type of confrontation.

"I haven't talked to you or anyone in two days! Everybody is laughing and I can't join in! I can tell they are talking about the mouse incident. You have been with your mother all day! And your niece told me that a man stood up and was insulting and publicly calling me names openly at the festival yesterday! Kamthibi, for all I know, your little trip to your mother's village was not to your mother's village at all, but probably to visit your wife Nora's parents. And…"

"Are you done? Are you done?" Kamthibi interjected, "is it a crime to talk to my mother now?" He responded, clearly getting annoyed at the piling on and for a moment thinking he was in love with a lunatic of a woman, "did you want me to drag you with me to my mother's village at six in the morning so you can be sure it's not Nora's village? My niece Misozi is only in tenth grade in a village secondary school. She wouldn't even know how to translate anything accurately into English besides "Good morning," or "May I have some water." If you can't speak Tumbuka, am I supposed to bring the whole of Ireland here in the village so poor Trish can have someone to speak to?" Kamthibi suddenly paused really steamed, stammering and out of breath.

"Look, all I want is to be with you for a miserly, not even half an hour," Trish said in a lower tone, "is that too much to ask? Maybe I should pick up a number to get my turn to see you," she said half sarcastically. She had not seen Kamthibi get this angry before. He had a quiver in his voice and a slight stammer.

"That's it, Trish! If you don't like it here, why don't you go?" Kamthibi said, slowly pouring the exaggerated sarcasm. Immediately the words came out, Kamthibi wished he had not said them.

"Ok, it's no use reasoning with you. I have had enough of this," Trish said angrily huffing away towards the *mphala* hut, "I am leaving this, this...little lousy village!" she yelled.

Kamthibi thought that was a joke because if she were truly leaving, she would have gone back to her *nthanganeni* hut and then left. But she wouldn't even know where to go at night. Trish disappeared behind the *mphala* hut. Kamthibi waited for a while because he expected her to re-emerge on the other side of the hut. But when she didn't, he walked around the hut to see if she was hiding there. But when he didn't see her, he got concerned. He ran around the hut again, and Trish was not there.

"Trish! Trish!" Kamthibi called, "where are you? This is silly now. It's dark and I can't see you. I didn't mean what I said."

He couldn't hear any rustling in the grass and bushes around the hut. The only way she could have run was the path toward Boyole School. 'This is ridiculous and dangerous', Kamthibi thought to himself as his anger was replaced by alarm and fear. 'There could be poisonous snakes, scorpions, and stinging ants on the path in the dark.' He briskly trotted on the path and stopped. He couldn't hear any noise, rustling in the grass or footsteps. 'She must be far ahead on the smooth footpath'. So, Kamthibi ran farther and faster on the path towards Boyole.

"Trish! Trish! Stop if you can hear me!" Kamthibi hollered as he ran on the path as fast as he could.

Kamthibi's worst fears were confirmed when he paused out of breath near the Denkhule creek. The crickets and the frogs at the creek suddenly went quiet, normally a sign at night that someone or something had just arrived there just ahead of him. He heard the quick splash, splash, splash of feet crossing the creek quickly. He knew Trish had to be close probably less than fifty yards away. He sprinted across the creek in his gym shoes splashing the ankle-deep water all over his legs and hands. Trish was weeping softly in the dark ahead of him. She leaned her forearm and head against a tree as she wept and moaned gently rocking her bosom up and down.

"Trish, are you all right?" Kamthibi asked still breathing heavily as he followed the direction of the soft moaning in the dark like sonar or radar. He plied her away from the tree and held her in his arms. She wept on his shoulder as he stroked her hair.

"It's all right. I didn't mean to say what I said. It was just in the heat of anger that I said that," Kamthibi soothed.

"Maybe you don't want me at the village or with you any more after all the mean things I said. You can put me on the bus tomorrow and I will go back to Lusaka."

"It's all right. I am surprised that we haven't fought more often. You have been such a good sport and I am proud of you," Kamthibi reassured Trish, "did you know that some women liked the way you behaved at the *Kulimizgha* ceremony?"

"Really?" Trish asked, "When was that?"

"You remember when we met in the grass, I overheard some women saying you behaved so well."

"That sounds like I am a little girl," Trish responded.

"Of course they didn't mean it in that way."

Kamthibi held Trish's hand as they approached the Denkhule creek. They waded through the cool shallow water in their already wet gym shoes. The bull frogs were quiet again. It would have been dangerous to cross on the precarious log bridge in the dark. Their water-filled gym shoes made sloshing sounds as they waded out of the water to the other side on dry ground. They followed the path as they talked and made up walking slowly as each profusely apologized to the other for the bad things they had done or what they had said. They professed their love to each other and how they expected to be alone again in another day or two.

As they neared the village *mphala* hut, they stopped and kissed each other with such intense passion that they felt aroused. But they knew they couldn't go anywhere to be alone long. In spite of this however, they were both soon beginning to approach the bridge of no return. Kamthibi kicked the thin wooden door of the *mphala* hut and pulled Trish inside. He closed it feeling the rough doorframe for the small nail latch and hooked it down securing the door from inside.

"We have a couple of minutes before my nephews come to bed," Kamthibi hastily whispered.

They kissed as their passions gushed out of the floodgate. They kissed and their lips slurped as they desperately grabbed each other all over in the pitch darkness of the hut. Their breathing was heavy, intense but erratic. Kamthibi pulled her down with him to the bare smooth mud floor. He could feel hot breath helplessly escaping from her hot open lips against his neck. He felt and searched for buttons on her blouse. She felt and found the buttons on his shirt. The fingers on the one hand quickly undid the top button, felt his chest hair, and paused. She abruptly slid her trembling hand all the way down to reach his groin. He grabbed her hand and froze. He suddenly held his heavy breath. He could hear footsteps approaching the hut.

"*Odi! Odi!*" Kamthibi's brother said in front of the hut.

"*Yeo!*" Kamthibi responded trying not to sound out of breath, "Wait a minute! Trish and I had just come in to chat for a while just before the boys come to bed. We were looking for matches and the candle. We couldn't find them in the dark."

"No, no, that's ok. I will come with the boys later," his brother walked away.

Kamthibi quickly grabbed a blanket and spread it on the floor. They kissed and kissed while standing and caressing each other all over the deeply intimate places of their bodies. They hastily discarded their clothes. They embraced and the ecstatic feel of their bare amber-hot skins sent them to the floor again. The vigorous wrestling and rapid but deep breathing was accompanied by small moans of passionate pleasure. They were soon engulfed in flames of passionate desire as they began to cross the bridge of no return. She begged him to take her across the bridge as she moaned and gasped his name that she was ready. When he finally obliged, the moaning got louder. They moved across the bridge in strokes; she on her back and he on top, locked in a primordial symbiosis. Half-way across the bridge, they slid and fell into the river below. They instinctively stayed locked together and tumbled in and out of the sweet fresh water. For a while they swam for the shore as they desperately synchronized their strokes together. She was too tired to last the short three feet to the riverbank. He made one big stroke and they both landed on the sandy riverbank and they moaned loudly as he collapsed on top of her and she instinctively clutched him very tightly in her arms, her fingernails digging into his back. They were drenched and exhausted. She laid her head on his chest and he held her in his strong arms. They lay down quietly for a while.

Kamthibi struck a match and lit the candle on the far end of the hut along the edge of the floor and the brown mud wall. They slowly got dressed. He whispered to her to button her blouse and straighten up. She covered her mouth with her palm. She smiled and snickered at the absurdity of the situation earlier at Kamthibi's lame attempt to disguise to his brother about what they were really doing. Soon his brother came back.

"I'm not coming in anyway," Kamthibi's brother said, "my wife and a few people in the village said they heard loud words exchanged between the two of you and that *mwanakazi waputhuka* towards Boyole School. Is everything ok?"

"Yes," Kamthibi replied, "as a matter of fact Trish will be going to bed soon to rest." His brother walked away wishing both of them goodnight.

"What was that?" Trish asked, "Something about Boyole?"

"*Mwanakazi wapunthuka* in Tumbuka means when a man and a woman have a fight and in anger, the woman storms away back to her home village. So they heard that this had happened between us. I told him things were all right between us."

"I would have *punthuka* to Gandy in Ireland. That would have been a long walk," Trish laughed, "tell him I only made it as a far as the creek." They both laughed heartily.

Soon after Kamthibi's brother had left, the nephews showed up in the hut to go to bed. Kamthibi and Trish kissed each other good night under the tree. They both tossed in their beds for a while in the pitch-dark huts, thinking and fantasizing what it could have been if they had spent the whole night together.

"*Odi! Odi! Awise* Pyera!" (Father of Pyera)

Kamthibi awoke to the unmistakable voice of his older sister Neliya outside the *mphala*. He had dreaded this occasion. He wondered whether her sister had travelled all night. Wasn't this a weekday when she would have been working, teaching at her primary school?

The Bridge

"*Yeo*! I will be out there in a minute," Kamthibi replied kicking his covers and getting up and out of his mosquito net. His sister was sitting on the edge of the hut. He shook hands with her and sat down. They exchanged *malonje*. Before he could finish explaining his side of the *malonje*, Neliya became impatient.

"I love you as my little brother. I would not say what I am going to say if I was not concerned about you and the welfare of everyone in our family. I took a day off from the Headmaster because I had heard rumours about what is going on. Last night, I was going to talk to you as soon as I had arrived in the bright moonlight. I had been cycling all afternoon. I have to go back later this afternoon."

"Don't beat about the bush, just go ahead," Kamthibi wanted to get the injection quickly and get the pain over with, just as when he was young and had to be given fourteen injections to treat bilharzias.

"This white woman is breaking up your family and is ruining your reputation in this entire family and all the villages around. Are you out of your mind? How can you bring a grown woman here when you have a wife and children? What about our children that you have with your wife Nora? Why are you ignoring the traditional custom? It seems Western life style has blinded you. You are not fooling anyone. The reason why nobody has mentioned this to you directly in your face is because they look at it as *munthondwe*; something that is unheard of in our village."

"You don't even know what happened between me and Nora," Kamthibi tried to defend himself against his sibling.

"That is irrelevant. We all know that Nora was unfaithful. All grown up men face similar problems in marriages. But those problems do not give you license to act in any impulsive way you want. This is not acceptable in our family and our village."

"You just don't understand," Kamthibi explained, "life is different in America. I was working very hard and feeling very isolated and lonely for a long, long time. What was I supposed to do? Would you have been happy if I had become suicidal and killed myself? At least this woman you call the white woman saved my life. We owed it to each other to share our love."

"What is it with you little brother? Can't you find a woman who is black? Are you attracted to her because she is a *muzungu* and has a long nose?"

"I'm not going to listen to this any more!" Kamthibi stood up angrily and stormed away on the path leading to the Lundazi River.

"You might not like what you are hearing Kamthibi!" Neliya yelled after him as the tall grass swallowed him, "you need to decide. Mother says there is a *mphala* for you tomorrow to look into your marriage problems!"

The loud voices had drawn everyone's attention. Trish had stood by her *nthanganeni* with the others including Kamthibi's parents, nieces, nephews, his brother, clan members, and onlookers. Although Trish could not understand Tumbuka, she knew it concerned her when she heard Neliya refer to *"muzungu."* She could see that Kamthibi was getting angrier but did not say much to challenge his sister. She felt sorry for him and for the first time felt guilty for bringing so much pain to Kamthibi and possible discord in his family and clan. Trish promptly followed Kamthibi on the path.

Kamthibi sat on the sandy river bank barely a couple of feet from the fast- flowing, lightly milky water. This was the exact place they used to lie on the warm sand when they used to swim in the cold river as young boys. Soon Trish was there asking if it was all right if she could sit beside him. Kamthibi agreed absent-mindedly as he stared at the water. The strong scent of fresh water and plants engulfed them. Some of the thick green trees that lined the river had fruits hanging from them and birds noisily feasted on them as they talked to each other in an incomprehensible language. The ten-foot *matete* reeds thickly grew along the edge of the river with some scattered in the middle. Men cut the reeds and used them to weave mats and baskets. The water was flowing so swiftly around some of the reeds in the middle of the river that they shook and looked like they were dancing. There was a cacophony of bright-coloured river birds continuously singing melodious sweet songs, flapping around, flying, and landing from reed to reed. Out of curiosity, some of them landed on the reeds in the middle of the river nearest to where Trish and Kamthibi were sitting as if they were waiting for a performance. The reeds swayed up and down and bent over in bow-shaped curves in the middle with the top touching on and off the surface of the swift-running water. *Sambi sambi*, dragon flies, and numerous other water borne tiny insects floated on the edge of the river where the water was calmer. Kamthibi and Trish sat in silence for a while.

"This is so beautiful, Kamthibi. I wish I had my house right here so that I could wake up to this beauty everyday."

"Why do you think I am drawn to the village? Why do you think I brought you here?" Kamthibi asked rhetorically.

"I am really sorry about the fight with your sister, Neliya," Trish put her arm around Kamthibi's shoulders.

"There was nothing unexpected there. It's amazing how sibling relationships never change. She used to tease me this same way when we were young. But some of what she said is right. Do you know one of the things she asked?"

"What?"

"Did I fall in love with you because you are white and have a long nose?" They laughed for the first time relieving the tension.

"The woman is nuts. Did you fall in love with me because of my long nose and white skin?" asked Trish looking at Kamthibi, smiling.

"Of course not. But we should think about some of the things she said. Let's go. I need to get ready for the *mphala* over my marriage which could be any day now."

They stood up, tightly hugged, and kissed each other passionately before they returned to the village.

CHAPTER SIXTEEN

The *mswela* rains which usually start in January, started a few days early. During the *mswela* rains, the whole sky is blanketed with a thick cloud and it continuously drizzles and pours alternatively all day and all night sometimes for a whole week. No one can come out to do anything. When the rains finally subside, the grass, weeds, and food crops would all have sprung up two feet or more.

The *mswela* rain started rather early on Christmas Eve. It drizzled and poured all night and most of Christmas day. As a result, they could not go to church at *Kanyanga* Catholic Mission. Kamthibi had wanted to take Trish to see a few traditional dances that take place on that day. This could not happen either.

Kamthibi's nephew had been sent on the new bicycle to the grocery store at *Boyole* School to do the Christmas shopping for the family. He bought goodies for Christmas such as several loaves of bread, margarine, sugar, tea, cooking oil, and rice. No one ate *nshima* on Christmas day if they could help it. All of that brought very dear fond memories of Kamthibi's very first Christmas as a child in the village.

Kamthibi remembered that his grandmother had saved twelve cents during the year. His aunt walked all afternoon to Hoya stores just beyond Boyole School and came back in the rain that evening. Whatever she had bought was dry and had been obviously carefully concealed all through advance contingency planning. Kamthibi could barely sleep in the *impala* hut with other boys that night with the anticipation about Christmas and whatever his grandmother was keeping secret.

Early the following morning, as the grandchildren jostled for position around the open fireplace, a large clay pot of water was boiled. From a small, brightly-coloured aluminium foil packet, his aunt sprinkled half the contents of some black dry floating substances never seen before. She then poured a whole three cents worth packet of sugar into the pot. She stirred it. The children sat near the pot as the adults – uncles, aunts, older cousins – sat a little distance away waiting and making commentary among themselves on how excited the kids were.

Kamthibi's grandmother had handed each child a small rusty metal cup. Adults had larger metal mugs. She carefully and slowly poured a little bit of the dark steaming liquid into cups enough so that the liquid could go around the many cups. His grandmother unwrapped pieces of golden brown, white and soft edibles, which were known locally as scones; pronounced in Tumbuka as *sikono*. She split each piece among four children while adults split halves.

Kamthibi had proceeded to slowly take a sip of the sweet dark liquid followed by a small deliberate bite of the *sikono*. The whole experience was known as drinking tea with a small piece of a bun and it sent all the kids bananas with profound sheer joy, pleasure, and bragado. As kids, this experience could not simply be bottled away.

Soon after most of this exhilarating event was over, Kamthibi had clutched, by that time, a rather small piece of bun he had saved in his hand and run outside the house, and had bragged to other admiring friends in the village: "We drank tea and ate scones for Christmas!" Kamthibi had yelled at the top of his lungs as he had pranced around. The other kids in the village had desperately begged for a piece of the Christmas. Kamthibi had given each of them a smitten of the bun. It was just enough to have wetted their appetites. But the kids had been thrilled all the same. That was what Kamthibi called his happiest Christmas ever. Later that morning, they had gone to church and in the afternoon had watched traditional dances like *chimtali, chitelele, dekesa* and *fwemba*. Kamthibi had always remembered that Christmas with a certain fondness and nostalgia.

So it was that on Christmas day, more than thirty years later, they all feasted on Kamthibi's mother's special *chikasu* spice rice, chicken, goat meat, tea, bread, and margarine. Trish said it provided her some good needed variety because she liked *nshima*. But eating it every meal would have to use some getting used to. It was the best Christmas the Simbazako family had had in years, no doubt because Kamthibi had bought the special foods. And they didn't know that it only cost him an equivalent of thirty American dollars to feed everyone that much plenty of food.

Kamthibi was happy because he only did what his dad had done all those years when he and his siblings were children. Their dad did not earn enough to buy his children expensive, let alone cheap Christmas presents. But he always made sure he bought enough special foods, which they had enjoyed tremendously.

On the day of Kamthibi and Trish's departure, there was a special sadness in the Simbazako family. The departure evoked powerful memories from younger years when all of them went away to school. Kamthibi's father was an elementary school teacher at the time near Chipata more than a hundred miles south of Lundazi on the Chipata road. Kamthibi identified with the pain mixed with fond memories since he had gone to a boys' boarding school at a tender age of ten. Packing was easy since he only had two pairs of shorts, two shirts, and two small blankets to throw into the small suitcase. He had no shoes, no towels, no bed sheets, no pillows and other things that would be considered necessities of life today. Two pairs of uniforms and a small bar of soap were issued at school. It was difficult to pack the food goodies. Kamthibi's mother made peanut butter and put it in a jar and threw it into the corner of the suitcase. But his mother had also wanted Kamthibi to take peanuts, fresh roasted corn, sweet potatoes, and many other home-made goodies. This is where his father would step in, arguing with his mother that

The Bridge

Kamthibi wasn't allowed to transport the Simbazako's entire kitchen with all its culinary delights to school. Kamthibi as a boy had to be tough.

The morning of departure was hard. Kamthibi couldn't eat the last meal as a frog was lodged in his throat. Because they were a family of nine, with several siblings travelling to distant boarding schools at the same time, the logistical arrangements were challenging and complicated. His father would always bark to "hurry up! We haven't got all day! Let's go!" While his mother would be trying to squeeze one more goodie into the suitcase and reminding young Kamthibi to put his fifty cents transport and pocket money in a secure place, his father would pile the entire luggage on his bike and ride ahead the six to eight miles of rough and bumpy bush paths to the bus station.

On one occasion, Kamthibi's father had escorted him to school and they arrived at the bus station by the main dirt road early in the morning. They waited all day. They could not afford to eat much of anything as they were saving the few cents for Kamthibi's bus ride to school. The Zambia Bus Company bus never showed up that day. It was cloudy and rainy and getting dark. His father had begged from total strangers for Kamthibi to spend the night at the stranger's house so that he would be able to catch the bus to school early the following morning. Kamthibi's father had to be at work the following morning at seven a.m. He did not have a raincoat. He was tired and hungry. It was sprinkling harder as Kamthibi watched his father ride his bike into the small bush path and was swallowed by tall African elephant grass. His father was going to ride ten miles home through a bush path, in the rainy, pitch-dark African night. No words could have expressed a father's deep love for his son. That's one memory Kamthibi had of his father that never failed to make him teary-eyed up to that day.

The first few times at school, Kamthibi had cried and had a frog lodged in his throat and sniffed all night. Reuniting with friends he had not seen all Christmas holidays injected some momentary diversion and excitement during the first night. Institutional food would never be better than Mom's home-cooked meals. The awfulness of the food could not be entirely blamed on the boarding school's lone village cook. Poor storage was most likely the culprit. The hundred-pound bags of dry corn, raw peanuts, and red beans were simply stack-piled high on the floor of a huge storage building. All kinds of weevils, rats, and bugs had a priceless feast. Students gave a special name to the black insect weevils that bored holes into the beans we ate; black Maria. All the sacrifice placed a very high price, appreciation, and value on education. The mostly poor Zambian African students knew it was going to make a big difference in their future.

Modern forms of communication did not exist then and even now. There was no electricity and Kamthibi and the students used kerosene lamps for two hours every night for studying. After being away from home for months, the last day of school was so exciting. Since Kamthibi's home was eighty miles away at the time, he rode the bus and walked or rode the bike the last six to eight miles. He found the last half mile from the house so heart-warming and comforting to spot his mother, *aNyaNthula*, walking about the house yard, laundry blowing gently on theclothesline. As he drew closer to the house he could smell his mother's cooking. At the sight of him walking, the young brothers and sisters would scream his name and sprint excitedly to welcome him home. One of those memorable years, Kamthibi's younger brother died after a short illness at home while Kamthibi was away to school. He has never forgotten the sad emptiness the whole family felt. For a long while, his mother kept calling his dead brother's name by mistake.

Kamthibi's mother said one of the worst days was when her children had all left for boarding school. She said she felt empty; she got depressed, and would not eat much for days after. She said she missed the noise, the hassle and bustle, and especially the laughter of the children. Despite having very little material-wise, Kamthibi's house was a household of laughter.

So it was that some of those memories were being relived when the entire Simbazako family walked to Boyole School bus station to escort and see their guests off -brothers, nephews, nieces, cousins, and even his mother and father now much older hobbled the five miles to the station. A second bicycle was borrowed, such that Kamthibi and Trish's luggage were tied on separate bicycle carriers. The nephews took pleasure in riding ahead such that they were already waiting at the station when the rest of the family arrived. Kamthibi gave the new bicycle to his parents as a Christmas gift to use for trips to the clinic and as general transport.

The goodbyes were hard as some of the little nephews and nieces wept. There was shaking of hands and clamouring from the children of, "a *Tirishi*! a *Tirishi*! a *Tirishi*! *Mulute makora,*" (Trish, Trish, Trish go well). Everyone had become fond of Trish in those few short days. In a way in which Westerners and perhaps other non-Africans would find hard to appreciate and understand, Trish was already a member of the family. Kamthibi was not surprised at all when his relatives told Trish she would be welcome even if she came alone to the village. These are the same Africans that welcomed and were genuinely kind to whites after the brutal slave trade in America, cruel colonialism in Africa, and vicious apartheid in Africa. The strong and sweet human social bonds were already firmly established between Trish and Kamthibi's family. Nothing would ever erase them.

Kamthibi was sad as he approached his mother and father to bid them farewell. The disturbing thoughts kept intruding in his mind that they were both so old that this could be easily the last time he would see either one or both of them alive. He was not the only one with the secret thought about the dreaded because his mother stated it out aloud later.

"My son," Kamthibi's father cleared his throat, "the *mphala* of elders to discuss your marriage problems was not called because both relatives from Nora's and our village agreed they could not discuss the case without your wife's side of the story. You need to think and make decisions about your marriage. We would favour that you stay with your wife and raise your children as a responsible father. They are still very young. But we realize these are changing times. Maybe you could consider coming back here with Nora and the children. Whatever you decide, we will support you."

"My son," his mother said in that familiar tone of intimacy only reserved for Kamthibi, "we are growing old now. You might not find us alive. If you can, bring Phyera my grand daughter and the two boys so I can see them before I die."

"Yes, Mother", Kamthibi replied choked, "I will see if I can raise some money so that I can fly home here with them."

"As for your wife, Nora." Kamthibi's mother continued, "although she comes from a good people of Basiti Village, marriages today are hard. There are so many things that tempt men to go so crazy that they rise up against and abandon their wives and small children. This is happening even now here in the villages. Even women are doing this. People are dying like flies because of this new AIDS sexual epidemic disease. Trish seems like a good woman even though she is not from here. She will learn many of our ways and you will learn hers. We as a family will not be involved much these days since you live very far. What matters is you send us a little money now and then to buy sugar. If you are happy with Trish, that is what matters. Although it was rare, even in the old days here in the village, people used to divorce each other if things were not going well."

"*aNyaNthula*," Kamthibi's father interjected, "you have said enough. He is now a grown man and not a little boy. Let him go otherwise the bus will leave them. The driver is blowing the horn."

With these last words from his mother, and a warm lingering handshake with both of them, Kamthibi and Trish's visit to Nkhorongo village came to an end. They boarded the Zambia Bus Company bus whose front destination sign said: "LUSAKA." They were lucky to catch a bus that was going all the way from Boyole School, through Lundazi, Chipata to Lusaka. They did not have to spend a night in Lundazi or Chipata. They would travel for eighteen straight hours arriving in Lusaka perhaps at dawn. That same afternoon at four, Trish's Air Zambia plane would be departing for Heathrow Airport in London.

CHAPTER SEVENTEEN

Filimoni slowly swung the two black gates to the house open.

"*Yendesa iwe*, Filimoni" (hurry up), Milika said to her son impatiently out of the rolled down window as she drove the car into the driveway.

"Is your father home?"

"Yes, he is watching TV."

Milika grabbed the *Zambia Times* newspaper and rushed into the house.

"*Awise* Filimoni!" (Father of Filimoni) she yelled excitedly, "your friend is in danger. Have you seen this story in today's paper?"

"Which friend? What story?" Teketa asked, "I didn't even read the paper today because I was too busy at work getting ready for the trip to Mauritius."

Teketa anxiously began to read the story that was on page six on the home news page. The headline read:

POLICE DETAIN IRISHMAN
By **Brown Siyamujaye**
Zambia Times **Reporter**

Lusaka - A middle-aged Irishman, Richard Butler, was briefly detained for questioning and later released by police yesterday afternoon at Lusaka Central Police station. According to police sources, it all started at the popular Green Elephant Bar and Restaurant located at the Northern end of Cairo Road. Mr. Butler had been drinking alone for most of the afternoon when he began to complain and shout loudly about his missing wife whom he had been searching for all over Lusaka for a week. One of the Zambian patrons suggested that Mr. Butler, who is white, just divorce his wife and marry one of the many beautiful Zambian women. Mr. Butler took exception to the comment and became agitated. He began to shout that his wife and all Zambian women were f***ing useless bitches.

"The *muzungu* was very drunk," said Stanley Phiri, a patron from Chawama West, "he was insulting everyone in the bar including the barman. He threatened to kill all women including the f***ing Zambian who stole his wife. Some of the people were threatening to beat up the rude *muzungu* if he did not shut his dirty mouth. It was then that the barman called the police."

Mr. Butler was taken to the Lusaka Police Station where he spent a few hours in police cells. Police discharged him on account of insufficient evidence to charge him with disorderly conduct. Lusaka police Chief Michael Chikoti confirmed that Mr Butler had been briefly detained and released.

"There wasn't enough evidence to detain or charge him," Mr Chikoti said speaking by telephone, "the police have to act professionally and sometimes have to act to prevent violence. Police removed Mr. Butler from the scene for his own safety. We cannot detain a man just for saying certain things in public. If we arrested and detained everyone who verbally threatened someone, the police cells would be full. His passport shows that Mr Butler is in Zambia on a visitor's visa."

The Ministry of Foreign Affairs and the British Embassy could not be reached for comment.

Teketa and Milika were alarmed. They discussed the issue most of the evening and late into the night. They were very worried for both Kamthibi and Trish. They discussed the best and worst case scenarios and the many options. The best case scenario was that Kamthibi and Trish would return from the village without Richard's knowledge. She would safely board the plane and leave the country. Whatever happened later in Ireland would be Trish's business. The worst case scenario was that Richard would discover that Kamthibi and Trish would be staying at the Crystal Rose Motel. If he wasn't successful getting at them at the motel, he could stake out the Lusaka International Airport terminal knowing that Trish would be flying back to Ireland. He could humiliate or harm her. They did not want to cause unnecessary publicity or alarm by going to the police since they were unsure whether Kamthibi and Trish would have approved of such possibly unwarranted actions which would have angered Richard even more.

Teketa was leaving for one week on a business assignment on the Island of Mauritius. They decided that Milika would cut out the newspaper article from *Zambia Times*, put it in an envelope and keep it in her purse. During the next few days, Milika would drive to the Crystal Rose Motel and check if the couple was back from the village. Trish's flight back to Ireland was any day.

* * *

The love between Trish and Kamthibi was so strong that both knew intuitively that parting was going to be one of the most difficult and painful things they will ever have done in their lives. None of them wanted the other to leave, especially with the future fraught with uncertainty. Life is not like spending hours building a beautiful sand castle on the beach only to knock it down in seconds. Human social bonds built of the strong foundation of love and deeply caring for the other's very souls are too precious to be built and then thrown away willy-nilly. This deep and nagging worry was in the back of their minds. The fear about Richard and whether he could harm or even kill both of them had been relegated to the margins of their minds.

As the hours ground on and the bus drew closer to Lusaka, Kamthibi and Trish clutched each other's hands tighter. They both stared outside the bus window at nothing for hours, not saying anything. Their private furious thoughts and worries tumbled endlessly like clothes in a dryer. Between the two of them, they must have let out a million sighs. They both thought, 'Why should loving someone be so painful?' Now that the exciting village trip was over in a predictable way, they felt depressed like the way drug addicts feel as they come down from their high and are experiencing severe withdraw, except this was worse.

They both wished they could crawl into the other's head to find out what the other was thinking. When and if either one of them initiated conversation, it was short sentences asking if the other was hungry. Are you cold? Are you hot? Did you want water or a drink? Are you tired? Are you ok? The answer was a curt "No" or "Yes."

Sometime after midnight, the bus crossed the Luangwa Bridge. Everything had a touch of familiarity because the heightened expectation for anticipating and experiencing something new was now a thing of the past on this return leg of their trip. The passenger conversations interjected with "*Muzungu*" "*Muzungu*" barely startled Trish. She was getting used to it as a mostly harmless reality of life among the wonderful Zambian people. They were both comfortable knowing the everyday Zambia.

An hour after the bridge, the driver pulled the bus over again. Everyone slept for more that two hours. Although both had not been concerned, Trish and Kamthibi recognized that Richard could still be in Lusaka and might have learnt that they had stayed at the Crystal Rose motel. Therefore, it was going to be stupid to stay at the motel even for a few hours. Since Trish's Air Zambia flight to London was later that day, they both thought it was safer to stay at Teketa and Milika's house.

They rode the bus past the Crystal Rose Motel and got off at the Chelstone Township water tank. They hired a taxi and were at Teketa and Milika's house within minutes.

Teketa, Milika, and the older children were all at work and school respectively. Mrs. Jere, the house servant, made Kamthibi and Trish comfortable because her bosses would expect her to do so for their close relatives and close friends who were guests.

In spite of Mrs. Jere's insistence, Kamthibi and Trish declined to sleep in the children's bedroom. They did not want to impose since their hosts were not home. They both crashed right away because they were so exhausted and deprived of sleep. Trish slept on the couch and Kamthibi on the floor. They woke up in the afternoon and took baths and changed. Mrs. Jere had delicious *nshima* ready on the table with Kafue bream fresh fish and rape. If there was one thing Kamthibi missed in the United States it was being able to hire a house servant for a modest pay per month.

Filimoni, the first-born boy and the younger daughter were both back from school. It was unfortunate that Teketa and Milika would not be able to see Trish off. At three in the afternoon, Kamthibi and Trish got into a taxi for the Lusaka International Airport. By the time they drove past the Chelstone Township huge blue water tank again, the knots in the pits of Kamthibi and Trish's stomachs were tighter and their hearts ached, begging for mercy. They were holding on to each other tightly in an arm lock in the back seat of the car. What broke the ice for a while was that Trish bent over holding her stomach as she grimaced in pain. Tears welled up in her eyes. Kamthibi stared rigidly straight ahead through the windshield. He was numb and his mouth so dry that he could not mouth the feelings that were lodged like a frog in his throat.

"I can't stand this Kamthibi," Trish finally broke the silence. The anguish wrung and twisted her face as her lips trembled. She tried to speak but words could not come out of her quivering lips, "I don't want to make a fool of myself at the airport," she finally forced the words out between hyperventilated, quick short breaths.

Kamthibi was quiet for a while as the taxi turned left from the Great East Road onto the airport road.

"What do you mean?" Kamthibi said just to say anything. He sensed he was also getting too tense.

"Maybe just drop me off quickly at the terminal curb and come back," Trish suggested hesitantly, "this way both of us can avoid the pain."

"Don't be silly," Kamthibi said as he squeezed and kissed her on the forehead. "I want to see you off."

Kamthibi tried to make conversation with the taxi driver to take both their minds off the impending inevitable tragedy that was now a matter of just an hour or two away. That failed miserably as the taxi driver might have sensed that the two lovers were in another zone. Kamthibi and Trish were in highly charged emotional state. They developed an emotional tunnel vision which only parting deeply romantic lovers experience. That was a state in which Kamthibi and Trish did not notice the normal noises, sounds, the grass, the trees, cows feeding in the pasture along the airport road, people riding bicycles and walking about, the taxi, and the taxi driver talking. All of these receded into the background. It was as if the whole world around was far away except for the throbbing emotional intensity of pain that engulfed them; gripping their bodies and churning their stomachs. Kamthibi thought he and Trish were like two goods trains headed for a collision that nothing could be done to stop. Trish thought it felt like they were going to a funeral or waiting to be executed and they could not back out of both.

They arrived at the departure terminal too quickly. Much as it was painful, they wanted to enjoy the last precious minutes together. They both knew life, if there would be any especially for Trish, would certainly not be the same. When deep love is cemented with strong memories together, it is a powerful event that alters life permanently. One can never do everything the same way after that. The world and life itself become different. It can be likened to eating the biblical forbidden fruit. If you never eat the fruit, you will never know that life could be different for better or for worse. So it is with deep romantic love. Once one experiences it, one's life is changed forever for better or for worse.

After they checked in her baggage, the two sat on a bench holding each other in the crowded and noisy public departure hall. Their eyes were red and blood-shot with grief.

"Kamthibi, there is something I want to tell you," Trish said, "I didn't want to ruin the whole trip by giving you blow by blow account of my health everyday. I was ok until the last two nights at the village. I had a pain in my right side and night sweats. Maybe it was because I had forgotten to take the medication some of those days."

Kamthibi was quiet for a while, not knowing what to say. He admired Trish's great courage but he couldn't bring himself to say it. Tears just welled up in his eyes. "Kamthibi, I want to thank you for changing my life," Trish could not understand where the words leaping out of her mouth were coming from, "It is the greatest gift you have given me. Just knowing and being with you and all that has happened between us is good. I will love you forever whatever happens."

They held each other tightly on the bench and Trish's contorted face experienced another wave of pain.

"All I can say," Kamthibi was surprised that he could say some words at all, "is that my life is different and a hundred percent better just by knowing and being in love with you. During the time I was with you, everyday was filled with passion. I admire your courage. I don't know whether I would have found the courage to do what you did if I had just been diagnosed with cancer. You practically put your life and faith in the hands of a total stranger. You shattered all the rules of the book. I don't know what life I will have once you are gone if I will have any life at all."

They sat quietly on the bench for the rest of the time as if sensing they didn't need to say any more perhaps, just like some condemned men are asked for their last words and refuse to say anything before their execution. Maybe there comes a point in life where words do not add any meaning any more to what has happened.

This was it. Kamthibi and Trish stood up holding hands and walked to the crowded security screening station leading to the exclusive international departure lounge where people without tickets are forbidden. Kamthibi and Trish hugged each other tightly for the last time as if they did not want to let each other go. They had a quick snappy kiss on the lips. Trish plied herself away from Kamthibi's frozen stiff arms. He slowly let her walk away until their arms stretched out and their hands and finally fingers snapped apart. Trish placed her carry-on bag and the fanny pack on the moving x-ray conveyor belt. The bags were sucked into the dark crevices of the x-ray security machine and popped out on the other side. Trish walked through the security screening gate and retrieved them. Kamthibi raised his hand and waved. Trish did not look back and was swallowed like quick sand into the throng of departing passengers. She was too afraid to look back.

Kamthibi rushed into the bathroom. It was empty. The big heavy frog that had been tightly lodged in his throat all day suddenly dislodged. He ran into a toilet booth and hastily placed the toilet seat and the cover down both making rapid banging sounds. He sat on it holding his head between his hands, elbows on his knees and wept like he had never wept before. He moaned as if Trish had just died. He had just lost what he had been looking for for more than forty years -true love. Why was this happening? What would he do now that Trish was gone out of his life? Should he go back to his marriage with Nora and assume the hard and mundane chore of raising his children? Tears poured as he gently sobbed and moaned softly. He sniffed quietly when someone walked into the bathroom. He got some toilet tissue and blew his nose. He wiped his eyes and cheeks. He stood up, lifted the toilet seat and threw the tissues in it. He flushed the toilet. He felt a little better. He made up his mind to get the last glance at Trish as she would walk to the plane. He came out of the toilet and stood by the large glass window with his arms crossed on his chest and waited.

* * *

Late in the morning on the same day Kamthibi and Trish came back, Milika drove to the Crystal Rose Motel. The receptionist who was by now familiar with Milika, anticipating the arrival of a couple, told her Kamthibi and Trish had not yet arrived. Milika drove to Chelstone Market to buy some vegetables for supper. She also checked on how her girls were doing at the small hair boutique she owned in the market. When she walked out of the market, she was irritated that the front left tyre of her little car was flat. She quickly asked one of the market boys to remove the flat tyre and replace it with the spare one from the trunk. If he could mend the flat one for her, she would pick it up later that afternoon.

Milika drove to the front of the big black gates of their house. Before she could honk, Filimoni quickly swung the gates wide open and impatiently beckoned to his mother to drive up into the driveway. When his mother did not respond, Filimoni rushed out before she could drive forward.

"Aunt and Uncle were here!"

"Which Aunt and Uncle?"

"Uncle Kamthibi and Aunt Trish."

"When did they leave?"

"About three hours ago. Aunt Trish said she had to catch her plane this afternoon."

Milika's heart sank. "Ok, I am rushing to the airport," Milika told her son Filimoni as she quickly put the car in reverse. She put it in forward gear and floored the accelerator. The rickety car took off like a rocket hurling stones against the metal gates. Filimoni wondered why his mother was suddenly driving like in the movies. Only his father drove like that sometimes, never his mother.

Milika's adrenaline was pumping and she was shaking. 'Both of them had no idea what possible danger they were in,' Milika thought to herself. She swore under her breath as she wished she had come to the house sooner to catch them before they had gone to the airport. She blamed the flat tyre for delaying her. 'If only she had come straight home,' she thought. She had to get to the International Airport quickly.

She quickly turned left into the main Great East Road as the car she cut in front of honked very loudly. The driver made rude gestures at her with his hand. She floored the accelerator. If something happened to Kamthibi and Trish she couldn't forgive herself. She didn't even hesitate to pass all the cars and trucks. Fortunately for Milika, there was little traffic coming from the airport.

Milika arrived at the front of the airport terminal and left the car right on the curb where large signs said: "No Parking or Waiting. Unloading Only." As soon as she parked, smoke began coming out of the edge of the hood of the little old car. She rushed to the departure terminal entrance. She dashed through the door. Her eyes quickly darted on the hundreds of people milling in the public departure lounge. She was looking for Kamthibi or Trish. She spotted Kamthibi standing with his arms folded near the large glass window facing the huge Air Zambia jumbo jet, which was a hundred yards away on the tarmac.

"Kamthibi! Kamthibi!" Milika called waving the brown envelope as she ran towards him.

"Am I glad to see you, Milika!"

"Quickly read this!"

"What is it?"

"It's an article from *Zambia Times*. It's Richard! Both of you might be in danger! Where is Trish?"

"She already checked in and went through security," Kamthibi said as he hastily read the article, "Oh, My God! She must be warned. She can't just walk to the plane."

Kamthibi and Milika rushed to the passenger security screening point. It was noisy and still jammed with passengers. They could not even get close enough to talk to the screening officials. They rushed to the courtesy desk to ask if any type of public announcement could be made. They were told of lengthy bureaucratic requirements including first seeking permission from her superiors before such a message could be conveyed on the public intercom. Kamthibi and Milika realized they were running out of time. If Teketa had been around, he could easily have gone to warn Trish. If Richard was going to do anything, the most likely time was when Trish was walking to board the plane. Kamthibi devised a plan.

Kamthibi's last desperate plan was to run and intercept Trish somehow as she was walking on the open tarmac with other passengers the hundred yards or so to the steps of the Boeing 747 plane. This was dangerous, as armed guards were everywhere after the beefing up of security all over the world's airports.

Kamthibi went upstairs to the second floor where there were restaurants. He had to be calm and not draw attention to himself. There were a couple of armed guards in military fatigue chatting and pacing leisurely up and down the terrace. One guard was on the roof of the airport as Kamthibi could see his shadow pacing along the roof. Would they shoot? He went through the glass doors leading to the open observation terrace where friends and relatives of departing or arriving passengers usually waved and called names to their dearly departing and arriving ones.

He sat in a chair and waited. He heard the intercom announce the departure of the plane and instructing passengers to proceed to the boarding gate. Kamthibi was so tense that his heart was pumping very fast. This was it. The plan had to succeed. There was zero room for error or no tomorrow. This was his last and only chance. He peered over the edge of the high terrace wall and observed the passengers as they emerged out of the gate. He didn't want to strike too early. Trish was not among the first passengers. Then there was a small white body wearing a colourful skirt made of African *chitenje* material, and long hair blowing in the gentle African breeze. Kamthibi quickly rushed downstairs through the empty arrival tunnel of the terminal where there would be the least security. The lone security guard with a button in his hands was probably stunned when Kamthibi out of the blue rushed by.

"Hey *Saa*!! Wrong way! Stop!" he yelled, "Departure is that way! You will be shot!" He pointed the other way and for awhile contemplated and hesitated chasing the unruly probably confused passenger. But that hesitation gave Kamthibi enough precious few seconds to bolt through the narrow door. He split two surprised armed camouflaged guards.

"*Mugwireni uyo*!!" (Catch him!) The security guard shouted at the armed military guards.

Kamthibi sprinted on the open terminal tarmac towards the line of passengers marching towards the plane. The armed guards corked their guns and both fired four warning shots into the air. They lowered their guns and aimed. The shots ricocheted against the metal baggage-moving cart, which at that instant was moving across the open tarmac. Hearing the shots, some passengers ducked and instinctively hit the tarmac screaming.

"Trish! Trish! Get down! Beware of Richard!" Kamthibi yelled raising his hands and waving them down as he ran the last thirty yards with his arms stretched out.

At that instant, a single loud rifle shot was heard from the top of the airport terminal building roof. Trish hit the ground as a bullet landed ten yards behind her. The trajectory of the bullet showed that's where her head would have been if Kamthibi had not yelled for her to get down. It was a narrow escape. There were more screams. Trish and Kamthibi were ten yards from each other lying down on their stomachs.

"Are you all right?" Kamthibi shouted.

"Yes, Yes," Trish answered.

There was confusion and screaming. They desperately crawled on their stomachs towards each other. A few seconds later, the irate security guard and the armed guards also bolted from the arrival tunnel after Kamthibi.

"*Imwe* Stop! *Imwe* Stop! *Muzapaisa ma* passengers!" (You Stop! You Stop! You will cause passengers to be killed) the guards yelled.

Kamthibi and Trish finally met. The two were like colourful ecstatic love birds in an exciting courting ritual. One felt the other was like a sphinx that had risen from the ashes. They tightly held hands with their elbows planted on the ground and kissed. He noticed the clear blue sky surrounding her head. For a split second he flashed back to the blue sky he saw in Gandy when he first met Trish. A dozen armed camouflaged guards suddenly surrounded the couple that was oblivious to what was happening. One guard roughly grabbed Kamthibi by the arm but paused as he came under the spell of the couple.

"Trish, honey, I am glad I got here just in time."

"What happened?" Trish asked.

"Richard might be here,"

"Oh, I can't believe it," Trish responded, "that son of a gun won't leave me alone."

Trish was completely stunned. She touched his head and once more felt the kinky, rough, greying hair. She looked around as the equally stunned passengers stopped to watch this strange crazy scene which none of them would ever see in a Hollywood movie thriller or maybe only in their wildest nightmares would any of them see this. An African man and white woman were kissing in the middle of all the commotion.

Kamthibi and Trish kissed with passionate desperation for the last time as the passengers clapped and cheered while some smiled and shook their heads. A number of armed military police were walking around saying it was safe. Kamthibi felt a tap on his shoulder.

"What you did was against regulations," the young security guard sternly said as he grabbed Kamthibi by the arms and roughly lifted him up. He had also stood there mesmerized and watched the whole thing. The armed guard dragged Kamthibi telling him he has to answer for what he did and he could go to jail for wanton breech of airport security. Kamthibi was handcuffed.

"I am sorry," Kamthibi apologized as he was dragged away, "as you can see, I can explain."

"*Mdala nchito zathu zizatha,*" (You will make us lose our jobs), the armed guard complained as he led Kamthibi away.

"Let's go back this way to the police station for questioning," the security guard said, "passengers are not supposed to be on the airport tarmac without permission. This is trespassing and you endangered so many people's lives. Don't you remember September 11 in America? Ha?"

Kamthibi looked back towards the plane. Another guard led Trish away. Her long brown hair, which he knew had lovely soft grey strands in it, was blowing gently in the soft afternoon breeze.

The most serious security incident at the Lusaka International Airport was five years before. A bomb had been planted in the men's toilet. It exploded killing one person and injuring five. Since then, airport security had been tightened and the new rules were strictly enforced. As is often the case with humans, after a while, the security became lax again. It was under these circumstances that the dramatic events happened on the airport terminal.

The Lusaka International Airport police post was a small room, which was a wooden cubicle with a desk, a phone, and six chairs. The security guard who had pursued and fired upon Kamthibi brought him handcuffed. He told Kamthibi to sit down.

"Good afternoon, Sir," the constable saluted.

"Yes constable. What is this man here for?" asked Langston Msimuko, the Officer-in-Charge of the International Airport police post, "I have heard the commotion out there and I want a complete and full report."

"Yes, Sir," the constable security guard was anxious to tell his story, "this man broke through the security barrier and ran toward a woman passenger who was about to board the plane. I fired warning shots. It appeared, Sir, there was another man firing at the passengers from the roof top of the airport terminal building."

"What?" Officer Langston Msimuko shot up from his chair, "this is a major security breach. Which officer was assigned to the roof top?"

At this point a distressed-looking Trish was ushered into the small office. Soon after, Richard was brought in handcuffed still wearing the dark Zambia Military Police uniform. He was wearing black gloves and a black ski mask. The shell-shocked Zambia military police officer in Richard's civilian clothes was led in with his hands still bound together in duck-tape. There were still duck tape marks around his cheeks and mouth. Richard glared at Trish. She stared straight ahead of her. Kamthibi slowly shook his head.

"There have been so many incidents. This is a very serious complicated case," Officer Langston Msimuko announced, "There are so many possible charges here. Attempted murder, trespassing, eluding police, kidnapping, and breaking immigration laws. We will take all of you to the Lusaka Central Police station. You will all give statements so that we can get to the bottom of all of this."

SUMMARY

THE BRIDGE

An African man is riding in a taxi north of Belfast on a dirt road in Northern Ireland with great urgency. A middle-aged Irish woman is driving south, on the same dirt road, from her small Irish village. The unlikely couple finally meets at their Internet secretly pre-arranged rendezvous on the rural road under the most inauspicious circumstances, in a romantic first face-to-face encounter. A Police Squad car and an ambulance soon arrive on the scene and the African man is arrested.

This is the dramatic beginning of the transoceanic love story between Trish and Kamthibi. Because of compelling circumstances beyond their control, Kamthibi agrees to take Trish with him to visit his boyhood village in Zambia in Africa. Trish had neither flown in a plane before nor been outside her small rural Irish village of Gandy. But since her childhood, Trish had always dreamt of adventure to foreign lands. Her abusive, cruel and jealous husband does not like the changes. Kamthibi emigrated to and lives in the US. But in spite of his being very educated, he still cherishes and yearns for his African cultural traditions. Kamthibi and Trish develop a deep passionate romantic love for each other, which leads them to cross so many bridges.

GLOSSARY OF TUMBUKA AND ZAMBIAN WORDS

Chipungu: a type hawk that flies very high circling an animal carcass on the ground before the birds descend on it.

Chitenje: a traditional colorful cloth Zambian women wear outside their dress or skirt below the waist wrapping it around their bodies. Also proudly used by women to carry babies on their backs.

Fontini: an expression Zambians use to describe someone who is not hip or shows unusual ignorance or lack of sophistication about modern urban culture.

Kamthibi: derived from a traditional sweet non-alcoholic drink brewed from finger millet. Also a sensuous traditional dance even adult men and women used to dance that died among the Tumbuka during the late 1940s with the arrival of European missionaries.

Kulimizgha: a traditional custom and ritual in which a household brews *kamthibi* non-alcoholic drink and beer and invite people from many village to come and hoe or till an entire household field in exchange for the drinks during the growing or farming season.

Kupunthuka: a very specific expression used to instantly convey that a woman has quarreled with her husband and has angrily left their home and returned to her parents' village.

Malonje: an elaborate greeting custom, after the initial greeting, in which the guest systematically describes the purpose of their visit and the guest describes the state of life in their family.

Munthondwe: an act that is unthinkable or breaks a taboo in an unimaginable way.

Mphala:	a physical structure with a thatch roof on the edge of the village where Tumbuka men gathered to eat, sharpen hoes, axes, carve wooden implements such as cooking sticks. This was also the place where men gathered to hear disputes and settle village disagreements.
Mphala:	also a hut in which all single young men and boys slept.
Muzungu:	a term used to refer to anyone who is white or of European descent.
Mwenye:	a term of endearment Zambian use for anyone who is from India or of Indian descent.
Nshima:	the Zambian staple meal eaten twice per day during lunch and supper. It is cooked using plain corn meal. Dining in the home eating nshima involves elaborate rituals and customs.
Nthanganeni:	usually a small round hut that young single women and girls slept.
Sowela:	a gift in form of money members of the audience give to dancers to express appreciation of their dancing. The money may be tossed on the ground, in a plate or handed to the individual dancer(s).
Sungununu:	a tiny black ant that roams the village hose floor or grounds.
Nkhoswe:	a village elder a married couple chooses to be a custodian of their marriage. He or she will offer wisdom, counseling advice or offer a listening ear to both or either partner in the case where couples have serious disputes or disagreements.
Mwambo:	customs deeply steeped in Tumbuka tradition that individuals are expected to live by.